TRUTH TO LIFE

TRUTH TO LIFE

THE ART OF BIOGRAPHY IN THE NINETEENTH CENTURY

❁

A. O. J. COCKSHUT

COLLINS

ST JAMES'S PLACE, LONDON

1974

William Collins Sons & Co Ltd
London . Glasgow . Sydney . Auckland
Toronto . Johannesburg

First published 1974
© A. O. J. Cockshut 1974

ISBN 0 00 216760 3

Set in Monotype Scotch Roman
Made and printed in Great Britain by
William Collins Sons & Co Ltd Glasgow

For Avril in affectionate gratitude

CONTENTS

❋

1	A neglected form	*page* 11
2	Sketch of a tradition	16
3	The death scene	41
4	The reassessment of the past	55
5	The milieu	64
	1 The Protestant ethos	64
	2 Oxford in 1832	79
6	Stanley's Arnold	87
7	Smiles as biographer	105
8	Trevelyan's Macaulay	125
9	Froude's Carlyle	144
	1 General	144
	2 Background and Religion	152
	3 Politics	159
	4 Marriage	164
10	Morley's Gladstone	175
11	Ward's Newman	193
	Appendix: Biographical summaries of leading figures	209
	Index	217

You may behold a Scipio and a Lelius gathering cockle-shells on the shore, Augustus playing at bounding-stones with boys, and Agesilaus riding on a hobby-horse among his children. The pageantry of life is taken away; you see the poor reasonable animal, as naked as nature ever made him; are acquainted with his passions and his follies, and find the demi-god a man.

JOHN DRYDEN
Preface to English version of *Plutarch's Lives*, 1683

Read no history: nothing but biography, for that is life without theory.

BENJAMIN DISRAELI
Contarini Fleming, 1832

1

A NEGLECTED FORM

✳

Literary critics have not been quick to take the hint offered one hundred and fifty years ago by Disraeli, and nearly three hundred years ago by Dryden. For nearly two centuries we have been living in a golden age of biographical writing; Johnson's *Lives of the Poets* and Boswell's *Johnson* come at the beginning; Froude's *Carlyle* comes in the middle; and admirable biographies have been published within the last fifteen years.[1] Yet everyone seems to know that the two centuries from Richardson to Lawrence constitute a great age of the novel; those who are aware that the same is true of biography have been curiously, perhaps even culpably, reticent.

The reason is not hard to find. Biographies are normally treated as historical records; and this is obviously right. Dealing with facts, and their interpretation, they can be judged by their accuracy and by their insight. We can ask of a work of biography, as we do of a work of history, does it illuminate the past for us? But we can also ask the question, is it a notable work of literary art? It is that question that this book is mainly concerned to ask.

But, of course, the biographer's necessary concern with facts involves difficulties. How can we judge him as an artist until we have first judged him as a historian? An accurate biography may be dull and lifeless; can an inaccurate one be a great work? A work of art must have an informing principle; what is the biographer's informing principle and what is its relation to accuracy?

The biographer plunges down into a mass of documents, testimonies and (sometimes) personal memories. He emerges

---

[1] For instance, Richard Ellmann's *James Joyce* (1959) and Quentin Bell's *Virginia Woolf* (1972).

with a view of a man's character. He then has to submit his interpretation to the pressure of facts. The difficulty of biography as an art lies mainly in this tension between interpretation and evidence. Some nineteenth-century biographers, admittedly, avoided this tension by having no central interpretation. They abdicated in the face of a mass of documents, and tried to let the story tell itself. But stories will not tell themselves; a batch of letters and dates is not a biography. Books written by authors who were uncertain of what they really thought of their subject, or afraid to say, are quickly forgotten.

But the opposite danger can be just as serious. The line of interpretation can be unyielding, unable to bend before the pressure of facts. Then the facts may break through and destroy it. A notable case is Froude's interpretation of Henry VIII in his *History of England* – (especially notable since, in my opinion at least, the same writer produced, in his life of Carlyle, one of the great classics of biographical writing). Froude convinced himself that Henry's character had been traduced by enemies of the Reformation. He reasoned in this way: the Reformation was the most glorious event in English history; more than any other man Henry brought it about. The man who conferred such a blessing on his countrymen cannot have been a wicked man. He refused to take refuge in a contrast between dark personal character and beneficent public deeds; for him Henry was all of a piece.

His difficulties were increased by the very detailed character of the work he had undertaken. Document follows document and fact follows fact; and constantly they batter against Froude's conviction that Henry was a man whose faults in youth were venial, and in later life largely excused by the terrible burdens imposed on him. Froude is defeated by his own vast learning. When he has finished, he has hardly a single reader left agreeing with him.

This is an extreme case; more often, there is no decisive issue in the contest between fact and interpretation. Various exceptions or anomalies remain unexplained. We are left half-convinced that the man really was the man the biographer saw. Often, too, in the lengthy works of the period, there are sections of intractable material, that seem to tell neither for nor against the author's interpretation. This material may be interesting and informative in itself. But, like a long digressive essay in the middle of a novel, it is artistically useless.

This conflict between evidence and interpretation is the great strategic difficulty of biography. The hardest tactical problem is that of time. A narrative, a mass of letters, a series of conversations do not in themselves give the sensation of time passing; still less do they convey the complex way in which time is experienced – that strange mixture of continuity, memory, anticipation, routine and surprise. Everybody knows that time seems to run fast or slow according to the nature of the experience; and everybody has moments when the past seems to be relived. Everybody dreams and broods and hopes. But mediocre biographies never capture this aspect of life. As a rule, they start their subject out on his steady progress through the years; they may skip and they may concentrate attention on events of special importance. But they do not show his memories and regrets. The great biographies – and it is one of their most obvious distinguishing marks – show

A lifetime burning in every moment.[1]

The second great tactical difficulty of the biographer lies in his own personal relationship to his subject. The majority of nineteenth-century biographies were written by people to whom the subject had been intimately known. Many were written by wives, sons or daughters or close relations; and many more were written by disciples of the dead man. How far should this be allowed to appear? The second part of this book will analyse the effects of this close personal involvement in particular cases. Speaking generally, we may say that there is a paradox here. The formal style of biographical writing which prevailed during much of our period encouraged suppression of the author's feelings. But we find that the more the feelings are suppressed the more obvious they are, and the more they tend to inhibit a detached view of the subject. Thus (to take an extreme case) Mrs Kingsley speaks of the birth of her own child thus: 'His

[1] T. S. Eliot: East Coker, section v.

youngest daughter, Mary St Leger, was born in June, and the day following he resumes his letters to Mr Ludlow. . . .'[1]

One is tempted to ask, how could a woman so suppress all her own memories, sufferings, hopes and fears about one of the most intense experiences of her life? She must have been a true Roman matron, and her book will be cold and unfeeling. Not at all; the book is one of the most emotional, and most ardently partisan of all the many records of wifely special pleading. But Froude, who presents himself as one of Carlyle's friends, and records private conversations the two had, achieves in the end a wonderfully detached, and in some ways shocking, portrait of the man he so profoundly admired. The true artistic detachment is achieved, not by suppressing the feelings, but by first giving them full play, and then bringing the disinterested intelligence to bear upon them.

One difficulty caused by the author's personal knowledge is particularly awkward. Almost always, the biographer is younger than his subject, and cannot have known him when young. The better he knew him in old age, the harsher is the contrast between mere evidence about the early years and haunting memories of later years. The more vivid the memory, the more brilliant its recreation, the bleaker the contrast; so it is, that Boswell, perhaps our greatest biographer of all, is peculiarly unsuccessful in the handling of this intractable problem.

In his biography of Leslie Stephen, Maitland quoted Ruskin's words in *Fors Clavigera*:

> The little pig was comforting to me because he was wholly content to be a little pig; and Mr Leslie Stephen is in a certain degree exemplary and comforting to me, because he is wholly content to be Mr Leslie Stephen; while I am miserable because I am always wanting to be something else than I am.[2]

We need not consider here whether Ruskin was right or wrong about Stephen. But the general question is perhaps the most exacting of all the biographer's problems. The tension between

---

[1] *Charles Kingsley: His Letters and Memories of his Life*, edited by his wife, 1884, p. 135.

[2] Maitland: *Leslie Stephen*, p. 258.

aim and personality can be seen as a constantly searing force, as in Froude's view of Carlyle, or as slight, as in Morley's view of Gladstone. But, in any case, it is the element that binds the everyday to the pattern of a whole life. General aims change slowly or not at all; personality is always revealing new facets, as the light of everyday experience falls here or there.

Finally, the biographer is left with the difficulty that any interpretation, however well-chosen, is over-simple. There is always something not accounted for. Perhaps the most difficult question of all is this: when we say a man acts out of character, do we mean that the character we have imputed to him is thus shown to be a slightly inaccurate version? Or do we mean that on certain rare occasions a man can act contrary to his character as it really is? Whatever the right answer to these questions may be, they are questions which the great biographers, like the great novelists, insistently force us to ask.

2

SKETCH OF A TRADITION

❀

Almost one hundred years separate Southey's *Nelson* (1813)
from Ward's *Newman* (1912); and to summarise the history of a
major literary form over such a period is a formidable task.
Formidable, but not hopeless, as it would be with poetry or the
novel. It is not hopeless because all variations can be seen within
a common frame of reference. Biography changed, but general
assumptions about its nature varied little. The student who
attempted to summarise the course of biography from 1900 to
1940 would confront difficulties not encountered in the present
task.

Certain features change hardly at all. There is a persistent
attempt to establish heroism. Standards of candour varied; the
scope of forbidden topics expanded and contracted. Some of the
heroes, like Nelson at the hands of Southey or Carlyle at the
hands of Froude, came in for shrewd and even stern criticism.
But the assumption remained that the fundamental reason for
writing a man's life was that he was admirable. Then there was,
throughout the period, a universal trust in documents. The
books are long because there is so much written evidence, and
selective processes are suspect. There is a paradox here, of
course. In one sense, twentieth-century lives are more inclusive.
One is no longer disposed, in reading them, to wonder how the
brothels avoided bankruptcy. But the omissions of the nineteenth century were determined by general public standards of
taste and reticence; these apart, the biographer felt bound to
include as much as he possibly could. And, while it was an age of
respect for documents, it was also an age when documents
tended towards the voluminous. Long letters were the rule, and
an extraordinary proportion of them were kept. The most
admired of all biographers was Boswell; but for most of his

nineteenth-century followers one half of his example proved much easier to follow than the other. Boswell had given thorough documentation, with many letters *in extenso,* interspersed with detailed records of living conversation. The first needed only conscientious industry; the second needed a unique combination of opportunity, genius and memory. In the circumstances, the failure to reproduce the Boswell formula was predictable.

All the same, it is doubtful if the implications of this half-following of Boswell were fully perceived. Obviously, it led to less intimacy and liveliness. Less obviously, it imposed certain unintended biases. The time when a man writes fewest letters is his boyhood; in his early childhood he writes none at all. The time when the lowest proportion of his letters is kept is the early time before his talents are known or his future fame suspected. Conscientious zeal for documents led the biographers, unwittingly, to the construction of top-heavy works. We learn very fully what a man thought between fifty and sixty when his attitudes changed little, and hardly anything of what he thought between ten and twenty when they changed much. One of the most intelligent and interesting of the many lives written by wives, Mrs Creighton's life of Mandell Creighton (1904), consists of more than 900 pages. On p. 7 we have already reached his seventeenth year, or well over a quarter of his total life-span.

This lack cannot be ascribed, as it might be in the eighteenth and earlier centuries, to a simple disbelief in the importance of childhood experience. We are dealing here with a period when the cult of the child flourished mightily. An age in which Wordsworth was the idol of the intellectuals, and Dickens of the crowd, can only have been keenly sensitive to the grandeur, the pathos and the comedy of childhood. An age of educational reform must be an age of serious inquiry into the principles of moral and intellectual training. Moreover, the contrast with autobiography is particularly striking. Who would hesitate for a moment if offered the choice of reading Mill's account of his years before or after twenty? Documents, of course, are useful in autobiography. But the broad contrast between memory as the source of autobiography and documents as a source of biography imposed another contrast, usually unintended and unnoticed, in the different times of life stressed.

In a sense then, the absence of childhood from the biographies is a fortuitous consequence of the fashionable method of composition. It cannot be ascribed to any undervaluing of the importance of childhood. Over-reliance on documents had another effect too. The process of writing is more deliberate, even in a way more artificial than speech or action. To draw mainly on written evidence involves emphasis upon conscious and deliberate mental activity, and a corresponding failure to emphasise impulse. In the jargon of our century it gives the ego an unfair advantage over the id. But here we are in the presence of a general tendency of the whole period, of all its literature, of all its assumptions about life and conduct. Nineteenth-century biographies, on the whole, and with certain notable exceptions, like Lockhart's *Burns*, describe men who did what they intended to do, men who either were not tempted by stray impulses, or who were successful in rigidly suppressing them. Some caution is advisable here. In any age, it is the exceptional men who are considered worthy to have their lives written; and exceptional men, frequently, are exceptional in their power to exercise the will. Nor should we dismiss too hastily the hypothesis that will-power was, in actual fact, wholly dominant in personality more often in this period than in others. The sense of national greatness, the high sense of destiny, whether religious or secular, which informed so many lives, the very high standards of conduct expected of men aspiring to heroic stature, the intellectual brilliance and moral elevation, especially in the middle period from 1840–90, of parliamentary struggles and of religious controversy – all these and other factors may indeed have meant that an élite possessed stronger powers of will than we easily accept as credible. And yet – and yet, when we have made full allowance for all this, we must be inclined to wonder whether any group of men, taken collectively, were ever so strong and inflexible in purpose as a reading of nineteenth-century biography would suggest.

This is not just a question of whitewashing. If the sudden,

18

unexpected power of sexual impulse and anger is forgotten, so too is the sudden force of moral inspiration. Wordsworth's 'spots of time' and Hopkins's moment of *The Windhover* are just as much absentees as masturbation or violent quarrels. And the absence of the high moments is more damaging, since in the impulses of the flesh men in the mass are much alike; but every moment of ecstasy is unlike every other, and what is uniquely personal is most of all suited to biography.

Even in the acknowledged supremacy of the documentary method, however, there will be occasional times when a significant moment in childhood comes to the biographer's attention. What does he do with it then? Few biographers can have had a more striking opportunity of this kind than Southey in his life of Wesley (1820). He tells how, when Wesley was six years old, the house in which the family lived was burnt down. John, one of eight children, was forgotten in an upper room while the others were rescued; and when his absence was noticed, the stairs had already begun to collapse. There was no time to fetch a ladder and he was rescued through the window by a man standing on the shoulders of another. Southey writes:

> John Wesley remembered this providential deliverance through life with the deepest gratitude. In reference to it he had a house in flames engraved as an emblem under one of his portraits, with these words for a motto, 'Is not this a brand plucked out of the burning?'[1]

And that is all. The whole work is some 700 pages long. The absence of comment derives for us an added piquancy from the fact that the writer is Southey, romantic poet and friend of Wordsworth and Coleridge. Had he never heard that the child is father of the man? What a missed opportunity, we are tempted to cry. And, after all, no straining of the evidence is required to find a connection between the event and Wesley's career as a preacher of salvation and damnation, since the words he used himself, 'a brand plucked from the burning', clearly show that he was aware of it. The phrase was a consecrated one in Methodist preaching, and would immediately be understood as

[1] Robert Southey: *The Life of Wesley* (ed. Maurice Fitzgerald, O.U.P. 1925) I, 11.

having a double reference to release from peril, physical and spiritual.

Naturally, Southey was just as much aware of this as we can be. Why then did he refrain? The salient point is that Wesley himself, tacitly backed here by Southey, saw the event as emblematic, not as formative. And to regard it as formative, that is to say to assert that, if Wesley had not been saved from a fire, he might never have preached about salvation from hell-fire, is soon seen to involve grave intellectual difficulties. Is the whole course of life really determined by a single incident? And, if so, how can we be sure of it when our knowledge of any man's life is so sketchy and uneven? How are we to balance an experience, like Wesley's fire, of which we have record, with another, possibly more significant, of which we have no record? And are we to assert a relation of invariable cause and effect? If so, would we not be well-advised to inquire into all cases of children being saved from dangerous fires? Do they all become famous preachers?

The emblematic view, which Southey adopts, and which most other biographers of the nineteenth century would have adopted here, has the advantage that it does not assert a dubious proposition as if it were a fact. But it does not deny the possibility that a real influence on the future may have been at work. It is an open view; it is poetically suggestive, but (provided that the actual facts are stated correctly) is incapable of being refuted. It preserves the mystery of personality; it preserves the salutary humility of all good biography in the august presence of another soul. Perhaps the theorists of psychological causation are abandoning more than they know.

But behind all this there is a more fundamental difference between the biographers of Southey's century and some (though not all) of the biographers of ours. Ultimately, the difference is a religious one, though it does not always correspond to the religious profession of the writer. Victorian agnostic biographers, like Leslie Stephen, tend to assimilate to Southey's view here; and perhaps some believing Christians of the twentieth century find the psychological causation in which they do not literally believe, a useful working model.

The difference is as difficult to define as it is important. Biographers of all schools, if their work has any value at all, have some general idea of direction or destiny in the life they describe. They all have some sense of a man struggling to achieve something, and of some other forces, separate from his will, at work to help or hinder him. The nineteenth-century biographer, whether Christian or not, inherited and seldom questioned an assumption that these forces could not be summed up simply in physical law and social pressure. There is, almost always, a further idea present, sometimes overtly expressed, sometimes vaguely adumbrated, of spiritual formation by forces beyond man's control, and indeed beyond his full understanding. Each life is felt to have a meaning, an objective meaning to which all interpretation is only a weak approximation. Emblematic events, such as Wesley's fire, are hints towards the meaning of the whole. It is possible to read a good biography as if it were a novel, paying attention to the author's mastery of form. But in the nineteenth century, another process was more common. The biographer himself reads the *evidence* of the life as if it were a novel, and God were the novelist. In that case, the finished biography is more accurately compared to literary criticism; it is a report upon an obscure but momentous work of art.

Opinions will differ about the value and the legitimacy of this procedure for biography. But, obviously, it leaves open a very important choice. Shall the subject be shown as dutifully subservient to the shaping spiritual forces, or shall he be shown as kicking against the pricks? Most people to-day, I imagine, would not hesitate to prefer the second alternative. And I must say that I agree with the prevailing opinion, if I have divined it correctly. The thesis that every man is his own worst enemy has many advantages for biography. It is fruitful in conflict, in drama, in surprise, in irony. But, above all, it is true to experience; and it is equally true whether it is understood in religious or in secular terms. It is true of the soul (always), and it is true of the worldly career (generally). The most serious criticism that can justly be made against the biographers of our period is that they concealed or evaded or forgot this truth. Men, even exceptional men, are not heroes; and you can only show that they are by one of two methods. You can show it, by evading the bitter truth, as most (but not all) biographers of the time were content to do; or you can show it by presenting what is tawdry as admirable, as in Lord Rosebery's maudlin hero-worship of Napoleon.[1]

II

Not all the biographers were hero-worshippers, and the second half of this book will deal with some who were not. Without anticipating, we have here to consider the various types of hero-worship that prevailed.

The first broad distinction to be made is between biographers who took a rosy view of human nature in general, and those who presented their heroes as solitary champions embattled against a hostile world. Many of the less distinguished ecclesiastical lives belong to the first group. Prothero's life of Dean Stanley may be taken as a favourable example, since it is accurate, lucid and readable. A boy such as Stanley was in the year 1832 can only be prevented from rising in the world by disease or sudden death. He was well-born, well-connected, serious, sensible and highly intelligent. A prize pupil under Dr Arnold at Rugby, he is about to become a prize pupil at Balliol. His opinions, formed by Arnold, but modified by a cooler, more detached mental faculty than Arnold could command, are developing in the direction of a decorous Broad Church liberalism. In due course, he will attract the favourable notice of Queen Victoria, and the admiring confidence of statesmen, who like churchmen to be men of the world rather than fanatics, and who are struck by the adroitness of a man who combines the talents of the populariser with entirely genuine pretensions to serious scholarship. In the fulness of time, but not too soon, he will marry Lady Augusta Bruce, a close intimate of the Queen.

The preceding account, I dare say, will appear to have a satirical ring. If so, it is the biographer and not Stanley himself that has attracted the satire. Stanley was a man of real and not

[1] Lord Rosebery: *Napoleon: The Last Phase* (1900).

merely of worldly eminence. He was, as we shall later see, himself a biographer of distinction; and his *Essays on Church and State* are still among the few reliable guides to the complex problems of Victorian religious history. But Prothero's unspoken assumption (and here he stands for many remembered and many forgotten biographers) is that since the world was kind to Stanley, and since Stanley deserved its kindness, the world must be a kind place. And we do not need the sour hindsight of our century to see that this was not so. We can appeal to the classic writers of Stanley's own time, to Newman, to Dickens, and to Ruskin.

Stanley had his being, of course, in a world of scholars and gentlemen; and, since he knew little of the world of *Hard Times*, it would be merely petulant to blame his biographer for omitting it. But Stanley's best friend in youth, and the chief mourner at his funeral, as Prothero duly records, was C. J. Vaughan. Vaughan was, to outward appearance, just such another as Stanley himself – prize pupil at Rugby, devoted admirer of Dr Arnold, headmaster of Harrow while still a young man, clergyman of the Church of England. But Vaughan's life was seared, and his ecclesiastical career halted by an uncontrollable tendency to paederasty, which led to his sudden departure from Harrow.[1]

I am not suggesting for a moment that Prothero's book, which was published while Vaughan was still alive, ought to have contained an exposé of his life. There was no scandal that involved Stanley himself who was, in all probability, just as respectable as Prothero made him out. I am merely using Vaughan's case as an illustration of a very old and very obvious truth, that no amount of intellect, education, wealth, sophistication or earnestness can exempt one of the sons of Adam from his inheritance. One of the reasons why Dr Johnson was a great biographer is that he was never tempted for a moment to forget this. Prothero, typical here of many others, did forget it; and the consequence was often, paradoxically, to reduce the stature for

[1] On Vaughan's public personality, see David Newsome: *Godliness and Good Learning*. On his private torments, see Phyllis Grosskuth: *John Addington Symonds*.

the reader of the heroes being celebrated. In the world of Prothero, it is easy to be good, if you are one of the *right set*; the right set is conceived as a subtle English mixture of class, intelligence, education, seriousness and sound opinions. Dr Johnson knew that it is very difficult indeed to be good whatever set you belong to.[1]

The assumptions exemplified by Prothero can be linked with important features of English national consciousness in the nineteenth century – with insularity, success, world power, the moral superiority of Protestantism and the prestige of Empire. The other assumptions, which turn the hero into a despised or neglected genius, are well seen in the work of Samuel Smiles, with whom a later chapter deals. And these assumptions also are linked with features of national self-consciousness, with the England of political change, technical inventiveness and material progress. Smiles writes in the aftermath of the heady excitement of the Railway Age, of which the great literary monument is *Dombey & Son*.

Different as they are, both sets of assumptions have a common element. They both appeal to the deep-rooted human tendency to smug self-satisfaction.

But it is important to emphasise that, in discussing these two types, we have been dealing with biographers of the second rank. The best and most memorable works fall into neither category;

---

[1] This feeble kind of optimism about the world seems to be particularly common in ecclesiastical biographies. This is intelligible in one sense, since, given talent and industry, the churchman's career was less at the mercy of sudden shifts of fortune, and involved less enmity and conflict, than did those of the politician or capitalist. All the same, it is paradoxical, that Original Sin should be most easily forgotten in writing of men whose professional duty it was to preach a system of doctrine that makes no sense without the basic idea of human corruption. This should be taken as a corrective to the passage earlier in this chapter in which it was suggested that in another respect nineteenth century biography showed a greater religious sensibility than that of the twentieth. Twentieth century biographers have not always chosen to call human corruption Original Sin; but under one name or another they have generally taken account of it. And the corruption of human nature is, in its essence, a religious idea. This should protect us from light-heartedly adopting the often parroted (and largely baseless) *idée reçue* that the nineteenth century was very religious and the twentieth is very secular.

and frequently they avoid it by adopting the idea of the flawed hero. Of this kind are Southey's *Nelson*, Lockhart's *Burns* (1828) and *Scott* (1838), Cottle's account of Coleridge (1847), and some others.

But this group is not homogeneous. It divides very clearly into two. Southey's *Nelson* and Lockhart's *Scott* present their subjects as men of heroic stature, who are truly admirable. The flaw is seen as inseparable from the man's peculiar impressive quality. Scott was, in Lockhart's view, a man of literary genius, who was at the same time honest, generous, loyal, forgiving and, above all, lovable. Moreover, Lockhart, partly through his own skill, and partly because he was fortunate in the nature of the man with whom he was dealing, thoroughly convinces us that Scott really possessed these qualities. His fatal flaw, financial irresponsibility, was inextricably linked with these fine capacities. It is a flaw, but not, strictly speaking, a weakness. Without it, Scott would not have been what he was, and what he was, on the whole, was great and admirable. In one wonderful passage, Lockhart synthesises all these ideas in a single picture, as Scott leads his guests up a winding and dangerous stair to gaze out in the moonlight over the broad lands which he so fatally desired to possess, and to fill with contented tenants. Here the whole Scott is present, the generous host, the high-spirited gentleman, the boyish adventurer, the romantic dreamer, the man attached to soil and roots, the landlord, the potential bankrupt.[1]

Rather similarly in a very much shorter work, Southey had shown Nelson's love of glory as at one and the same time the essence of his greatness and of his weakness. Thus at Trafalgar, he would not protect himself from French snipers by wearing an ordinary coat over his distinctive admiral's uniform and medals. And:

> he consented at last to let the *Leviathan* and the *Téméraire*, which were sailing abreast of the *Victory*, be ordered to pass ahead. Yet even here the last infirmity of this noble mind was indulged; for these ships could not pass ahead if the *Victory* continued to carry all her sail; and so far was Nelson from shortening sail, that it was evident he took

[1] Lockhart: *Scott* IV, 190.

pleasure in pressing on, and rendering it impossible for them
to obey his own orders.[1]

What would you? Southey asks in effect. The man who would
not have behaved so illogically here would not have disobeyed
orders at a vital moment, and would not have had the daring to
win at Copenhagen.

Flawed heroes of this sort make no exception to what was said
above about the favouritism enjoyed by the ego at the expense
of the id. For these flaws are *willed* flaws, composite parts of
formed characters. Scott and Nelson suffered, as their biographers present them, from an excess of ambition, energy and
will.

Coleridge and Burns, obviously, offer very different opportunities and difficulties to the biographer. In each the will failed
to control impulse; intermittently in Coleridge, and habitually in
Burns, the id triumphed. Lockhart's *Burns* (1828) was, of course,
written before the extreme sexual reticence of the mid-century
had become customary; and I go on in a moment to deal with the
wider question of changing standards of reticence. What concerns us here is not so much that Lockhart does not evade words
like *brothel* when his narrative requires them. It is rather his
general interpretation of character. His defence of Burns's
essential decency is robust: 'of all Burns's failings, it may be
safely asserted that there was more in his history to account and
apologise for them, than can be alleged in regard to almost any
other great man's imperfections.'[2]

In his paradoxical way, then, Lockhart is following the general
practice of presenting his hero as admirable. He had three
choices open to him. He could have ignored the evidence for the
dissipated conduct of Burns. All the indications are that he did
not wish to do this. But, in any case, it would have been an
ineffective procedure, since Burns's brother had already published (in Lockhart's words) 'a book, in which almost everything
that should be (and some things that never should have been)
told'[3] had been included.

The second course Lockhart could have taken would have

[1] Southey: *Nelson* (Hutchinson's Standard Lives) p. 323.
[2] J. G. Lockhart: *Burns*, p. 186.   [3] Op. cit., vi.

involved a rigid separation between work and life. 'He was a poor sort of *man*, but, in spite of that, he was a great poet.' Lockhart considered, and here one can only agree with him, that Burns was not the right man for such treatment. His poetry was too personal, too impulsive; and in Lockhart's view, was apt to be at its best when its moral content was most dubious.

The third choice, then, to present the poet, lecher, drinker and serious moralist in Burns as all of a piece became inevitable. But this decision still left open different possibilities. To justify Burns's conduct altogether would have been inconsistent with Lockhart's own character and moral conviction. But he could have presented the sensual failings simply as weaknesses incident to human nature. This, perhaps, is what Johnson would have done. Lockhart goes further than this in two ways. He suggests that the poetic temperament gives special temptations to, and therefore, special excuses for, sensuality. His judgment, though certainly not more humane than that of Johnson in the partly similar case of Savage, is actually milder. And the reason for this is interesting. Lockhart was altogether a cooler and less generous man than Johnson; and he had not been a personal friend of Burns as Johnson had of Savage. So that natural expectations are confounded here, until one remembers certain fundamental changes, between the time of Johnson and that of Lockhart, about what a poet is. Johnson assumes, admirably and rightly as it seems to me, that since one is a man before one is any particular kind of man, so moral principles apply to one's basic human status, not to one's function in society, or one's natural bent. So, when one has performed the very difficult task of arriving at a view of fornication or drunkenness which is both moral and humane, which makes all due and no undue allowances, *then* it applies to anybody. To plead that a man was a poet is entirely beside the point. Lockhart, sober Scots citizen and family man that he was, is yet influenced by the current of thought that issued in phrases like 'unacknowledged legislators of the world.' A poet cannot quite be judged by ordinary standards.

The second way in which Lockhart goes beyond Johnson is in blaming the society that adulated Burns, and then neglected him, that invited him to grand social occasions without giving him anything serious to do or any money to live upon. Johnson, too, is severe upon some people who did not treat Savage well; but he would never have maintained that any of these could be held responsible for fornication or drunkenness, which concern only a man's personal moral identity, and his duty to God. By comparison with Johnson, then, Lockhart is here seen to be very slightly sentimental; and he is detracting from his hero's dignity and moral freedom. If you choose to fornicate under a hedge, you must take the responsibility on yourself; it is no use saying that you would not have done it if the Edinburgh drawing-rooms had been kinder. Not that Burns would have said any such thing, one imagines; but Lockhart very faintly insinuates such an excuse for his hero.

This admitted, Lockhart's achievement here is notable. He has given a sympathetic and intelligible picture of a man of genius whose will was incapable of mastering random impulse. This is a very common human type, among men of great talent and among men of no talent. And, as we have seen, it is a type generally neglected by the biographers of a whole century. It is striking, too, that the same man is the biographer of Burns and Scott. The contrast between the two books can only enhance our sense of his versatility and his fairness. The formula of 'id defeating ego' is appropriate to the case of Burns; the formula 'flawed hero' is appropriate to Scott. There is an underlying harmony between Lockhart's strategy and his detail; and it is such works that endure.

Cottle had a different problem. He was fortunate, perhaps, that Coleridge's vices were not sexual, for the twenty years or so that intervened between Lockhart's *Burns* and the appearance of Cottle's book in 1847 saw a remarkable revolution in agreed standards of literary decency. All the same, Coleridge's weaknesses were humiliating enough. In part, Cottle reverts to the old idea of the moral *exemplum*.

He asks:

Is it expedient; is it lawful; to give publicity to Mr Coleridge's practice of inordinately taking opium? which to a certain extent, at one part of his life, inflicted on a heart naturally cheerful, the stings of conscience, and sometimes almost the horrors of despair? . . .

And he answers:

if he could now speak from his grave, retaining his earthly, benevolent solicitude for the good of others, with an emphasis that penetrated the heart, he would doubtless utter, 'Let my example be a warning.'[1]

In part the difference of treatment by Lockhart and Cottle is determined by the nature of the two cases. Burns is seen as the sort of man who drinks and fornicates, because his will is weak; and this weakness of will is a salient point in the whole poetic personality. Cottle sees Coleridge's weakness as less inherent in his nature, more accidental. Coleridge might never have tried laudanum. If his medical history had permitted him to avoid severe physical pain, he probably would not have tried it. Cottle was no profound psychologist; he was in every way a less thoughtful man than Lockhart. And so, his portrait lacks the tragic grandeur of Lockhart's *Burns,* and the reader may be reluctant to believe that the course of a great man's life was determined so much by chance. What was it in Coleridge that made him a victim to a dangerous experience which other men met coolly? Indeed, it is important to remember how usual a medical prescription laudanum was in the nineteenth century.[2] Some strong characters, like William Wilberforce, became addicted, as a result of medical treatment, but never increased the dose, or suffered any adverse moral consequences.[3] Coleridge, according to Cottle, became a liar, though his natural love of truth was exceptionally strong. His life work was only half-done. But Cottle is able to comfort himself and the reader with the reflection that Coleridge died penitent, and even happy, and is able to quote a moving letter to a godchild, written very near the end, in support of this.

With both Cottle and Lockhart, the reader feels that they are

---

[1] Joseph Cottle: *Reminiscences of Samuel Taylor Coleridge and Robert Southey,* 1847, p. 348–9. There is a useful facsimile of this edition by the Lime Tree Bower Press 1970.

[2] On this, and related points, see Alethea Hayter: *Opium and the Romantic Imagination.*

[3] R. I. & S. Wilberforce: *The Life of William Wilberforce,* 1838, i, 173–4.

performing a duty reluctantly, when they show the hero's weakness. It may be that they have not always been read in the spirit that they wrote. For in later times, many would come to feel with Yeats's admonition to Katharine Tynan: 'Remember it is the stains of earth colour that make man differ from man and give interest to biography.'[1]

An even rarer case than these is that of the *misguided* hero – not the man betrayed by what is false within, like Burns, but the man who, with deep seriousness and at great personal sacrifice, aimed at a false goal. At first sight the rarity of this type seems surprising. It is so easy to think of cases. The high Anglican, thinking of Newman, the Liberal Unionist thinking of Gladstone, must surely have taken some such view? No doubt; but as a rule such thoughts did not lead to the writing of biography, since, as we have seen, the celebration of the hero was throughout our period its constant aim. But one notable, and still underrated, author, wrote two such books separated by thirty years. Mrs Oliphant's life of Edward Irving appeared in 1862, and her life of her kinsman Laurence Oliphant in 1892. The two stories had something in common. Irving and Oliphant were both religious enthusiasts, whom the established churches and sects could not satisfy. But Irving was a leader, and personally founded the church known as Catholic Apostolic, which exists to-day 140 years after his early death in 1834. His story had an added interest for the Victorians, and for us, because of his close association with Carlyle, when both were very young, and because of the two men's rivalry for the hand of Jane Welsh. Laurence Oliphant's religious enthusiasm made him an ardent disciple of another man, whose strange sect has left no trace (so far as I know) upon the American scene. Mrs Oliphant's anger against this leader, Harris, was very bitter. In the preface to the second edition, which appeared in the same year as the first, she wrote, commenting on attacks on her original account, that Harris was a 'spiritual tyrant'. And she went on to speak of:

> disciples whose argument is simply that all things he has
> done are right, that all his motives are pure, that Laurence

[1] *Letters of W. B. Yeats*, edited by Allan Wade, 1954, p. 155.

Oliphant having been in the later part of his life rebellious to the Master's authority, was righteously, he and his wife, swept out of his path and given over to desolation – arguments to which, as I conceive it, there is no answer, since those who can put them forth are beyond the limits of reason.

Oliphant, in his biographer's view, was betrayed by his virtues, not his vices. His idealism, his high ascetic character, his childlike trust made him a victim of a monstrous fraud. The case of Oliphant is interesting but tantalising. Here, one feels for once, is an entirely different kind of man; he cannot be assimilated to any recognisable type of the Victorian hero. There are hints that Oliphant's craven submission to Harris was occasioned by remorse following sexual indulgence. Harris's system permitted marriage provided the approval of the community was sought and obtained. But husband and wife must live together without sexual relations.

On this she writes:

That the relation ought to be strictly Platonic, to use a comprehensible phrase – a union as of brother and sister, though distinguished by an absolute oneness of spirit, peculiar to the 'sacred tie', 'the most sacred of ordinances', in which, as they believed, the being of the dual Godhead was displayed and imitated – was, I believe, this strange creed. That it was not always consistently carried out was, of course, inevitable. What is much more wonderful is that it *was* sometimes carried out with unflinching resolution, neither the most tender affection, nor the usual circumstances of confidential intimacy between married persons affecting the self-imposed rule. *It is not a question which can be entered into further.* . . .[1]

The last italicised words lead us on to the whole question of reticence and propriety in the biography of our period. And they have a sad ring; for, however much we may admire decorum and restraint, we must see that the point that cannot be discussed is the very point here of most intense biographical interest. A writer whose knowledge of the human heart was considerable,

[1] Margaret Oliphant: *Laurence Oliphant*, 1892, p. 214, my italics.

as her best novels show, is handicapping herself in the full deployment of the biographer's art.

We must now attempt some assessment of the whole period in this matter. In rough terms, the course of the years between 1813 and 1914 can be seen as a parabola of prudence and restraint. It is at its height from about 1840 to 1875. It is less marked before and after these dates. For the prevailing ethos of biographical decency before 1840, Moore's *Byron* (1829) is a good example to take. Byron still retains for us the special interest of a unique case; and it is not difficult to recreate the breathless curiosity about his career that existed when Moore's book appeared about five years after his death in 1824. Here was a man of European celebrity as a poet, whose life was admittedly scandalous, but also, in part, impenetrably obscure. Immensely attractive to women, he had proved unable to persuade his wife to live with him, though she was evidently untouched by passion for any other person, had lived apart from him in chaste seclusion, and had refused to explain the true reason for the separation. Moreover, some documents had been solemnly burned after Byron's death as unfit for the world. Moore was an intimate friend of Byron, who had seen him in the penultimate period of his life in Italy (prior to the brief, final Greek episode) about which English curiosity was strongest.

We are not here concerned with the main lines of Moore's interpretation of Byron's character, except insofar as they relate to the general questions of reticence and decency; but one part of his judgment of Byron is relevant. Moore took Byron, mistakenly as it may seem to us, as a true romantic. The eighteenth-century-style nobleman, the devoted admirer of Pope, the comic-obscene rhymer of *Don Juan*, are muted presences in Moore's very long book. To some extent, then, his refusal to give prominence to Byron's love of ribaldry is in keeping with the main lines of interpretation, instead of being simply dictated by good taste.

When this allowance is made, we find that, except on one single point, Moore is very outspoken about facts. He is not afraid to quote Byron's account of the moral condition of Milan, of 1 November 1816, which includes a sketch of a mother and son, believed to be of the 'Theban dynasty' – that is to say, practising incest like Oedipus and Jocasta.[1] On another occasion, he has a highly-coloured, and surely exaggerated, description of a theatre, divided into professional tarts, on one side of the proscenium arch, and amateurs on the other.[2]

Nor is he afraid to quote Byron's more outrageously flippant remarks, such as: 'Not a divorce stirring, but a good many in embryo in the shape of marriages' (12 June 1815).[3]

The subject about which he is reticent is homosexuality; or perhaps, he is not simply reticent, but rather puzzled and uncertain. It is not always possible to decide just what he really thinks himself. Thus he makes reference to an episode when a girl was made to dress in boy's clothes, without indicating whether he thinks it very significant.[4] He quotes a passage that seems to hint at the Lesbian temperament of Lady Eleanor Butler, but without making it clear whether he himself understands it in this way. These are small points, but Byron's feeling for Lord Clare at Harrow, and the extreme emotion with which he encountered him unexpectedly in Italy many years after, present a real challenge to the biographer, which he is hesitant of accepting. It may well be that he provides evidence which induces us to go beyond any interpretation that he himself would have countenanced, in an age when the subject was little discussed in print.

This apart, Moore's principle is that almost anything may be said, provided it is phrased with a certain delicacy, and (very important) provided it did not wound the reputation of individuals, especially English ladies.

Over delicate phrasing, Moore was sometimes in a dilemma, since a large part of the book consists of the letters and speeches of Byron, who despised delicacy of phrase. Still, he applies the principle when he can. Thus he tells how one of Byron's plebeian Italian mistresses was very pious, and crossed herself whenever she heard the church bells. Moore made an omission here of a passage which indicated that she did this even if she was in bed with Byron at the time.[5] This is delicacy, not falsification. The

---

[1] Moore: *Byron*, 2nd ed. 1833, Vol. II, p. 271.   [2] Moore: op. cit., I, 583.
[3] Op. cit., II, 152.   [4] Op. cit., I, 184–7.   Moore: op. cit., II, 438.

reader of Moore's text would not be surprised to hear that she behaved in this way; but he might feel that he would rather not be told.

This is a small point. Much more important, both in itself and the contrast presented with the mid-Victorian ethos, is the attitude to personalities. Moore's sense of delicacy is a development of the idea of personal dignity, not of an idea of moral soundness. Like any gentleman of his time, he had to consider the personal dignity of other gentlemen. Aristocracies are always touchy; and duelling was only just dying out of the world. More pressing even than this was the obligation of chivalry. Most of Byron's secrets concerned women, and many concerned English ladies, the sisters and social equals of the people one met at the club, or had known at school. A gentleman must be careful of a lady's honour, even when she had none to lose.

Such an attitude, of course, rests on various unexamined assumptions of national and class superiority. Moore does not conceal these; so that when Byron finally departs for Italy, and the virtue and reputation of English ladies ceases to be at risk, Moore shows obvious relief. Italy is a country where social morals are less strict, where a woman can hold her place in society even though a known adulteress.[1] Moreover, most of Byron's Italian loves were low-born girls, who perhaps could not read, and certainly did not know English. They would suffer nothing from anything Moore wrote about them in a far country and in a foreign language. Granted his assumptions, Moore's logic here was sound enough, though it may conceal a touch of contempt for foreigners. But, obviously, the case of Byron's last mistress, Teresa Guiccioli, was a different matter.[2]

It was different in two ways. First, she was noble, and engaged Moore's respect as a born lady with a position in society, just as much as earlier English participants in Byron's drama. Second, and more important, there was between her and Byron a bond that showed signs of permanence at the time of Byron's death. Moore's handling is delicate; he does not name her, referring to her as Mme G., though many of his English readers must probably have known her name. And he makes a very sharp

[1] Moore, op. cit., II, 273.   [2] See Iris Origo: *The Last Attachment*, 1949.

moral distinction, similar to that made in Shelley's letters about Byron,[1] between the reckless dissipation of the first phase of Byron's Italian life, and the sober, quasi-marital, devotion of his life with Teresa Guiccioli, whose husband had, in Moore's view, forfeited all claim to her loyalty or even forbearance.

It is not easy to disentangle the strands of varying assumptions within Moore's total attitude. He was not deeply reflective, nor a profound moralist. In his view of Teresa, there is a subtle mixture of class respect, sentimental fondness, and a slightly tainted moralism. Byron and she were so truly domestic together that it was pleasant to fancy that they were as good as married, though, in fact, each was married to somebody else. Like many good-hearted men of the world, Moore adheres in general to strict moral principles, but makes certain allowances for the pressures of the world; pity, sympathy, realism, sentiment, chivalry may combine in various unknown proportions to determine them.

Elusive as Moore is in some ways, yet the main lines of the contrast between his attitude and that prevailing thirty years later is clear. Moore has regard in his own way both for morality and for decency, but his fundamental canon rests on the delicacy of personal relations in a limited élite society, where everybody knew everybody. The difference brought by thirty years can best be illustrated thus: in 1829, Moore would rather have referred without names to some gross or unnatural physical acts than have said that a named lady had been unfaithful to her husband. Thirty years later *topics* had become unmentionable; the moral welfare of the reading public was the issue rather than the personal dignity of individuals.

The mid-Victorian ethos of decency is a subject full of pitfalls; to judge by the general run of comments on it to-day, it is especially easy to misunderstand. The essential thing to grasp about it is that it was something felt and lived by, not just a hypocritical façade. Let us take an instance from a review of a novel published in 1848:

But there still remains the question – important to all Art
that addresses itself to the laudable business of scourging

[1] *Letters of P. B. Shelley*, ed. Frederick L. Jones, Vol. II, esp. pp. 58 and 363.

the foibles and criminalities of mankind – is there any den
of vice so utterly depraved, any round of intercourse so
utterly hollow and deceitful, that there is not some
redeeming feature lurking somewhere, under rags or tinsel?
This revolting reflex of society is literally true enough. But it
does not shew us the whole truth.[1]

The book upon which this passage comments is *Vanity Fair*.
It is hard, and yet necessary, if we are not to abandon all effort
of historical imagination, to realise that this was how its mild
satire, its sugary sentiment, its careful reticences, really did
strike this reviewer, and very many other readers. A similar surprise awaits us when we find *The Mill on the Floss* (of all books)
described as 'dreary and immoral'.[2]

But, of course, like all dominant standards of moral sensibility,
Victorian decency had its half-hearted and unwilling adherents,
as well as the great mass of people for whom it was simply the air
they breathed. And perhaps the most useful Victorian figure to
set against Moore is one of these; since the willing adherents of
the prevailing ethos will be slow to give us any idea of what they
are concealing. Leslie Stephen was born in 1832, and so had no
memory of the time before Victorian decency became *de rigeur*.
He prided himself on his love of truth; he gave up his Anglican
orders, and consequently his academic career at Cambridge, on
the point of conscience, since he ceased to be a believer. His own
most notable biographical work (apart from his editorship of the
Dictionary of National Biography) was his life of his brother
Fitzjames Stephen (1895). Fitzjames was a notable criminal
jurist, and his life and writings, especially his *Liberty, Equality,
Fraternity* (1873) were characterised by an outspoken iconoclasm.
The idols of the age, especially progressive and optimistic ones,
were the objects of his relentless scorn. Leslie Stephen did not
always agree, but he heartily approved the outspoken candour
of his brother. Leslie's own *Essays on Freethinking and Plain-
speaking* (1873) are almost offensive in their pride of candour in
attacking accepted religious ideas.

[1] Fraser's Magazine, Sept. 1848. Quoted in *Thackeray: The Critical Heritage*,
edited by Geoffrey Tillotson and Donald Hawes, 1968.
[2] Cf. Gordon Haight: *George Eliot: A biography*, 1968, p. 327n.

Now this is the man, who, in the following year, wrote as editor of the *Cornhill Magazine* to Thomas Hardy, whose *Far From the Madding Crowd* was being published there, as follows:

I have ventured to leave out a line or two in the last batch of proofs from an excessive prudery of which I am ashamed; but one is forced to be absurdly particular. May I suggest that Troy's seduction of the young woman will require to be treated in a gingerly fashion when, as I suppose must be the case, he comes to be exposed to his wife? I mean that the thing must be stated but that the words must be careful – excuse this wretched shred of concession to popular stupidity; but I am a slave. . . .[1]

Stephen's distaste for the current ethos of decency seems plain enough here; yet the passage does not represent fully the complexity of his attitude. Like many people, who dissent from the spirit of the age, he was influenced by it more than he knew.

When this happens, even clear-sighted men become confused; they are inwardly uncertain how far to carry their opposition to the *Zeitgeist*. Stephen's confusion appeared most obviously in his essay on the *Browning Love Letters*. These were not published until 1899, when our parabola of decorum was already well into its downward curve. Here, of course, the issue was different from the one about which Stephen had written so anxiously to Hardy a quarter of a century before. Fanny Robin's had been a sad and sordid little affair; but here Stephen was dealing with the written record of something he deeply approved and admired, a passionate and highminded monogamous union, lasting for life. Yet he is distinctly uneasy. One part of his mind is playing with the idea of decency, so that he is inclined almost to assimilate interested readers (including himself) to Peeping Toms. Another part is wondering whether love at this high level is not too *sacred* for the public gaze, even though ten years had passed since Browning's death, and nearly forty since the marriage had been ended by the death of Mrs Browning. The result is (and this is most unusual for Stephen) that the essay is thoroughly incoherent; and he takes refuge in a paradox to which no real

[1] Leslie Stephen (letter of 12 March 1874). Quoted in Laurence Lerner and John Holmstrom: *Thomas Hardy and his readers*, 1968, p. 24.

meaning can be attached: 'The best books to read . . . are the books that ought never to have been written.'[1]

In general, Stephen is fairly typical of independent intellectual opinion among his contemporaries in exhibiting a kind of petulant docility in the face of the public demand for decency at any cost. Thus the reviewer of Hardy's *The Return of the Native* (1878) in *The Athenaeum* wrote:

> Eustacia Vye belongs essentially to the class of which Madame Bovary is the type; and it is impossible not to regret, *since this is a type which English opinion will not allow a novelist to depict in its completeness,* that Mr Hardy should have wasted his powers in giving what after all is an imperfect and to some extent misleading view of it.[2]

But Stephen's idea of the sacredness of married love, though confused as he presents it, should not be dismissed as an excuse for prudery simply. Maitland, another very honest man, in his treatment of Stephen's own married happiness, is equally reticent.[3] And many years earlier, Carlyle had taken a similar position on a matter not sexual at all, when he wrote of his friend John Sterling:

> Four days before his death there are some stanzas of verse for me, written as if in star-fire and immortal tears; which are among my sacred possessions, to be kept for myself alone.[4]

Naturally, it was the men of strongest sensibility to whom such reactions were natural. Their genuine feeling merged with the evasive falsities of the crowd, often unnoticed and undistinguished.

But sometimes, of course, what we are apt to mistake for prudery was a simple absence of curiosity. Hallam Tennyson's account of his father, the poet, provides a notable example.[5] The point that would be seized upon by a later biographer is this, 'What was the nature of Tennyson's feeling for Arthur Hallam, and what were his first experiences of bereavement in

[1] Leslie Stephen: *Studies of a Biographer*, III.
[2] Lerner & Holmstrom, op. cit., p. 44, my italics.
[3] Frederick W. Maitland: *Life and Letters of Leslie Stephen*, 1906.
[4] Carlyle: *Life of John Sterling*, 1851, Part III, chapter VI.
[5] Hallam, Lord Tennyson: *Tennyson, A Memoir*, 2 vols., 1897.

1833 and 1834?' No such question concerns the son. To him it was simple. The two men were close friends; Tennyson was upset when Hallam died, and eventually he published a poem about it. There is not a trace of defensiveness or concealment in this attitude; there is nothing to hide because there is nothing of interest to say. His handling of Tennyson's marriage, which assuredly contained no dark secrets or unorthodox behaviour, and no infidelities on either side, is in marked contrast. He writes:

> I have not felt able to include the many passages which would show the intensity of feeling expressed in these letters, but have burnt them according to my father's directions.[1]

But we are dealing here, of course, with a rather unimaginative writer, who would probably never have written a biography if he had not been the son of a great and much-revered father.

This example illustrates the student's greatest difficulty in dealing with biography in its most reticent period. How much really is reticence, how much is concealment amounting to falsification, and how much is simple unawareness of what has been omitted?

Often the answer can only be a guess. An intriguing problem of this kind arises in Hallam Tennyson's account of the marriage of the Prince of Wales. Tennyson, as Poet Laureate, had written a poem *Welcome to Alexandra*, which was first published in *The Times* on 10 March, 1863. The circumstances of the marriage were sordid enough. The Prince was 21, and was being hastily married off to forestall further dissipation. Given his character, the marriage was most unlikely to have the desired result; a detached observer at the time, had there been one, would probably have predicted what actually followed, a lifetime of callous marital infidelity for the Prince, and uncomplaining endurance for the Princess. And, of course, 1863 was a time which cannot in general be accused of treating marital infidelity lightly. But the charm of royalty covers a multitude of sins. Hallam quotes a letter to his father from a lady of the royal household, Lady Augusta Bruce, who later in the same year was to marry A. P. Stanley, the biographer of Arnold.

[1] Hallam Tennyson, op. cit., I, p. 169.

She wrote:

Dear Mr Tennyson,

Last night, a few minutes after the advent of the lovely Bride, while I felt my heart still glowing from seeing the look of inexpressible brightness, confidence, and happiness, with which she alighted on the threshold of Windsor Castle and threw herself into the arms of her new family. . . .[1]

And more, much more to the same effect. How much did she know? How much did she deceive herself and more important, how much did Tennyson know, and what did he really think and how much did Hallam Tennyson know or guess of the answer to these questions?

Such questions must be asked, but certainty in answering them may be impossible. We know that Tennyson combined a deeply sincere belief in the marriage bond, with a firm adherence to monarchy. We also know, though we could not learn it from his son's book, that he was, in male company, a coarse, salty man of the world; and among his favourite anecdotes were ribaldries about royal personages. Which part of his nature would have been uppermost here? We do not know.

On the other hand, when the biographer[2] of the eighth Duke of Devonshire, better known to political history as Lord Hartington, speaks of his marriage to the Duchess of Manchester, we know what to think. The duchess had lived openly as his mistress for many years, when at last legal marriage became feasible after the death of the lady's husband. This was generally known. In speaking of the marriage as if there was nothing unusual about it, the biographer can hardly have been intending to deceive. Right at the end of our period, we are back with a more dignified and polite version of the standards of Moore's *Byron*. One does not, as Bertie Wooster was still saying many years later, bandy a woman's name.

[1] Hallam Tennyson: op. cit., i, 489.
[2] Bernard Holland: *Devonshire* ii, 213–14.

3

THE DEATH SCENE

❖

If a man's life is seen as a work of art shaped by forces outside his control, and partly outside his knowledge,[1] then the moment of death has a peculiar significance. Not only is it the last line of the play, the long-prepared aesthetic climax, but it is the moment of launching into another world, mysterious but unavoidable. At the moment of death a man is nearest to that other world; possibly (as it was natural though not wholly reasonable to suppose) he even has a glimpse of it. Perhaps his last words indicate his future.

Now, when these two ideas — the curtain line, and the adumbration of the future — are explicitly stated, they are seen to be distinct. It is clear, too, that they may conflict, as in the famous epitaph:

> Betwixt the stirrup and the ground
> Mercy I asked, mercy I found.

Inconsequent and unconvincing as the end of the play; granted Christian assumptions, admirable, heartening and entirely feasible as a prelude to eternity.

At first sight it seems odd how seldom this distinction is clearly found in the biographies of our period. Most of them write death scenes which seem, without any exact intention, vaguely designed to fulfil both needs. Sometimes a fitting end to the life is sought for its own sake, and adumbrations of eternity are treated as beyond the proper range of biography, as in Southey's *Nelson*, where the dying hero's mind strays back to Lady Hamilton and to their child, back also to naval duty well-performed. Yet even this is not an absolutely clear case, since he also says to the chaplain, 'Doctor, I have *not* been a

[1] See chapter 2.

41

great sinner.'[1] Many secular-looking death scenes in our period
will be found to have some such shadowy spiritual content as
this. Sometimes, and more commonly after 1880, as agnosticism
became fully respectable, and worthies such as Bradlaugh and
Huxley died and were celebrated by like-minded children or
friends, the idea of a future life is deliberately excluded. Even
then the dying person will often be conscious of diverging from
the traditional norm of many centuries, and be anxious to show
himself steadfast in the conviction that death is the term of
consciousness.

Death scenes of this last kind, though increasingly common,
remain the exception; and in the others, one comes to see that
one's first surprise at the blurring of the distinction between
earth and heaven is not wholly reasonable in view of the general
character of the age. For it was an age much less confident of its
spiritual assumptions than it appears to be. The note of real
conviction is often absent from confidently-phrased statements,
as in the deaths of Dickens's doomed children; and this may be
due either to inner uncertainty, as with Dickens, or to simple
insincerity.

Of course, if the subject of the biography is treated as a
flawless spiritual hero, there need be no conflict, and the right
curtain line can also be the fitting first line of eternity's prologue.
Since, as we have seen, hero-worship is a normal attribute of
nineteenth-century biographers, and since hero-worship and
spiritual admiration were seldom as well distinguished as they
ought to have been, this is a common case.[2] The life of Kingsley
by his wife is an example typical of many. His whole life had
been a beneficent spiritual warfare. So near the end, he murmured
'No more fighting – no more fighting'; and later:

when conscious of no earthly presence, true to his own

[1] Southey: *Nelson* (ed. cit., p. 331).
[2] But some Victorians were well aware of the consequent falsifications. Thus
in chapter 38 of Charles Reade's *A Terrible Temptation* (1871) a little girl
wandering in a churchyard asks: 'Can you tell me where all the bad people
are buried? for that puzzles me dreadful.' Told that they are in the
churchyard, she says she has read every word on the tombstones, and
'there are none but good people buried there; not one'. She concludes that
the bad are probably buried in gardens.

words written years before, 'Self should be forgotten most of all in the hour of death' his daughter heard him exclaim, 'How beautiful God is.'[1]

And here the biographer-wife is able to enforce the theme of inner consistency by recalling that twenty years before, when still almost a young man he had expressed a longing for death and said 'God forgive me if I am wrong, but I look forward to it with an intense and reverent curiosity'.

This is impressive; and though the biography cannot be called a good one, because the author is unaware of his faults, and grotesquely unfair to his opponents, the death scene is a triumphant success. Why is this? It is surely because for once the formula exactly fits the case. Kingsley may have had obscure and contorted urges of which his wife knew nothing. He may have been the most unfair controversialist of his age. But he really did mean what he said about death; and he really did have the rare courage to act and to feel as if it were true, when the final agony approached. We are far away here from the conventional world of half-sincere piety. But for one final chapter of this stamp there are several embodying vague gestures in the direction of the spirit, often reduced to unconvincing formulae.

Sometimes the holy death formula is applied with a breath-taking baldness and brevity which make coherent comment difficult. Thus, in Dean Stanley's essay on Archdeacon Hare,[2] his end is described as follows:

> One sign, eminently characteristic, broke the all but entire unconsciousness of his last hours. When asked to change his position, he only answered, pointing with his finger as he spoke, 'Upwards, upwards.'

If the scene is accurately described here, it is hard to avoid the suspicion that the dying man himself was collaborating in his own biography. The words seem remote from the actual religious preoccupations of a dying man, just as the public statements of

[1] *Charles Kingsley: His Letters and Memories of His Life,* edited by his wife, 1884, pp. 348–9.

[2] A. P. Stanley: *Essays on Church and State,* 1870, pp. 554–5. Reprinted from *Quarterly Review,* July 1855.

politicians are remote from the real issues of politics. Instead we
have a pseudo-religious equivalent of the wedding-bell chapter
at the end of the novel. Indeed, it is possible that the end of
David Copperfield, still fresh in the minds of everybody, actually
influenced the phrasing.

But then, if there was such influence, did it work upon the
dying man or on the biographer? In this case it is impossible to
say. But there are other cases where such a question is easier
to answer. A striking case is the life of the celebrated hero of the
Indian Mutiny, Major Hodson. Hodson died of a wound
sustained while recklessly entering a room full of armed men in
the Begum's palace, a rebel stronghold.

> 'Where are the rebels?' he said. I pointed to the door of the
> room, and Hodson, shouting, 'Come on!' was about to rush
> in. I implored him not to do so, saying, 'It's certain death.
> Wait for the powder. I've sent men for powder-bags.'
> Hodson came a step forward and I put out my hand to
> seize him by the shoulder to pull him out of the line of the
> doorway, when he fell back shot through the chest. He
> gasped out a few words, either, 'Oh, my wife!' or, 'Oh, my
> mother!' – I cannot now rightly remember – but was
> immediately choked by blood. . . .[1]

Obviously, since the words 'wife' and 'mother' do not sound
in the least alike, a man who was not sure which had been used
was not really sure that either had been used. It is a startling
fact, full of implications about the practice of biography, that
this obvious point was not perceptible to an experienced and
competent biographer, writing, not in the immediate glow of
admiration and regret, but more than forty years after the event.

But if Hodson had been unmarried, no doubt he would have
been confidently reported as having called upon his mother; and
there would have been no particular reason to question the truth
of the account. Therefore caution is indicated whenever the
death scenes are being treated as historical sources. Fortunately,
our concern is rather with their nature as literary artefacts.

[1] Lionel J. Trotter, *Hodson of Hodson's Horse* (published 1901), Everyman
Edition, p. 253. The narrator quoted was an officer called Forbes-
Mitchell.

Often, then, a literary formula may have influenced not only the written account of death scenes, but even the memory of observers from whom biographers collected evidence. But it would be recklessly over-simple to suggest that the formula was generally applied in this unimaginative way. Some writers, while accepting wholeheartedly the idea that the death scene was a uniquely significant pointer to the quality of the life, allowed it to appear ambivalent. This was, of course, most likely to occur when the biographer's own attitude to his subject was a synthesis of conflicting emotions.

Of this inner conflict Purcell's life of Cardinal Manning is a notable case. Manning was 84 at the time of the scene described:

> He had expressed a belief that what turned out to be his last illness was merely one of his usual colds in winter. His hopeful clinging to life up to the very last is illustrated by the last words he spoke to his friend and doctor, Sir Andrew Clark. 'Is there any use in your coming to-morrow?' 'Certainly there is use,' was the reply. 'Then mind you come, Sir Andrew, at nine to-morrow.' 'To-morrow' never came to Cardinal Manning.

But in the next paragraph but one we are told that:

> Cardinal Manning manifested on various occasions in the night his perfect resignation to the Divine will, and his implicit trust in the love and mercy of God.[1]

There is, strictly speaking, no inconsistency between trying to preserve life as long as possible, and humbly accepting death when it comes as a manifestation of Divine Will. Yet it is surely no accident that each of the two passages expresses in miniature one part of what this lengthy, enigmatic book conveys as a whole. On the one hand, Manning was a wilful, imperious careerist; on the other, he was a genuine servant of God, conscious of his own imperfections, and capable at times of curbing them wonderfully by force of will, guided by an intense religious conviction. 'As in life, so in death' is the implication of Purcell's death scene, as of so many others. But he maintains at the same time a sense of the conflict which must exist in the lives of all men who try to guide themselves by lofty principles that

[1] Edmund Purcell: *Life of Cardinal Manning*, 1896, II, 806.

are at war with their egoism. Slovenly and prolix as it often is,
Purcell's book conveys a truer impression of the difficulty of all
spiritual attainment than most biographies of its time; he is free
from the characteristic Victorian illusion that it is easy to be
good.

Purcell's account may not have been consciously designed to
be ambivalent. His was not a profound or very analytical mind,
and he was writing near the event about a man he had known.
A much clearer, because conscious, case of ambivalence is
provided by Morley's account of Cromwell. Morley, of course,
was a latecomer to the field of Cromwellian biography.[1] It was
his task to give his own interpretation to dying words, already
consecrated by time, and already known to many of his readers.
He gives it thus:

> ... he put the moving question, so deep with penitential
> meaning, so pathetic in its humility and misgiving, in its
> wistful recall of the bright, bygone dawn of life in the soul:
> '*Tell me, is it possible to fall from grace?*' '*No, it is not possible,*'
> said the minister. '*Then,*' said the dying Cromwell, '*I am
> safe, for I know that I was once in grace.*'[2]

The barrier against despair was a single doctrine; a doctrine
which is contrary to orthodox Christian traditions and subversive
of social order, since it appears to give an unlimited license for
crime after the all-sufficing conversion experience. At the
moment of truth, Morley means to say, such a barrier will seem
to a man in agony flimsy indeed. Was it splendid that he could
still cling to the doctrine, or was it just a childish wilfulness?
Or does the urgency of Cromwell's question indicate an inner
doubt that could not be crushed?

Was he admitting that if it was possible to fall from grace,
he would have done so? Was he remembering some of the
terrible crimes he had committed in the firm conviction that he
acted as the Lord's instrument? We do not know; and Morley

[1] On the general relation of Morley's view of Cromwell to other Victorian
ones, see chapter 4.
[2] John Morley: *Oliver Cromwell* (pub. 1900), 2nd Edition, pp. 506–7,
Morley's italics.

does not profess to know either. But he writes with the intention of making the reader ask such questions.

Morley is tactful here; he does not insist upon his own settled conviction that Cromwell was setting out on a journey into nothingness. He rightly sees that the crucial issue here is the same for those who agree with him, and for those who believe, as Cromwell himself did, that he was about to appear before the Divine Judge. What we want to know is, what did Cromwell really think of himself and of his past life in those terrible moments? Morley suggests, cautiously but definitely, that he saw himself at the last as a wicked, misguided man, who might yet be saved by his faith. Morley's handling is so successful because it can be read with equal appreciation by men in any and every state of conviction, doubt or denial of immortality. It is a case where the last line of the play of life and the prologue to eternity can both be accommodated in a single, strong and memorable but enigmatic scene

Morley, then, does not insist on his agnostic principles here.[1] But abstinence of this kind was not usual. The agnostic death scene comes to be a separate genre with conventions of its own parallel to the religious ones. An early example (which perhaps attracted little notice because its deviations from the religious formula were so delicately made) was the account of Goethe's death by G. H. Lewes:

> His speech was becoming less and less distinct. The last words audible were: *More light!* The final darkness grew apace, and he whose eternal longings had been for more Light, gave a parting cry for it, as he was passing under the shadow of death.[2]

That eyesight often fails as death approaches is a familiar fact, of which Tennyson had made a beautiful use a few years before in *Tears, Idle Tears*.[3] 'More light' is a phrase perfectly adapted to any of three kinds of death scene, the merely clinical, if it is

[1] For Morley's treatment of Gladstone's Christian faith, see below, chapter 10.
[2] G. H. Lewes: *The Life and Works of Goethe* (published 1855), Everyman, p. 576.
[3] Ah, sad and strange as in dark summer dawns / The earliest pipe of half-awakened birds / To dying ears, when unto dying eyes / The casement slowly grows a glimmering square. (From *The Princess*, 1847.)

taken only at the literal level, the Christian, if it is taken to suggest a hope of heaven, and the agnostic, if it is taken as a poignant moral sentiment *in extremis*. The single word 'final', which Lewes attaches to the darkness, is the only definite indication that it is the last type we are being offered here. And the phrase 'eternal longings' quickly following, which is ambiguous, perhaps deliberately so, may have distracted many readers' attention from an epithet that is not particularly striking. The agnostic death scene makes an unobstructive first appearance.

Thirty years later, when a kind of agnostic orthodoxy had had time to develop, the consort of Lewes, who had played a notable part in developing it, was given a different treatment. Her biographer, J. W. Cross, was also her faithful disciple, and, at the very end of her life, her husband. One part of his account is, no doubt unintentionally, vivid and characteristic of her personality, as he tells how, just before she lost consciousness for the last time, she whispered, 'Tell them I have great pain in the left side.' There is the dauntless blue-stocking, and the creator of Lydgate. But more significant for our topic is the exact reflection of the great novelist's own considered view about death, which can be found also in her poems, and in the last paragraph of *Middlemarch*. Cross writes:

> Here the letter is broken off. The pen which had carried delight and comfort to so many minds and hearts, here made its last mark. The spring, which had broadened out into so wide a river of speech, ceased to flow.

And a paragraph or two later he adds:

> Her spirit joined that choir invisible 'whose music is the gladness of the world'.[1]

Cross was not inconsistent in using phrases derived from Christianity to express an agnostic message of bleak comfort. For George Eliot's whole moral and quasi-religious agnostic system had done this too. Indeed, in using the phrase 'choir invisible' to mean not the joy of heaven but the ennobling memory retained of the unconscious dead, he is actually quoting her. His point is similar then in moral intention, though opposite

---

[1] J. W. Cross: *George Eliot's Life as Related in Her Letters and Journals*, 1885, III, 438–9.

in doctrine, to that of many Christian biographers. He is showing his heroine firm in her considered faith as the death-agony approaches.

Cross's method was found generally useful. More than twenty years later, Maitland is still following it exactly in his life of Leslie Stephen. Passing lightly over the circumstances of the death itself, he ends his book with a quotation from Stephen's own writings about 'the good done by a noble life'.[1]

II

From one point of view, obviously, the Christian and the agnostic death scene are opposites, since they enforce opposite views of death's nature. Yet their literary tone and moral intent is often curiously similar, as the foregoing examples will have shown. And the omissions are similar too. To ordinary men[2] death is terrifying. It is often preceded by a weakening of the mind and will, which makes it hard to maintain a firm sense of lifelong convictions.[3] There may be intense spiritual struggles. Then, death is sometimes physically sordid and aesthetically distressing. All this is absent from the vast majority of biographies of our period. But there a few exceptions. A very striking one is the life of F. D. Maurice by his son.

> During the night of Easter Sunday he suffered greatly from difficulty of breathing, and from cold death perspirations all night. He was in great anguish of mind. Once he said to me, 'Ask that these nervous fears may be taken away. *Pray.*' . . . Later he said, 'I have two voices, but I cannot silence the second voice as Tennyson did.'

A little nearer the end:

> A barber had been engaged to come and shave him, and at this moment it occurred to my father that he would not be able to keep the engagement, and that he ought to apologise for breaking it. He turned to Mrs Maurice and

[1] F. W. Maitland: *The Life and Letters of Leslie Stephen*, 1906.
[2] And sometimes to extraordinary men, too – Dr Johnson, for instance.
[3] One devout Christian and man of literary genius who railed in delirium against the faith by which he had lived was Manzoni. See Archibald Colquhoun: *Manzoni and his Times*, (1954), p. 258.

said, 'You will explain to the barber why I cannot see him.'[1]
The pain and the lack of spiritual assurance here are striking
because Maurice was a man of deep faith and piety. To judge as
the world judges, he had little to reproach himself with. One
wonders how many others had doubts and struggles that their
biographers omitted to record; and one wonders, too, how many
of those who had no doubts or struggles might have been held
guilty of the sin of presumption.

But quite different, and equally arresting to the reader already
steeped in the biographical literature of the time is the barber.
How splendid, one may irreverently feel, to have a touch of
comedy at last in a Victorian death-scene. And this shallow
desire for comic relief is perhaps susceptible of a more serious
defence. For the more seriously we take man's spiritual nature,
the more incongruous death becomes, at the same time as it
becomes more momentous. There is nothing either tragic or
comic in the death of an animal. But there are unlimited
possibilities for tragedy and for comedy in the idea of mortal
remains of an immortal soul. Neither the gravediggers nor
Yorick must be left out of *Hamlet*. From one point of view,
death can be called too serious for undue solemnity.

As we might expect, it was that sombre comic genius, Carlyle,[2]
who made the most of death's ridiculous incongruity with human
dignities. In his life of Sterling, he quotes from a letter dated
28 August 1831. He goes on, quite inconsequently:

> Which is otherwise a day of mark to the world and me – the
> poet Goethe's last birthday. While Sterling sat in the
> Tropical solitudes, penning this history, little European
> Weimar had its carriages and state-carriages busy on the
> streets, and was astir with compliments and visiting-
> cards. . . .[3]

[1] *Life of F. D. Maurice chiefly told in his own letters*; edited by his son
Frederick Maurice, 1884, II, 640. The first quotation is from Mrs Maurice's
account, quoted by the son.
[2] Hopkins, in a letter to Dixon of Sept. 24, 1881 (a few months after
Carlyle's death) wrote: 'always to be affected, always to be fooling, never
to be in earnest (for as somebody said, he is terribly earnest but never
serious – that is, never *in* earnest) is not to fight fair in the field of fame.'
A strangely neglected truth about Carlyle.
[3] Thomas Carlyle: *The Life of John Sterling*, 1851, chapter XII.

For Carlyle the incongruity of the details of social life with the purposes of destiny was a constant feature of his consciousness, only felt more acutely when he thought of the death of a revered master. And much later, we may catch an echo of the Carlylean tone, so contrary to ordinary English compromise, moderation and good taste in the words of Fitzjames Stephen:

'Why mankind was created at all, why we continue to exist, what has become of all that vast multitude which has passed, with more or less sin and misery, through this mysterious earth, and what will become of those vaster multitudes which are treading and will tread the same wonderful path? these are the great insoluble problems . . .'
The death of a commonplace barrister about this time makes him remark in a letter that the sudden contact with the end of one's journey is not unwelcome. The thought that a man went straight from the George IV Hotel to 'a world of ineffable mystery is one of the strangest that can be conceived.'[1]

It was a thought too strange for most biographers to admit to their final chapters, or perhaps even to their minds.

But there were others, who perhaps felt the incongruity just as much as these last, and yet found quite a different literary treatment appropriate. They chose to focus attention on the survivors, not on the dying man; and examples of this type can be found both among the Christian and among the agnostic writers. One of the first biographers to use this method in our period was Southey in his life of Wesley. Southey presents Wesley's death in extreme old age without any drama. The emphasis is on *continuity*, not on change. Wesley simply went on to the end as he had lived, writing letters, giving sermons. He knew he was near to death, and warned those who had anything to say to him to make haste. But the death is hardly an event at all in Southey's narrative. Instead he places at the centre of his account the funeral – preparations and instructions for it before the death, and the conduct of it afterwards:

The crowds who flocked to see him were so great, that it was thought prudent, for fear of accidents, to accelerate the

[1] Leslie Stephen: *The Life of Sir James Fitzjames Stephen*, 1895, p. 181.

funeral, and perform it between five and six in the morning. The intelligence, however, could not be kept entirely secret, and several hundred persons attended at that unusual hour. Mr Richardson, who performed the service, had been one of his preachers almost thirty years. When he came to the part of the service, 'Forasmuch as it hath pleased Almighty God to take unto himself the soul of our dear *brother*,' his voice changed, and he substituted the word *father*; and the feeling with which he did this was such, that the congregation, who were shedding silent tears, burst at once into loud weeping.

Mr Wesley left no other property behind him than the copyright and current edition of his works. . . .[1]

At first this handling is very surprising. If anyone might have been expected to give his biographer a genuine opportunity for an edifying death scene, Wesley was the man, supreme as he was in faith, in steadfastness and in eloquence. Southey austerely refuses the proffered opportunity. Why?

He refuses because the idea of continuity brought richer literary rewards. For a man so immersed in the world of the spirit as Wesley, death becomes a transition rather than a crisis. The inner meaning of his death has already been sufficiently recorded in his life. To aim at a higher reach of spiritual intensity might be to court failure and anti-climax. But the significance of the death, as of the life, lies in the lasting influence upon others; and here this idea is by no means the mere pious aspiration it so often becomes in other biographies. It is a plain fact of history that this man influenced decisively the lives of many thousands. The mourners, therefore, representing all the ecstatic hearers of sixty-five years, most of whom, perhaps, will have died before him – the mourners are the true index of his greatness. He has no need of dying words, because, unlike the common run of men, he always lived as if he was to die next day.

And how exactly the funeral gathering corresponds to those far-flung congregations of sixty-five years. He had always preached early in the morning, and the funeral, most unusually, was in the early morning. He had always excited tears from his hearers, and so he did now. He had always given away nearly all

[1] Robert Southey; op. cit. II, 333.

his possessions, and he died with none. All this is obvious, but something less obvious is also present in the narrative. The central paradox of Wesley's career was that the loyal Church of England man was the great architect of schism. The new wine would not be contained by the old bottles. How fitting that the hallowed words of the liturgy should be altered because of the reverence in which this man was held. His followers looked for authority not to a living church but to a dead leader. The future history of nineteenth-century Methodism is adumbrated in that momentous alteration. So, Southey, too, in his own way, is following the consecrated formula, 'As in life, so in death.' And he only obtains a subtler and more original effect by transferring the idea from the deathbed to the graveside. It is not surprising that Southey is an underrated literary artist. His worst passages are strident; his finest touches are easily missed. I know of no example so fine as this in agnostic death scenes. But the life of Bradlaugh by his daughter (1894) has another impressive burial scene:

> At his express wish . . . the burial was perfectly silent – an arrangement which caused some regret among his friends, and some characteristic phrases about 'being buried like a dog' from others, who could not feel the pathos and solemnity of the silent sepulture. . . . As he had always disliked the shows of mourning and the badges of grief, those who knew his taste wore none. But the grief of the thousands who filled the trains from London to the burial-place was such as needed no other attestation . . . soldiers' red coats and the bronzed faces of a handful of Hindus gave a wide significance of aspect to the throng . . .
>
> Over an hour after the coffin had been laid in the earth, when it was thought that the multitude had passed away, the immediate friends and mourners of the dead went back to take a last look, and they found a lingering band of devoted men had got the shovels from the workmen, and were one by one obtaining the last sad privilege of casting their handful of earth into the grave.[1]

Bradlaugh's daughter was right, as Southey was, in presenting

[1] Hypatia Bradlaugh Bonner: *Charles Bradlaugh*, 5th edition, 1902, II, 421.

her subject as a man who must be judged by the quality and the extent of his influence upon others. And each account corresponds exactly to the kind of influence the hero exercised. Wesley's being inward and spiritual, the tears and the significant substitution of 'father' for 'brother' convey it. Bradlaugh's influence was practical, and involved a denial of the reality of the spirit, and so the sad remnant seizing the workmen's shovels were his fitting monument.

But, similar in some ways, the two scenes are opposite in their reasons for eschewing the expected deathbed scene, and concentrating instead on the funeral. For Southey the deathbed was unnecessary just because the transition of a soul like Wesley's into eternal glory involved none of the usual struggle; he had hardly anything to regret. For Bradlaugh's daughter, death was important only because of its influence on the living, since for the dead man himself there was nothing to follow.

Not all agnostics were as rigorous in restricting the natural human emotions about death entirely to the survivors. T. H. Huxley's son, who equally eschewed the death scene, was able to find an effective compromise:

> He was buried at Finchley, on July 4 1895, beside his brother George and his little son Noel, under the shadow of the oak, which had grown up into a stately young tree from the little sapling it had been when the grave of his first-born was dug beneath it, five and thirty years before.
>
> There was no official ceremony. . . .[1]

This captures something that is missing in the Bradlaugh account. Huxley, a brave, strong man, who would never express regrets or fears about his own approaching death, had felt the death of the child intensely. The growing tree is a symbol of a deeper kind of continuity than is to be found in the idea of a life-work carried on by devoted followers when the leader is gone. It is the continuity of the life-process itself, of the mysterious cycle of which death itself is a part. Agnostic as he is, and as his father also was, the younger Huxley here achieves a touch of religious awe.

[1] Leonard Huxley: *Life and Letters of T. H. Huxley*, 1900, II, 402-8.

4

THE REASSESSMENT OF THE PAST

✻

We have been dealing so far, in the main, with biographies written within a few years of the subjects' death; and, as we have seen, the great majority of these are adulatory in tone. But every age has also to reassess the great figures of the past. And here the characteristic assumptions operated to different effect. Even the most pessimistic Victorian was apt to think that his own age was an improvement on the eighteenth century. 'Lifeless', 'mechanical', 'unfeeling', 'formalist' were the epithets thought suitable to the age of Swift, of Johnson and of Blake. In 1880, the SPCK issued a book entitled *Wrecked Lives*,[1] an account of the lives of Rienzi, Wolsey, Swift, Savage and Chatterton. The essay on Swift is the longest, and its condemnation is severe:

> Swift lived without Christ in the world; not indeed as one who denied that Christ had risen, but as one who never realised to himself the example and the work of Christ, and the obligations it entails. . . . No great man, it may be added, ever so wallowed in filth. He has written whole pages of unpardonable bestiality.[2]

Swift's last months were unusually painful and distressing to onlookers, since he was paralysed and hardly ever spoke. We see here how easily the usual strategy of the deathbed scene can be reversed. His sufferings are called an 'awful moral lesson'; strange indeed that a professedly Christian writer could treat a painful death as evidence of an ill-spent life. What about the martyrs? What about Christ himself? Such questions were not answered, and probably were never asked.

Despite this sombre and illogical conclusion, the treatment of

---

[1] W. H. Davenport Adams: *Wrecked Lives* or *Men Who Have Failed.*
[2] Op. cit., p. 225.

Swift's character is less stern than that accorded to him a generation earlier by Thackeray. The moral superiority of the nineteenth to the eighteenth century was a fixed idea to which writers of all schools could appeal. And it is often strong enough to blot out human sympathy altogether. So, in Adams's book, the almost unbearable pathos of Savage's last hours, as Johnson describes them, is lost without being noticed. The author does not *dispute* Johnson's wise and humane judgment; he brushes it aside while professing to agree. The reader who had not seen Johnson's account would infer that it was similar in tone to this with which Adams ends:

> Be sure your sins and follies will find you out; be sure that of every blunder you make your own shoulders must bear the consequences; be sure that if you sow tares you will not reap wheat; and that though the wheels of God grind exceeding slow, they grind exceeding small. If you waste your powers as Savage did, your life, like Savage's, will be a failure.[1]

Harsh and unfeeling as this is, it is doubly shocking in a professedly Christian publication. The prevailing Benthamite morality and deterministic cosmology are being insinuated under the aegis of Christ himself. We return with relief to the truly Christian understanding of Johnson.

Nearly everyone agreed about the eighteenth century; and superficial or inaccurate views of it were seldom challenged. But the seventeenth century was a different matter. In the Civil War, Victorian writers were able to recognise burning issues of their own time played out on the stage of history. It was sensed that as you judged Cromwell, so you would judge the men of your own time. The argument about Cromwell became an argument about general truths. When Carlyle edited Cromwell's letters and speeches, he attempted a frontal attack on the values and preoccupations of his own time. It would, indeed, be difficult to overrate the importance of Carlyle's work, but its revolutionary character as an assessment of Cromwell has sometimes been exaggerated. It is not true that before Carlyle everyone happily acquiesced in Hume's opinion that he was 'an artful and

[1] Op. cit., p. 283.

audacious conspirator'.[1] Macaulay had challenged this as early as 1828, when he said 'though to praise would long have been a punishable crime, truth and merit at last prevail.'[2] But this does not detract from the originality of Carlyle's portrait, since he was trying to comprehend Cromwell's soul, and Macaulay only his political influence.

Carlyle's *Cromwell* was published in December 1845, and no better moment could possibly have been chosen to make the issue topical. Newman's reception into the Roman Church just two months before gave Carlyle his cue to enforce the rightness of Cromwell's anti-catholic spirit; while at the same time, the discovery that the principles of the Oxford Movement did, or at least might, lead to Rome after all could be used to discredit the seventeenth-century High Churchmen in the eyes of Protestant England. The Irish famine was not indeed a deliberate massacre like those of Cromwell; but it was an event that might have stimulated a sense of guilt in English hearts, if the Irish had been regarded as fellow-citizens, with the ordinary rights and dignities of subjects of the crown. Carlyle seems to waver between saying that Cromwell's massacres never really took place, and saying that they were fully justified. A failure of logic is sometimes a tactical gain in argument. It was a soothing message to those English readers who wished to believe that there was no serious famine in Ireland, but that, in any case, the Irish were to blame for it.

Carlyle was fortunate not only in the topicality of his message but in the unconvincing character of the accepted view of Cromwell. Life is busy, and its concerns are multifarious. There is a powerful tendency in human nature to refrain from thinking about any question which does not impose itself as urgent. The idea that Cromwell was both a hypocrite and a fanatic clearly *could* not be right. This had not been generally perceived, only because as A. E. Housman said in another context: 'Thought is irksome and three minutes is a long time.' Carlyle's eloquent and passionate book made an urgent claim to those minutes. But

[1] Hume: *History of Great Britain*, chapter LIX.
[2] Macaulay: *Essay on Hallam's Constitutional History*, Albany Edition, VII, 195.

there is an equally strong tendency to suppose that a man who has refuted a wrong view must by the same process have shown a correct view. Carlyle's view of Cromwell, though professedly a restoration of seventeenth-century thinking, really derives from the assumptions of the romanticism of the early nineteenth century. He assumes that Cromwell, because he was a genius, was in some special, intimate way in tune with the harmonies of the whole universe and that, for this reason, he was not to be judged by ordinary moral standards. Thus he writes, describing Cromwell's native fen country:

> Here of a certainty Oliver did walk and look about him habitually, during those five years from 1631 to 1636; a man studious of many temporal and many eternal things. His cattle grazed here, his ploughs tilled here, the heavenly skies and infernal abysses overarched and underarched him here.[1]

In itself this is unexceptionable; in the context of the whole three volumes, the plain implication is that a neighbouring royalist squire was not so overarched and underarched. The sky itself is credited with a party preference.

This is sad – sad at least for admirers of Carlyle's genius. For only a few years before, in very different mood, he had written: 'The Sanspotato is of the selfsame stuff as the superfinest Lord Lieutenant.'[2] Something in the intervening years had led him to forget this.

Carlyle's account also provides an instructive illustration of the difficulty of assessing a period of history in its general nature. To-day both those who adhere to Christianity and those who reject it agree, as a rule, in calling the early Victorian period an age of strong religious influences. Carlyle, contrasting it with the seventeenth century, saw it as altogether godless. Commenting upon a day of prayer and fast in 1645, just two hundred years earlier, he writes: 'Consider it; actually "praying". It was a capability old London and its Preachers and Populations had; to us the incrediblest.'[3]

We have to wait over fifty years before the reassessment of

---

[1] Carlyle: *The Letters and Speeches of Oliver Cromwell*, edited by S. C. Lomas, 1904, I, 77.
[2] In *Chartism*, 1839.   [3] Carlyle, op. cit., I, 196.

Cromwell which Carlyle caused led to some interesting second thoughts. In the years 1897–1900, three able writers, two of them distinguished historians of the seventeenth century, and one a distinguished biographer, gave their reserved judgment. S. R. Gardiner was the first to speak.[1] Writing in the high imperialist days of the Diamond Jubilee, he disagreed with Carlyle's view that the Cromwell type had died out in the seventeenth century. On the contrary, he said that Cromwell was the archetypal Englishman of all periods. It was because our whole national character was Cromwellian that foreigners respected us, feared us and distrusted us. He clearly makes the connection between Ireland in the seventeenth century and the Jubilee empire on which the sun never sets. Foreigners think that we want an empire to gratify our love of wealth and power; we think we want it for the good of others. So with Cromwell's Irish policy. Gardiner does not say which view is right, or whether either is right.

Firth saw the issues in less far-reaching terms, and so focuses his subject more clearly. He quotes Cromwell's words about a 'righteous judgment of God' in speaking of the massacre at Drogheda, and he comments:

> Cromwell, in short, regarded himself, in Carlyle's words, as 'the minister of God's justice, doing God's judgments on the enemies of God!' but only fanatics can look upon him in that light.[2]

This passage must surely make us pause before we accept the judgment of G. M. Young that 'the Cromwell of Gardiner and Firth is in all essentials the Cromwell of Carlyle'.[3]

Morley, a less learned and in some directions a more cultivated man than either Gardiner or Firth, takes a more general view, though all three men are like Carlyle in taking a long perspective of time. Quoting one of Cromwell's fiery denunciations and calls to the solemn duty of shedding blood, he writes:

> Even such sonorous oracles as these do not altogether escape

[1] S. R. Gardiner: *Cromwell's Place in History*, 1897.
[2] Sir Charles Firth: *Oliver Cromwell* (published 1900), World's Classics, p. 255.
[3] Firth, op. cit. (Young's introduction, p. vii).

the guilt of rhetoric. As if, after all, there might not be just
as much of sham, phantasm, emptiness, and lies in Action
as in Rhetoric.[1]

Morley puts his finger unerringly, too, on the weak point of
Carlyle's success ethic. Cromwell, Carlyle had argued, must have
been a man of God because he triumphed over his enemies.
Morley neatly disposes of this argument, *on its own terms*, very
early in his book, by saying: 'To ignore the Restoration is to
misjudge the Rebellion.'[2] Carlyle's tactics in evading this point
had indeed been curious. The temporary success of the causes he
believes in proves them to be infallibly right, since success is
always a God-given reward for doing right. The lasting failure of
the same causes only proves the decadence of later centuries.
But Carlyle was really a poet, and his admirers must agree to
dispense with logic.

The reconsideration of men of earlier periods brought one
rather unexpected gain for the reader – a gain in humour. The
disappointed barber barred from Maurice's deathbed is almost
the only instance of humour we have encountered in this account
of the biographies of men recently dead. With the further past it
is different; and here the romantic poets of the early years of the
nineteenth century yielded a rich harvest. They were near
enough to seem accessible and interesting; they were far enough
away for the biographer's reverence to be weakened. In writing
the life of John Sterling (1851) Carlyle turned aside to demolish
Coleridge in a single chapter. The humorous method is a clever
one. First, a sonorous, tongue-in-cheek tribute to the sage and
philosopher, then a judicious doubt about consistency or the
practicality of his thought, and then a touch of downright
knockabout absurdity. It is these last that are most telling:

in walking he shuffled rather than decisively stept; and a
lady once remarked, he could never fix which side of the
garden-walk would suit him best, but continually shifted,
in corkscrew fashion, and kept trying both.[3]

---

[1] John Morley: *Cromwell*, 1900, 2nd Edition, p. 309.
[2] Morley, op. cit., p. 4.
[3] T. Carlyle: *The Life of John Sterling*, chapter VIII. The following quotations
are also from this chapter.

Emblematic of course of his (to Carlyle) tedious intellectual irresolution. In the next quotation, false sentiment and sham humility are imputed:

'Ah, your tea is too cold, Mr Coleridge!' mourned the good Mrs Gilman once, in her kind, reverential and yet protective manner, handing him a very tolerable though belated cup. – 'It's better than I deserve!' snuffled he, in a low hoarse murmur, partly courteous, chiefly pious, the tone of which abides with me: 'It's better than I deserve!'

Having so skilfully made Coleridge ludicrous, he ends his hatchet-job with a neat mixture of humour and prophetic seriousness:

here once more was a kind of Heaven-scaling Ixion; and to him, as to the old one, the just gods were very stern! The ever-revolving, never-advancing Wheel (of a kind) was his, through life; and from his Cloud Juno did not he procreate strange Centaurs. . . .

These middle years of the century saw a series of reassessments of the romantic poets. Monckton Milnes's *Keats* had appeared in 1848, and the '60's were to see the beginning of serious interest in Blake. But the most interesting case to the general public, and the one that provided the best opportunities for humour, proved to be that of Shelley. Shelley died young in 1822, and his friends and contemporaries mostly survived him by more than a generation. Hogg, Trelawny and Peacock, by a curious process of mutual stimulation, were all moved to write on Shelley at the end of the 1850's. It is Hogg's fascinating, eccentric and inaccurate volume that concerns us here because of the quality of its humour.

Hogg had felt long ago, it would seem, a keen resentment against Eliza, the sister of Harriet Shelley, and deeply distrusted her as a disintegrating domestic force. But, mellowed by time, he preferred to rely on ridicule.

Eliza was vigilant, keeping a sharp look-out after the nerves; yet she was frequently off-duty; her time was chiefly spent in her bedroom. What does that dear Eliza do alone in her bedroom? Does she read? No. – Does she work? Never. – Does she write? No. – What does she do, then?

Harriet came close to me, and answered in a whisper, lest peradventure her sister hear her, with the serious air of one who communicates some profound and weighty secret. 'She brushes her hair!' The coarse black hair was glossy, no doubt; but to give daily sixteen hours out of four-and-twenty to it, was certainly to bestow much time on the crop. Yet it was by no means impossible, that whilst she plied her hair-brush, she was revolving in her mind dearest Harriet's best interests. . . .[1]

And a little later:

Harriet assured me, most probably on the authority of her sister, that the Duke was quite charmed with Eliza; and, if his Grace admired black hair well brushed, it could hardly have been otherwise. . . . Unfortunately, the noble admirer was married already, although only to an insane Scudamore. . . .[2]

But Shelley himself is not spared either. There is a scene very characteristic both of Shelley and of Hogg, when Shelley called at Southey's house and saw him eating buttered currant-cakes.

'Why! good God, Southey!' Bysshe suddenly exclaimed, for he could no longer contain his boiling indignation. 'I am ashamed of you! It is awful, horrible, to see such a man as you are greedily devouring this nasty stuff!'

'Nasty stuff, indeed! How dare you call my tea-cakes nasty stuff, sir?'

Mrs Southey was charming, but it is credibly reported that she was also rather sharp.

'Nasty stuff! What right have you, pray, Mr Shelley, to come into my house, and to tell me to my face that my tea-cakes, which I made myself, are nasty; and to blame my husband for eating them? . . . Nasty stuff! I like your impertinence!'

In the course of this animated invective, Bysshe put his face close to the plate, and curiously scanned the cakes. He then took up a piece and ventured to taste it, and finding it very good, he began to eat as greedily as Southey himself.[3]

[1] T. J. Hogg: *The Life of Percy Bysshe Shelley*, 1858, chapter 14.
[2] Ibid.   [3] Ibid.

Hogg goes on to describe how Shelley then demanded a fresh supply of cakes, gobbled them up until no more were to be had, and went home to his wife and told her they were to have similar cakes every day for ever. And so the solemnity characteristic of most mid-Victorian biography was not universally maintained. These dips into the more distant past remind us that we are still in one of the greatest ages of English humorous writing, the age of Dickens, and of Mrs Poyser and of *Barchester Towers.*

5

THE MILIEU

✻

1. *The Protestant Ethos*

Victorian England was a world in which class differences were
very important, and a lord was dearly loved. But it was also a
world possessing a classless élite. Dickens and Thackeray
quarrelled partly because they belonged to the same club.
Reading the correspondence of Lord Derby and Disraeli, you
would not easily guess how different their origins were. Acton,
the cosmopolitan aristocrat, was subservient to the merchant's
son, Gladstone. The people the élite themselves most reverenced,
Carlyle, Newman, Dickens, George Eliot, were nobodies by
birth.

A world in which class is important, and yet, in this odd way,
unimportant, is one where formative influences are hard to
define. Are we to look to the nursery, to the school, or to the
university to find the key to a man's development? We can only
say that each case is different. If we are to judge by his siblings
the nursery can have had little lasting effect upon Newman;
Holland House seems more important than Clapham in the case
of Macaulay. But for Carlyle, perhaps all his voluminous reading
was less significant than the lessons his mother gave him before
he was seven years old. In reading of Dr Arnold we are tempted
to wonder whether he was ever influenced by anybody or
anything. He seems to have created himself in that time of
solitary reading and coaching which preceded his appointment
to Rugby. School was a major influence on Clough and Stanley,
perhaps on Gladstone. But Trollope was a Wykehamist, like
Dr Arnold, and a Harrovian, like Sir George Trevelyan. But the
Latin grammar was about the only thing which was the same for
all of them.

The class label may be as misleading as the school label. Two men could hardly be more different, not only in character, but in background, habits and assumptions, than the third Marquess of Salisbury, who was Prime Minister, and the eighth Marquess of Queensberry, patron of boxers, and father of Lord Alfred Douglas. James Mill and James Stephen belonged to the same world of trusted, responsible officialdom. But the upbringing described in Mill's *Autobiography* is in a different universe from that described in the life of Fitzjames Stephen. The assumptions of class here become insignificant compared with grand, controlling principles – with the authority of Bentham or of Evangelical Christianity. But in all this variety, there is a thread of continuity. The intellectual and spiritual history of Victorian England is, in the main, the history of developments from Evangelical Protestantism. In a world of conflicting ideas, startling new developments in science, profound religious controversies, it remains true that most notable men of all schools of thought came under this powerful influence and were mainly shaped by it in their earliest years.

A sentence in the life of Cardinal Manning is one that could be repeated, *mutatis mutandis,* of the majority of famous Victorians: 'At Totteridge he learnt of the Book of Judgment, and endeavoured to conceal himself from God under a writing-table.'[1]

Of course there were exceptions. Dickens's upbringing was slack and vague with the Church only an occasional presence in the background. Mill grew up thinking Christianity of no more direct concern to him than the idolatries of ancient Greece, of which he actually learnt at an earlier age. Keble was brought up as a High Churchman, and Acton was a born Catholic. Yet they were, and usually knew themselves to be, exceptions; and some who did not feel the evangelical pull directly were (like Virginia Woolf) formed by parents who had been formed by it.

There are many theological schools in Protestantism, and, theologically speaking, there is a world of difference between the Calvinism that affected Newman in 1816, and the creed held by William Wilberforce. Yet in England doctrines seldom have as

[1] Shane Leslie: *Henry Edward Manning,* 1921, p. 8.

much power as precepts, habits and social tones. It is possible, with due caution, to generalise about the formative influence on the young of Evangelical Christianity. It was an influence full of paradoxes.

There was a powerful and roughly equal stress on two opposite ideas – the idea of authority and the idea of personal responsibility. The sense of God as an active, ever-present, terrifying authority is well conveyed by the anecdote of Manning's childhood just quoted. The Bible was an unquestioned authority; the father of the family was an authority, not indeed infallible or beyond question, but very difficult to question in practice. The absence of any belief in priesthood meant that the natural authority of the parent and the spiritual authority of the expositor and exemplar of the Word of God were virtually indistinguishable. Perhaps, since the Oedipus complex is ineradicable, the system involved a psychological error. And it may help to account for a further paradox of Evangelicalism, that while the training given was profoundly influential, it failed, in many notable cases, to retain the next generation within the Evangelical fold.

But the stress on personal responsibility was equally strong, and in some ways more terrifying. The central act of the child's religious life was not a ritual or sacramental act, not something which was the same for everybody and thus bound him to the community of the faithful. It was the act of private prayer; and though certain forms of prayer (such as the Lord's Prayer) were taught, yet the child was soon encouraged to wander alone through an uncharted spiritual universe, in which he was told that God was seeking him, and would speak to him directly.

This might have led to a kind of Quietism. But it seldom did. For the world of the Victorian middle-class, from one section or other of which most eminent men came, was an active, energetic world, conscious of the challenge of rapid changes in society, in technology and in the world of thought. More often than not, the child would transpose the idea that God might find his soul and convert him, into the idea that it was his own duty to find God and get himself converted. Very often an intense strain developed in the constant search for an ineffable but unmistakable experience of spiritual illumination.

A further paradox was that this frightening spiritual freedom went with a highly-disciplined moral and social setting. The child was free to find God for himself, but not to leave the prunes upon his plate, to criticise his father, or to choose his own books. Since people in general, and children especially, proceed from the concrete to the abstract, and from the particular to the general, this usually meant that the idea of authority was carried over into the realm of freedom. That is to say, the child, though told to pray in his own way, would be seeking a spiritual experience of the approved kind. He would be told what to expect in the free realm of the spirit. Then one of three things might happen. He might really find just what his father had found; he might persuade himself that he did, though he did not; or he might pretend that he had while he had not. Here again we may discern a psychological weakness in the system. Introspection is a very difficult art; and to give a coherent account of what introspection reveals is more difficult still. With perfect good intentions on both sides, parental and filial, there was a strong tendency to over-strain, over-excitement and insincerity. The following account by Edmund Gosse of the practical consequences of the doctrine of direct Inspiration tells of an extreme case, certainly, but it was an exaggeration of something very characteristic:

> My father prayed aloud, with great fervour, that it might be revealed to me, by the voice of God, whether it was or was not the Lord's will that I should attend the Browns' party. My Father's attitude seemed to me to be hardly fair, since he did not scruple to remind the Deity of various objections to a life of pleasure and of the snakes that lie hidden in the grass of an evening party ... As I knelt, feeling very small, by the immense bulk of my Father, there gushed through my veins like a wine the determination to rebel. Never before, in all these years of my vocation had I felt my resistance take precisely this definite form ... My Father, perfectly confident in the success of what had really been a sort of incantation, asked me in a loud

wheedling voice, 'Well, and what is the answer which our
Lord vouchsafes?' . . . He positively beamed down at me;
he had no doubt of the reply. He was already, I believe,
planning some little treat to make up to me for the material
deprivation. But my answer came, in the high-piping
accents of despair: 'The Lord says I may go to the Browns.'
My father gazed at me in speechless horror. He was caught
in his own trap, and though he was certain that the Lord
had said nothing of the kind, there was no road open for him
but just such sheer retreat. Yet surely it was an error in
tactics to slam the door.[1]

This little scene, rightly understood, is ominous for the future
of Evangelical Christianity. We notice first that the word *father*
is given a capital letter so that it becomes indistinguishable from
the form used in addressing God. The father's shock and surprise
at the outcome show how easy it was, even for a very sincere and
devout man, like Philip Gosse, to confuse God's authority with
his own. Really, he was appealing, like all fathers, to his natural
parental authority, and to his greater experience of the world.
Children may at times resent this, but it is honest, and hardly
dangerous, since such authority gradually and insensibly declines
as the child matures and begins to know the world for himself.
But Philip Gosse, with a perfectly honest piece of self-deception,
chose to cloak this natural authority in a pure authority of the
Spirit. He was thwarted because he could not but admit that in
the world of pure Spirit, the child was equal to the father. The
father's deception was sincere. but the son's was not.

II

All students of the Victorian scene agree in emphasising its
intellectual variety. T. H. Huxley and Cardinal Manning could
meet at the Metaphysical Society and argue amicably without
any basis of fundamental agreement on the nature of life. How
then can we justify putting such emphatic stress on the
Evangelical milieu as the key to all the others? To answer this
question, we need first to see why the very powerful enthusiasms

[1] Edmund Gosse: *Father and Son*, 1907, Heinemann, 1909, pp. 253–4.

and energies which the Evangelical Movement released were directed in the following generations into many different channels, why the Evangelical Movement became the unwilling father of the Oxford Movement, of the reverent agnosticism of George Eliot, of Gladstonian Liberalism and of other tendencies far removed doctrinally from itself.

The key to the instability of the Evangelical tradition lies in the paradox just discussed – while the Evangelical tone and ethos were authoritative, yet there was ro living depository of authority. The Bible was an absolute authority, but the Bible can be interpreted in many ways. The characteristic Evangelical use of the Bible was to select a given text and build a whole doctrinal or ethical structure upon it; and this made matters worse. Obviously, you would get a different result according as you selected your text from the book of Deuteronomy, or from Isaiah or from St Paul. In practice the authority of the Bible was generally taken to mean the plenary authority of a few texts. There was little attempt at a Biblical synthesis, no interest in comparing and reconciling, for instance, what St James and St Paul say about faith and works. In this sense, the unlimited reverence accorded to the Bible probably worked against the serious reading of it. To consider the history of different books, to speculate about the authors and the circumstances in which they wrote might have seemed impious.

The unsatisfactoriness of the Bible as sole authority was inherent in the nature of the case. It existed independently of what soon came to make it more evident still, scholarly doubts, historical and textual questionings, the complex and troubled legacy of the German critics.

Dean Church well summarises the causes of the dissatisfaction with the Evangelical Movement, despite its splendid achievements and the manifest sincerity and power of its leading adherents, about 1832:

> It shrank, in its fear of mere moralising, in its horror of the idea of merit or of the value of good works, from coming into contact with the manifold realities of the spirit of man: it never seemed to get beyond the 'first beginnings' of Christian teaching, the call to repent, the assurance of

forgiveness: it had nothing to say to the long and varied process of building up the new life of truth and goodness: it was nervously afraid of departing from the consecrated phrases of its school, and in the perpetual iteration of them it lost hold of the meaning they may once have had . . . Yet it kept its hold on numbers of spiritually-minded persons, for in truth there seemed to be nothing better for those who saw in the affections the main field of religion.[1]

This account conveys two salient points very well. The Evangelical Movement was coming to seem by the 1830's a growth without any adequate soil or a grand building that lacked the necessary foundations. It needed new intellectual supports. But then we may be inclined to wonder why the men of the next generation did not simply reject and pass on. The key to the answer is conveyed, rather casually and unobtrusively, in the last phrase of my quotation. The appeal to the affections in religion and morality was the essential feature of the Evangelical Movement; and successors of varying schools wished to preserve it at all costs. Nearly all serious-minded Victorians considered the Evangelicals abundantly right in their rejection of the supposed coldness, formality and 'rational' selfishness of the eighteenth century. Their enthusiasm was admirable; it was also effective, as the crusade against slavery had shown. A large part of mid- and late-Victorian intellectual history consists in the careful transplanting by reverent hands of this precious enthusiasm, grown in the Evangelical hothouse, into different intellectual soils.

Dean Church was writing, of course, as the historian of the Oxford Movement, and as a High Churchman. But the characteristic Victorian agnostic schools were equally developments from the Evangelical source. The most eminent agnostic of them all, George Eliot, made a similar critique at greater length and with greater subtlety in her portrait of Bulstrode in *Middlemarch*. She, too, had responded with deep emotion to the Evangelical influence in her early years.

The men of the Oxford Movement sought a basis in the

[1] R. W. Church: *The Oxford Movement* 1833-45 (pub. 1891), Macmillan, 1904, pp. 7-8.

70

traditions of Catholic Christendom; George Eliot in Feuerbach. But they were alike in wishing to preserve the Evangelical insights as they understood them. Newman and George Eliot would, naturally, have given different accounts of what was valuable in these, and what needed to be discarded. But they could have agreed on some points. Each valued the Evangelical sense of the momentousness of personal choice, the deep awareness of responsibility before conscience. The lasting achievement of the Evangelicals, more important even than their practical impact upon legislation, was that they banished cynicism from any respectable position in educated society. Few leading Victorian figures could regard the wickedness of the world with equanimity. Those who could were either, like Lord Melbourne and Surtees, mere survivals of an earlier age, or else, like Disraeli, brilliant eccentrics.

The so-called Clapham Sect shows the Evangelical ethos at its finest hour. It was a great powerhouse of effective public action; it was the nursery of great and distinguished men – Macaulay, Fitzjames and Leslie Stephen, Robert and Samuel Wilberforce, and, in a later generation, E. M. Forster and Virginia Woolf. It was immensely influential, but it failed in the task which the men of Clapham themselves would have considered the most important of all. It failed to pass on Evangelical Christianity to future generations. Macaulay became a Whiggish Erastian; Robert and Henry Wilberforce became Roman Catholics; Samuel Wilberforce became a High Church bishop; Leslie Stephen became an agnostic, and his brother Fitzjames adopted an austere stoical doctrine which is hard to categorise, but was at any rate not Evangelical Christianity.

But this failure will look much like success if judged by other criteria than those of Clapham itself. The doctrines changed; but the spirit, the impulse, the enthusiasm remained, as well as the hereditary ability and energy. The dissident children were far from being rebels. Two of the Wilberforce brothers wrote their father's life at immense length in the most adulatory terms. Leslie Stephen's account of his father, contributed to the *D.N.B.*, is a model of filial piety. Macaulay, as we shall see in a later chapter, lived his whole life bewitched and even maimed by nostalgia for the delights of childhood. In some cases – this applies especially to the Wilberforces – the children felt that they were developing and completing the parental principles, and providing a more solid intellectual basis for deeply-reverenced parental insights. The parents, who often did not live to see the children's heresies in their final form, would not have agreed.

What was Clapham? In the first place it was not a sect; it is universally known as one, because as often happens, a joke happened to stick, and with the passing of time was taken over-seriously by people who forgot how it had first been made. Macaulay, reading Thackeray's rather ill-tempered account in *The Newcomes*, complained, very justly, that he had underrated the Anglican allegiance of the worthies of the earlier generation, such as his own father, Zachary, Sir James Stephen and William Wilberforce. But when we have noticed this, we are driven to ask, what then was so distinctive about it? The ruling groups in England had for centuries adhered, with more or less of fervour or sincerity, to the Established Church, as they had every reason of prudence and convenience for doing. Certainly, the Clapham men were much more devout than most people, and granted that they drew comfort and influence from their close connection of friendship, residence, and sometimes of intermarriage, what is it that makes us distinguish them as a separate culture? This is not an easy question to answer, though a few obvious preliminary points can be made. First, they combined an intense Christo-centric devotion, often in the past more characteristic of Protestant sects than of Anglicans, with a solid worldly position, exceptional energy, and an impressive array of varied intellectual talents. Then they conceived of their faith and devotion as bound to issue, not only in acts of charity, but in the forwarding of great public causes. This was an idea unfamiliar to the first readers of William Wilberforce's *Practical View of Christianity* (1791).[1] Samuel Johnson, who died in 1784, may be

---

[1] The full title is *Practical View of the Prevailing Religious Conceptions of Professed Christians in the Higher and Middle Classes in this Country Contrasted with Real Christianity*. A long title, but the words are not wasted. It is an attempt to form an Evangelical educated élite. Here lies

quoted as typical of the devout eighteenth-century intellectual at his best. His religion involved him in deep moral struggles; it made a man, naturally haughty and proud, active in charity towards the poor; it gave him complex and coherent canons of moral judgment by which to weigh public as well as private events. In a real sense Johnson's religion and its moral precepts pervaded his political judgment. All this is true; but still the contrast with Wilberforce is clear. Johnson does not believe that the world as such is capable of being changed for the better. He believes with sad sincerity that schemes of improvement are generally absurd. Clapham, though well aware that the world is always corrupt, believed that it could be changed. Taking their work as a whole, especially on the slavery question, we are forced to admit that they were not wholly deceived.

We must now turn to more obscure and less tangible facts. The idea of a self-perpetuating, hereditary intellectual élite is in itself a strange one. If it is not strange to us, that is only because through the efforts of a few strong groups like the Clapham Sect, it has become familiar. But the earlier traditional idea that a man 'founds a family' by bequeathing land, money, perhaps a title, seems at first sight much more realistic. If I have land I can make reasonably sure, granted a settled and civilised social order, that my son and my grandson will get it. But if I have ability, I must trust to luck (mainly) about its transmission, though perhaps intermarriage with like-minded élite families may help.

And then, how to preserve the tradition? An eccentric aristocrat will often be kept more or less within the tradition by the practical demands of landed property. Money in gilt-edged is much more easily diverted to purposes which its first compiler never thought of. The men of Clapham attempted, of course, to maintain the tradition by education; and the education they offered was a subtle and powerful synthesis. The main elements in it were a constant sense of the presence of God and of His providence, an active love of the best literary culture, especially

one of the clearest contrasts with Wesley, who preached mainly to the poor.

the Latin and Greek classics, a keen and often precocious interest in politics and public affairs, and a quasi-aristocratic idea of service derived from an unshakeable position of worldly privilege. All this combined with very strong family affections, family jokes, high jinks and pleasant intellectual games.

Enough has already been said to show that Clapham was very fortunate in transmitting to later generations intellect, energy and public distinction. But it would not be easy to find a doctrinal proposition on which Lord Macaulay, Leslie Stephen and Samuel Wilberforce agreed. They agreed, certainly, in various moral attitudes. They all believed that sin was sinful; but it is hardly necessary to ascribe views so generally held by their contemporaries to a special family influence. Where then (apart from intellectual eminence and worldly success) does the element of continuity lie? First, I think, in a peculiar combination of strength and sensitiveness. Leslie Stephen wrote of Sir James:

> My father, however, was a man of exquisitely sensitive nature – a man, as my mother warned his children, 'without a skin', and he felt very keenly the attacks of which he could take no notice. In early days this had shown itself by a shyness 'remarkable,' says Taylor, 'beyond all shyness that you could imagine in anyone whose soul had not been pre-existent in a wild duck.' His extreme sensibility showed itself too in other ways. He was the least sanguine of mankind. He had, as he said in a letter, 'a morbidly vivid perception of possible evils and remote dangers.'[1]

A very familiar type of character, of course – Jane Austen's Mr Woodhouse, for instance. But such men do not usually shape the fate of empires. Stephen did. His sons were the same. Fitzjames's *Liberty, Equality, Fraternity* (1873) disputes with some of the more bitter works of Ruskin for the distinction of being the most pessimistic book on public affairs written in an age in which common opinion tended to complacency. But Fitzjames was no solitary, brooding prophetic force, as Ruskin

[1] Leslie Stephen: *The Life of Sir James Fitzjames Stephen*, 2nd Edition, 1895, pp. 50–1. He could not reply because he was debarred from replying by his status as a civil servant. The Taylor quoted is Sir Henry Taylor (1800–86) an official colleague of Sir James, who had at one time some reputation as a poet.

was. He was a distinguished lawyer, and successful man of the world. Leslie's pessimism took a more comic form than that of his father and his brother. Readers of Mr Quentin Bell's life of Virginia Woolf will remember the recurring and ludicrous horror of the household accounts; and it may even be true that he really was in the habit of muttering: 'I wish I were dead – I wish my whiskers would grow.' At any rate he was capable of it. For the extraordinary combination of energy and morbid sensitiveness in Macaulay, the reader is referred to the later chapter on Trevelyan's *Life*. Yet both Macaulay and Leslie Stephen were strong, dominating men. Leslie Stephen in old age was felt to be distinctly terrifying.[1]

But, it may still be asked, was any of this really a continuing *ethos*? Was it anything more than a group of inherited psychological tendencies? Perhaps it is impossible to distinguish these two things with perfect exactness. But there are certainly some features which must be put down to training and tradition. There is a continuing sense, running through several quite different sets of doctrinal attitude, of the deep seriousness of life, of the overriding strength of evil, of the deep cosmic and personal significance of our struggles against it. All this finds its most eloquent expression in *Liberty, Equality, Fraternity*. But Fitzjames spoke in his own way for them all.

I have said that E. M. Forster and Virginia Woolf, descendants in a later generation, are still recognisably of the same type. Obviously, in saying this, we must allow for many changes, theological, moral and social. As a rough generalisation we may say that the order in which the changes occurred was the order given in the last sentence. Leslie Stephen and Macaulay retained the moral assumptions of their fathers almost unchanged. Indeed, they may be thought to have intensified the deep inherited Protestant sense of the sinfulness of sin, the paramount duty of service and self-control, the deep disgust at frivolity, waste, irresponsibility, dandyism, posing, and at licentious or abnormal sexual behaviour. They differed with their fathers' view of God; and they tried to live and write as if this made no

[1] For a full account of the corresponding traits in the Wilberforce family see David Newsome's admirable book, *The Parting of Friends* (1966).

difference to their view of man. A man like Leslie Stephen seems constantly to be appealing to a sacred void where the absent God of his father still leaves behind the tablets of Sinai. His father, if he had lived longer, would have sadly felt that his son was an infidel, a victim of the vices of pride and rebellion; but he would never have been driven to doubt his sense of honour, his robust normality, his reliability as husband, father or citizen.

In the Forster-Woolf generation moral principles have changed quite as much as beliefs about the ultimate. If Sir James Stephen could have read *Maurice*, he would not only have been grieved, he would have been startled and bewildered; and the agnostic Leslie Stephen might have been much more shocked than his devout father. For the father the book would have furnished a sad instance of the general corruption of human nature; for the son it would have been a base betrayal of the high agnostic tradition by a man who ought to have been one of its most distinguished representatives.

In his social and public personality, Forster seems to have been very much an old-fashioned gentleman, and, if he could have taken a time machine to the Clapham of the early days, would have dined comfortably enough. Virginia Woolf would have startled her father less by her moral outlook than by her social manner. Seasoned pessimist as he was, it probably never occurred to him in his gloomiest moments that he might have a daughter who would come to pronounce the word 'bugger' with easy jocularity.

But, particularly in Forster's case, it is worth emphasising that this moral shock is reciprocal. That is, not only would Clapham probably have been shocked by Forster, but Forster was actually shocked by Clapham. In his life of his great-aunt Marianne Thornton, daughter of a leading Clapham figure, he writes with sharp distaste of an emotional death scene of 1814, and of the subsequent literary embroidery of grief: 'He was ill. He died. His family and his friends were with him. Why cannot his daughter leave it at that . . . ?'[1]

We remember that in Forster's own novels the characters often die in relative clauses. The prudery of our century about

[1] E. M. Forster: *Marianne Thornton*, 1956, p. 67.

death would have seemed as strange to the Victorians as their own variety does now. But the principle on which reticence is based seems to be identical; sex (or death) is held to be so important that one must never speak of it. And this startling paradox is usually presented, as Forster presents it here, as if it were a truism.

The differences between the generations, then are clear. The vital thread of continuity is less easy to trace. It is best approached, perhaps, by asking were the men of Clapham, and these descendants and successors worldly, and were they cliquy? In reading of Clapham, as of Bloomsbury, one has a very strong sense, certainly, of a self-sufficient set; and in each case it is in some ways separate from high society, and from the values of the great world. Why is it that in either case, the word 'cliquy' seems inadequate and indeed unfair? Since most people normally prefer the company of those who share their tastes and interests, the gravamen of the charge of cliquyness lies in the attitude of hostility or contempt shown to those outside. The exclusiveness of Clapham is well described by Sir James Stephen himself:

> It is not permitted to any coterie altogether to escape the spirit of coterie. Clapham Common, of course, thought itself the best of all possible commons. . . . If the Common was attacked the whole homage was in a flame. If it was laughed at, there could be no remaining sense of decency among men. . . . A critical race, they drew many of their canons of criticism from books and talks of their own parentage; and for those on the outside of the pale, there might be, now and then, some failure of charity. Their festivities were not exhilarating. New faces, new topics, and a less liberal expenditure of wisdom immediately after dinner, would have improved them.[1]

It is worth noting, though, that this critique comes from one of the elect. Great powers of detachment were needed to write thus. One may compare it with the witty, delightful but very partisan defence of Bloomsbury by Virginia Woolf,[2] and conclude

[1] Sir James Stephen: *Essays in Ecclesiastical History* (published 1849), Longmans 1907, ii, 200.
[2] Virginia Woolf: *The Death of the Moth*, 1943, pp. 113–19.

that detachment was more difficult in the atmosphere of Bloomsbury than in that of Clapham.

And yet, neither group was altogether cliquy, because the exclusiveness of each, like their coherence, rested on a principle. A man belonged to Clapham or to Bloomsbury, not by being well-born or clever, or handsome or rich, but by accepting a doctrine, an ethical code and a way of life. The strange word *saved,* constantly used in *The Longest Journey* instead of nice or 'socially acceptable' neatly reminds us that the Clapham spirit remains. Arrogance, rather than cliquyness, is the charge that can be made to stick.

Both sets proclaimed that certain beliefs, attitudes or habits were needed for salvation. This implied an invitation to others to come in if they could; both sets try, from the citadel of their exclusiveness, to reach out to the mass of mankind. And here, it must be said that Clapham was more successful than Bloomsbury and perhaps more in earnest in the attempt. This is not surprising. Their creed, after all, for all its local peculiarities, was a version of historic Christianity. The Bloomsbury one was a local and temporary secular variant. The comfortable incomes of the men of Clapham were useful for their own material well-being and for the causes they served. But there need be no doubt that they would have held to the same ideas, and lived as far as possible the same lives if they had been poor men. Material comfort seems an indispensable prerequisite for the Bloomsbury life. The continuing ethos of the élite has subtly changed; it has become more exquisite, more rarefied, a little more scornful.

The sensitive strength with which we began is still there, but the proportions are different; and in the case of Virginia Woolf the strength, though real enough, cannot quite cope with the sensitiveness. But perhaps the most striking of all points of continuity is a certain determined, solid, serious unconventionality. Success in the world never prevented any of them from questioning the world's standards. A characteristic daughterly memory of Leslie Stephen is recorded by Maitland:

> At the end of a volume my father always asked our opinion as to its merits, and we were required to say which of the characters we liked best and why. I can remember his

indignation when one of us preferred the hero to the far more lifelike villain.[1]

Here the evangelical administrator,[2] the ritualist archdeacon,[3] the lapsed clergyman[4] and the homosexual novelist[5] are recognisably of the same school.

2. *Oxford in 1832*

Political historians have shown in detail what readers of Trollope's political novels already knew, that the Reform Bill of 1832 left abundant power in the hands of the aristocracy. As a great turning-point in this history of the constitution it would seem that 1832 has been much exaggerated.[6] Yet it may be that the prominent position 1832 has taken in the text-books can be justified in another way. Perhaps 1832 did not change England fundamentally; but it made people think. One is aware in reading of this time, and of the next few years, of an unusual depth in public controversy, an almost un-English reaching after first principles.

This was particularly striking in the traditionally pragmatic Church of England. 1832 was perhaps the first moment since the seventeenth century when the Church was really felt to be in danger. The situation is well summarised by Wilfrid Ward:

> Immediately on the passing of the Reform Bill a general attack seemed imminent on the sacredness of tradition in every shape. The men who despised tradition in philosophy as unauthorised sentiment, who waged war against the old-fashioned deification of the English constitution and the English law, now meditated a blow at the historical ordinances and institutions of the English Church. The Church like the State was to be dealt with on utilitarian and radical principles. Her position, too, was to be defined, in all

[1] F. W. Maitland: *The Life and Letters of Leslie Stephen*, 1907, p. 474.
[2] Sir James Stephen.   [3] R. I. Wilberforce.
[4] Leslie Stephen.   [5] E. M. Forster.
[6] Perhaps Bagehot gave the best-balanced view in a single phrase when he spoke of the Act 'which really changed so much, and which seemed to change so much more' in his essay *Lord Althorp and the Reform Act* (*Fortnightly Review*, November 1876).

consistency of logic, as the Servant of the State. The
indefinite views afloat as to the nature of the Anglican
Church, as on the one hand, a political body of Christians,
whose government and discipline were in the hands of the
State, or, on the other, the direct successor, independent in
essentials, of the Church of the Apostles, from whom her
pastors held their commission and inherited their pre-
rogatives, were to be cleared up in favour of the former and
to the exclusion of the latter. It was reported that Parliamentary committees were to revise the Prayer Book and
remodel the Creeds. A measure was in progress for suppression by Act of Parliament of ten Irish bishoprics. The
moving spirits of the triumphant faction were opposed to
the very existence of the Church. 'Next to an aristocracy,'
writes John Mill, 'an Established Church or corporation of
priests, as being by position the great depravers of religion,
and interested in opposing the progress of the human mind,
was the object of my father's greatest detestation.' The
younger Mill himself in 1832 addressed himself to the direct
consideration of the rights of the State over church property; and there were serious fears afloat that Church Reform
might end in the actual abolition of the establishment.[1]

Ward is right to stress the alarm excited by the Mills and the
Westminster Review. Few they might be, but they had the look
of winners. They were learned, serious, systematic and practical.
And utilitarianism, whatever it was in theory, could, when
applied to a practical issue, be made to look like good old
English empiricism and common sense. A point that Ward does
not mention is stressed by Bagehot. The peaceful revolution of
1830 in France 'seemed to prove that change, even great change,
was not so mischievous as had been said'.[2]

It is natural, perhaps, to focus attention on Oxford here, since
both the founders of the two leading schools of Anglican
opposition to the secularist trend were Oxford men. Arnold and
Newman were linked in other ways too. Arnold had been up at
Corpus with Keble, who appears to have had a deep moral,

[1] Wilfrid Ward: *W. G. Ward and the Oxford Movement*, 1889, p. 48.
[2] Bagehot, loc. cit.

though not theological, influence upon him. Keble was the co-founder of the Oxford Movement. Keble represents more clearly than anybody else what the bitterly opposed schools of Arnold and Newman really shared. Keble appropriated the romantic inwardness of Wordsworth and Coleridge, the sense of mystery deep in the heart of man, and disciplined them in the service of religion. Newman conveys Keble's transposition of romantic poetry into traditional theological terms when he speaks of him teaching 'the sacramental system; that is the doctrine that material phenomena are both the types and instruments of real things unseen'.[1]

A disciplined romanticism is one of the keynotes of early and mid-Victorian England. It was opposed, of course, by the utilitarians, and by others instinctively alien to it. But its assumptions were hardly questioned from within, until the early writings of Pater, culminating in *The Renaissance* (1873).

Before discussing the conflicting views of Arnold and Newman, we may pause to recall the position in 1832, in relation to Oxford, of several of the men who will be prominent in the second half of this book. Arnold himself had been headmaster of Rugby for four years, and was already sending to Oxford (usually to Balliol) the first of a stream of distinguished pupils. Stanley was to arrive in 1834, Clough in 1837, and his own son Matthew a few years later. His article against *The Oxford Malignants* was to come in 1836. Shortly before his death in 1842, Arnold was to return to Oxford as Regius Professor of History. Then he and Newman met for the second and last time, at an Oriel dinner in a party of only three. They were perfectly friendly, and talked with animation about African natural history. They were both, after all, very English.[2] In 1832, Newman had been a fellow of Oriel for ten years, and Vicar of the University church for four. He had, as he phrased it, 'come out of his shell' about 1828, and had begun to influence some of the younger fellows, including Hurrell Froude, who had been Keble's pupil, and Robert Wilberforce, son and biographer of the great William. At this

---

[1] Newman: *Apologia*, chapter 1.
[2] See Meriol Trevor: *Newman: The Pillar and the Cloud*, pp. 263–5, for full account.

point the shadowy connection between the Clapham sect and
the Oxford Movement becomes palpable. Robert Wilberforce,
like Newman, eventually became a Roman Catholic. Hurrell
Froude, though still under thirty in 1832, had only four years
to live. But Newman always emphasised his cardinal importance
in the beginnings of the Oxford Movement; and he said himself
that his one good deed was bringing Keble and Newman
together. A connection of quite a different kind is that he was
the elder brother of the biographer of Carlyle, who was in 1832
still a miserable, underfed schoolboy at Westminster, but who
was to come up to Oriel before Newman left it, and come
temporarily under his influence, before that of Carlyle proved
stronger.

Despite all that has been written, it is still not easy to focus
Oriel College in 1832. It was an élite institution in a university
still tender towards easy eighteenth-century ways. The prize
fellowship, judged by written examination on intellectual merit,
was the goal of many of the cleverest and most serious under-
graduates. The senior common room was felt by others to be
oppressively intellectual and disconcertingly ascetic. It had not,
as yet, any distinctive party flavour in church controversies.
Keble was not resident, though his connection with the university
had been made closer by his election to the Chair of Poetry in
1831. Whately, the dominating personality of Oriel in the 1820's,
left Oxford in 1831. He seems to have been the first person to
sense the approach of the Oxford Movement, at a time when
Newman and his friends had no inkling of their own future
course. He was opposed to the spirit he saw forming, agreeing
more nearly with Arnold.

Whately is one of those men whose importance lies in the
strength of personality, and who therefore become shadowy
figures to posterity. But his significance for us lies in the neat
way he illustrates the surprise of liberal, progressive thinkers at
the course taken by Newman. He had early sensed Newman's
intellectual power. He looked to him as a valuable recruit against
the vices of the old Oxford, idleness, ignorance, entrenched
privilege, unthinking two-bottle orthodoxy. Of course, Whately
thought, a clever and serious young man, with no aristocratic

connections and no interest in field sports, will be on the side of reform. And reform to Whately meant both the liberalising of doctrine and more serious attention to teaching and intellectual pursuits.

What he overlooked, perhaps, was the essential unlikeness between the old High Church movement and the new. It was a fundamental difference, not merely one of talent and genius; it is best illustrated by the attitude to State control. The two-bottle orthodox, who were still generally dominant in the Oxford of 1832 seem to have made only a shadowy separation in their minds between the idea of the Church and the idea of the State. 'Church and King' as a motto satisfied them. The phrase represented in their minds a whole corpus of traditional customs and assumptions, to which they were strongly attached by sentiment, rather than by thought. It was an intensely English, even insular, view. They were unworried by abstract questions about the relation of the Church of England to the Roman Church, or to the Church in England before the Reformation. But as good Englishmen they thought it a duty to be hostile and suspicious to popery, and contemptuous of Irish Catholics.

Newman and his friends rejected all this as intellectually muddled, and as hopelessly complacent in the sharp winds of 1832. They asserted that the essence of the Church was prior to any connection with the state. They turned the quiet Erastianism of the old High Church on its head, and said that the State ought to obey the Church. By stressing the forgotten doctrine of the Apostolic Succession, they raised the whole issue of the Early Church, the nature of the Reformation, and relations with Rome. They were, at first, it is true, just as anti-papal as the old High Churchmen. But ideas have their own logic, and move with their own power, while a religion based on habit and instinct, like the old Oxford High Churchmanship, remains the same. The two were bound to diverge more and more.

The central paradox which so puzzled Whately, was that it was Arnold, the liberal latitudinarian, not Keble and Newman, who took over and developed the Erastian spirit of the old High Churchmen. He changed its aspect a good deal certainly. He was for comprehension, not exclusion. He wished to see every doctrine that was an obstacle to a unified Protestant national church muted or dropped. Arnold's Erastianism was open and welcoming; and his eager, active, rather superficial mind approached the question without any deep theological study. The Bible for doctrine (interpreted as each believer privately thought best) and the State for cohesive organisation were his guiding principles. But he made one vital stipulation. The private interpretation of the Bible must not strike at the fundamental Christian doctrine – the Divinity of Christ.

To argue the merits of these contrasted theologies lies outside my scope. But in terms of practical prospects, the weak point of each was the same. Both Arnold and Newman were planning the future of the Church of England. And the Church of England is a complex historical growth. Its members do not *experience* it as a separate portion of a once undivided Catholic Church, or as a Protestant sect, which happens by accident to have bishops, but has the immense advantage of being national.

Both Arnold and Newman saw the weak point in the other's approach. The Oxford Movement led to Rome; Arnold's system led to infidelity. Arnold was aware of the first fact years before Newman suspected it, and Arnold died without seeing the second, which Newman had seen from the first. But if Arnold had lived to be ninety, as Newman (almost) did, he would have seen the line of succession of his ideas, passing through men like Stanley and Kingsley, on to *Essays and Reviews* and Benjamin Jowett.

Of course, we must not exaggerate here. The Oxford Movement was the parent of late Victorian ritualism and modern Anglo-Catholicism as well as of the Catholic revival; and Arnold had more genuinely Anglican successors than Jowett. Yet each man was in his way right to say that the other was trying to lead the Church of England on an unknown path where the bulk of its members would never follow.

And what meanwhile of Gladstone? He missed being in Oxford in 1832 by a few days only. He took a double first, as Peel had done twenty-three years earlier, in December 1831, and did not allow the examinations to prevent him from going to hear Newman preach 'a most able discourse of a very philo-sophical character' on December 11th.[1]

Both the Reform Bill and the Oxford Movement were still in the future. Not long after this both Gladstone and Newman set out for Italy, and for each the journey was momentous. On 31st March 1832, Gladstone entered St Peter's in Rome, and experienced 'his first conception of unity in the Church'; and a few weeks later, in Naples, he had a sudden new impression of Christianity as a 'ministry of symbols, its channels of grace, its unending line of teachers from the Head: a sublime construction based throughout upon historic fact. . . .'[2]

This is the very language of the Oxford Movement, but it was not learnt (at least consciously) in Oxford. Gladstone had to go to Italy to find his own version of what the Oxford of his time had been pointing vaguely towards, but had not yet articulated. Gladstone's Oxford of the late '20's was a world of revived learning and new enthusiasm for a small élite, only slightly affecting an inert mass. The enthusiasm came first and the principles on which to base it came later. It is a strange fact that the most anti-Roman (eventually) of all famous Victorian High Churchmen had to go to Italy to achieve his intuition of what Oxford was about to bring forth.

At the end of the same year Newman set out for Italy, and was out of England for more than six months, during which time he had a nearly mortal illness and spent long hours brooding on the theory of the Church, and the political problems of the day. A few days after his return to England, Keble attacked the Government for interfering with the Irish bishoprics. The movement that led towards Rome began as a protest against interference with the ultra-Protestant Church of Ireland, and against the Whiggish intention to take some slight note of the wishes of benighted Irish papists.

1832, then, is a striking moment in the lives of several great men, as well as in general religious and secular history. And its story reminds us how unforeseeable the future is. Arnold, Newman and Gladstone were all men of exceptional ability and determination. They were all natural leaders of men. But none

[1] Morley, I, 79.   [2] Morley, I, 87–8.

of them dreamed of the destinations to which they were being carried by the inner logic of their ideas. Only they had a sense of being led down a path they could not see. Newman spoke for many others when he wrote, about this time, 'The night is dark, and I am far from home.'

II

The men whose biographies are studied in the chapters that follow are very various. They include a Scots atheist of Calvinist leanings, a Broad Churchman, a high Anglican and a Catholic convert. And the biographers range from liberal agnostics like Morley to liberal Catholics like Ward. Apart from the talent and energy without which they obviously would not figure in such a selection, they all have two things in common, and perhaps only two. They all believe that traditional moral principles in some form are right, and necessary to society, though they justify this belief in totally different ways. And they all prefer an appeal to conscience to an appeal to reason. This is true even of Newman, one of the subtlest reasoners ever known. It is true even of Macaulay with his devastating weight of remembered facts. It is yet more obviously true of Stanley and Arnold, of Smiles, of Froude, Carlyle and Gladstone. Here again we see, that over and above its direct influence, the Evangelical tradition was the dominant one, the one to which others instinctively conformed when they could.

6

STANLEY'S ARNOLD

✼

There are three kinds of fame. The first (and least interesting from a biographical point of view) is due solely to events. In our period, Grace Darling, the lighthouse-keeper's daughter, who helped in a rescue, attained a national fame that persisted through three generations. The second kind is the fame earned by being truly exceptional in intellect, in genius, in virtue or in wickedness, or simply in the possession of a rich personality. The third kind, the kind that confronts us when we consider Dr Arnold, is more elusive. It lies in a peculiar combination of the typical and the influential. If a man is merely typical of a large class of people in his time, he will not be remembered. If he is influential enough to shape the destiny of nations or initiate new thoughts or modify the sensibilities of men, then he will claim a place in the second category. But if he is both typical and influential, if he appears influential to contemporaries, but later appears in retrospect much more typical than he seemed at the time, he may be a member of our third group.

It is always useful, before considering in detail what a man really was, to consider his myth; and perhaps most people who have never read or thought much about Dr Arnold would, if challenged, describe him as a great Victorian headmaster, who changed the face of English education. Making due allowance for the inadequacy of any rough, short summary, we might say that only one word here is incorrect – the word *Victorian*. Arnold died in 1842, at about the time the Queen celebrated her twenty-third birthday. He became headmaster of Rugby in 1828, before Catholic Emancipation, before the Reform Bill, before the Oxford Movement, when the Waverley novels were still being published. In 1828, Tennyson had not yet gone up to Cambridge, and that very un-Victorian best-seller *Pelham* had not yet been completed. Now the reason for the mild surprise these facts excite is surely linked with Arnold's influential quality. He was not a Victorian, but he trained Victorians. His son was one of the most eminent of all Victorians. His pupils changed the face of education. In an odd way he seems more typical of the decade that followed his death than of any period in his own lifetime.

There are some men, perhaps, who achieve fame of this kind by shrewd guesses about the way the world is going. To conjecture what people will say next year and say it this year requires, no doubt, some talent; but it is a talent essentially akin to those of the racing tipster and the stock-exchange columnist. And indeed, these last, if they do their job well, have as much claim as others to the accolade which a certain class of historian loves to give – the Man Who Was Ahead of his Time. But racing tipsters do not (or ought not to) influence the results of horse-races. Dr Arnold (all the evidence suggests) really was an influential man. And, beyond any doubt at all, he was a sincere man. He said what he thought, not what he thought people would like to hear.

Part, though perhaps not a great part, of his influence may indeed be ascribed to chance. By the accident of having a country cottage near Wordsworth, he got to know him well, and was able to introduce Matthew to him. This meeting between a Poet Laureate in his seventies and an undergraduate had some interesting repercussions on the future of literary taste. And while some of his more famous pupils may be counted products of the Arnold system, others, especially Arthur Hugh Clough, would have been just as remarkable, perhaps in a slightly different way, if they had never met Arnold. We must beware of giving the teacher all the credit for the inherent quality of his pupils – a mistake some writers on Arnold have tended to make. As a brisk corrective, we may remember that no one gives the notorious Dr Keate, headmaster of Eton, much credit for Gladstone's achievement. Yet Gladstone was as loyal, and even as sentimental, an old Etonian as some of Arnold's famous pupils were old Rugbeians. Finally, without raising the difficult question of a man's responsibility for his chromosomes or for those of his wife, we may be content to say that it was chance that ensured that one of Arnold's sons should have had the talents of Matthew. On the other hand Matthew's lifelong reverence for his father, who died when he was an undergraduate, and the peculiar quality of his tribute to him in the poem *Rugby Chapel*, may fairly be credited to the father as much as to the son. Here Arnold stands quite alone among the great men whose biographies are studied in the second section of this book. Carlyle, Newman and Macaulay left no descendants, and those of Gladstone made no claim to greatness.

Stanley's Arnold created a new type of hero in biographical literature. One can read dozens of volumes of *Life and Letters* written in the fifty years that followed its appearance in 1844, and recognise that with greater or less skill, with greater or less truthfulness, the Stanley formula is being copied. And, almost always, as is fitting, the prevailing impression is that the imitators do not equal the pioneer. But, of course, Stanley could not thus have influenced the future course of biography, and the whole manner in which his contemporaries ordinarily thought of character, if he had not been dealing with a legend possessing an independent life. Stanley was exceptional in the degree and in the discriminating intelligence of his Arnold-worship. But he did not invent it. A mass of evidence could be produced to show this; but only two items need be mentioned. *Tom Brown's Schooldays* has an abiding interest because it shows the power of Arnold's personality in enforcing his spell upon ordinary boys. Hughes did not know Arnold well, and was not an especially clever man. His hero will obviously settle down into the sort of squire who may possess a library, but will only really read about four books, one of them about hunting, and one about estate management. The book stands, then, as a remarkable testimony that this ordinary unimpressionable English clay could be moulded, and even improved, by a schoolmaster.

Another of Arnold's pupils, Hodson of Hodson's Horse, wrote from India of the death of Arnold as:

a national misfortune . . . As it is, the influence which he did produce has been most lasting and striking in its effects. It is felt even in India; I cannot say more than that.[1]

[1] Lionel J. Trotter: *The Life of Hodson*, Everyman, pp. 83–4.

But what was so new about the type of hero? First, and most obviously, he was a schoolmaster. This is not such a trivial point as it may appear to be. Arnold was other things besides a schoolmaster; he was a learned, though perhaps not an immensely gifted ancient historian. He was a religious controversialist. Stanley chose to make all those talents and interests secondary, almost nugatory. Indeed, as we shall see, he was unhappy about Arnold's role as controversialist.

To turn a schoolmaster into a hero involves a whole set of assumptions, most of which were unfamiliar in previous generations. No doubt the groundwork had been laid by the romantic poets of the generation before Arnold's with their glorification of the child. But the Wordsworthian child, and even more the Blakean child, functions independently of teaching. The schoolroom is either an irrelevance or a prison-house; and above all, they are *children*, not adolescent boys. Though Arnold exhibited a certain manly tenderness towards little boys, and said (no doubt with perfect truth) that he could not receive a new boy from his father without emotion,[1] his real interest lay in the development of the conscience and intellect (in that order) of the clever sixth-former. The assumption that the years from fifteen to eighteen are the crucially formative ones was a new one, entirely distinct alike from eighteenth-century commonsense and from romantic idealisations. It was a further step, and an even more surprising one, to suppose that the training of one particular sixth form was a work of the highest national importance. Both Arnold and Stanley believed that Arnold's extraordinary personal force would have been less effective for good in the highest places of church and state than they were at Rugby.

The second new feature in the type of heroism presented is that it was neither worldly nor spiritual but *moral*. In this it stands apart both from the long tradition of hagiography, and from the tradition of recounting the deeds of the heroes of this world. Two great sixteenth-century biographies, Roper's *More* and Cavendish's *Wolsey*, may serve as splendid examples of the

[1] A. P. Stanley: *Life of Thomas Arnold, D.D., Head-Master of Rugby*, (1844), Murray, 1904, p. 155. All quotations are taken from this edition.

types from which Stanley diverged. And he diverged equally far from the later tradition, initiated by Boswell, where the stress is on the uniqueness and thus on the strangeness of personality.

Arnold was, of course, a devout Christian, and an amateur theologian. Despite his loyalty, Stanley was too intellectually acute, and too learned not to see that Arnold was an incompetent theologian. His religious system has hardly any definable content; and the portrait Stanley paints is emphatically not that of a saint, any more than it is that of a great theologian. For Arnold, religion was interesting because of its moral consequences. (For Stanley, especially in later times, after he had written the *Life*, religion was much more than this.)

Nor is Stanley's Arnold a unique individual *à la* Boswell. Very intimate in one sense the book is, since the author feels so close in spirit to the subject, and since he spent his own most impressionable years as the cleverest pupil in Arnold's little Rugby élite. This proximity of author to subject is also the key to the book's lack of another kind of intimacy. What is felt by the reader is what Stanley had felt as a boy – the intensity of Arnold's *effect*. His private conversations, his deepest thoughts, his intimate hopes and fears – all the things that make every page of Boswell's Johnson fascinating – these are absent. Many letters are given, but mostly without comment or analysis; and, in any case, Arnold was not an outstanding letter-writer. Arnold's family life, which could have been endued with absorbing interest, receives perfunctory treatment. Striking incidents, which we know from other sources that Stanley remembered, such as Matthew, aged seven, picking roses from the garden to represent Lancaster and York in the Wars of the Roses, are excluded by Stanley's rigid classical restraint.

II

Stanley himself is not perhaps as widely remembered to-day as he deserves to be. There may be several reasons for this. His own life, by Rowland Prothero,[1] though perfectly sensible, and full of useful information, lacks any compelling literary quality, and

[1] Later Lord Ernle.

will never be much read except by scholars. A great deal of his intellectual energy was expended on the topical, and thus many of his writings are deprived of any strong appeal to men of later times. His leading quality was a balanced intelligence, a wish to see every side of the question. He saw his mission as Dean of Westminster, and as the most learned and lucid ecclesiastical journalist of his day to reconcile parties and to correct excess. Though, as I have said, his writings are mostly topical – about the Gorham case, *Essays and Reviews,* Colenso and so on – he always sees the topical in a long perspective of history. He is easily the most distinguished writer of the Broad Church school in his time; and he helps to mitigate the reproach, paradoxical yet just, of fanaticism and violence which lies against some of those who agreed with him on principles, but who were so different from him in spirit. No ultramontane, no fundamentalist, no atheist of the Victorian age is so violent, so reckless, so libellous, so self-righteous as Kingsley is in the name of moderation, fair play and Broad Church principles. Arnold, too, as we shall see, could be violent. Stanley had those very rare and precious gifts, sympathy with people who disagreed with him and an intelligent grasp of their mental processes. An aristocrat both by birth and intellectual formation, he lacked the common touch. His eloquence was a literary eloquence, a chiselled mastery of prose rather than an invitation to the feelings. A revealing anecdote about his first sermon after his ordination is recorded by his biographer:

> After the service, two old women of the parish were overheard discussing the sermon and the preacher. The first old woman observed to her friend, 'Well, I do feel empty-like!' 'And so do I,' returned the other; 'that young man didn't give us much to feed on.'[1]

This was in a Norfolk village. Stanley was a man for Westminster and Oxford, not for Norfolk villages; and it is worth remembering that the very greatest Victorians could stir the feelings of villagers as well as those of senators.[2]

All the biographers accorded detailed treatment here were in

[1] Rowland Prothero: *Life and Letters of Dean Stanley,* I, 243.
[2] Carlyle and Gladstone, for instance.

varying degree disciples of the men they wrote about, though, of course, this general term covers wide differences of attitude. It allows for Trevelyan seeing Macauley as pathetic, for Froude seeing Carlyle as boorish and unintentionally cruel, for Morley seeing Gladstone as totally mistaken on religious questions. Stanley is the most complete and loyal disciple of them all. Yet he is the only one who could seriously be reckoned by an impartial posterity superior to his subject. No one would suggest that Ward was a greater man than Newman, or Morley than Gladstone. But Stanley was most certainly a cleverer man than Arnold, and certainly a better writer. Whether we call him greater will depend on imponderable factors, like our assessment of Arnold's lasting educational influence, or the relative importance we ascribe to intellect and feeling in human life. But Stanley's subservience to Arnold, taken with our sense of his superiority to him at many points, is the central paradox of his book; and the study of it can be fruitful.[1] In a letter of 2 March 1828, which Stanley quotes[2] and which has very often been quoted since, Arnold wrote: '. . . My object will be, if possible, to form Christian men, for Christian boys I can scarcely hope to make.'

This is a key sentence in Arnold's thinking, and thus in the whole tradition of Victorian education, and it has been much misunderstood. This is not very surprising, because, if it really meant what it said, it would be nonsense. If the word *Christian* meant here what it usually means, that is, one who believes and practises the Christian religion, then common experience will show that a boy is just as likely to be a Christian as a man. Neither belief nor devotion is an uncommon feature of early years. But Arnold was primarily concerned with morality, not with religion. And by Christian, here, he meant, one who can stand by his conscience against the threats, or the mockery, or the seduction of the crowd. And Arnold seems to have been justified in supposing that, while the ability to stand firm in this way is exceptional in adults, it is rarer still in children. For

[1] For a fuller treatment of Stanley as a theologian see my *Anglican Attitudes*, Collins, 1959.

[2] p. 75.

this kind of misunderstanding, Arnold himself must be held partly responsible, since he would use words in a Humpty-Dumpty spirit, and was determined to be the master and not the servant, especially of words like the word *Christian,* which had powerful emotional force for him.

Another kind of misunderstanding is less excusable. Some writers, who seem to possess an amazing power of oblivion over their own early years, make out that Arnold was culpably pessimistic about the nature of boys; and one writer, whom it would be uncharitable to mention by name, actually contrives to blame this upon an entirely imaginary 'Calvinism' in Arnold. It is possible to think that Arnold expected too much, and was too much horrified by the vices of adolescence. It is possible to think that his ideal was faulty, and his educational method unsound. One may consider the following overstrained and undesirable:

> At the very sight of a knot of vicious or careless boys gathered round the great school-house fire, 'It makes me think,' he would say, 'that I see the Devil in the midst of them.'[1]

But that he was substantially correct in his estimate of the conduct of boys in the lump does not admit of serious dispute.

And here we touch on one of Arnold's great strengths. Most people who are as enthusiastic and idealistic about education as he was (and few are in that degree) are prone to illusions about the innocence of children. Most people who are as realistic as Arnold about the nature of youth (a larger number) are prone to wary cynicism, or at least to pessimistic views about the moral results of the educational process. But it is most unusual to combine the loftiest aims with the earthiest realism.

Yet another important aspect of Arnold's system lies hidden in the quoted sentence about Christian men and Christian boys. Boys left Arnold's care at the age of eighteen. If he had been a don, he might have been content to believe that the manhood, and thus the potentially 'Christian' character came after that age. But Arnold was not a patient man. It galled him to have to

[1] Stanley, op. cit., p. 103.

think that the fruits of his work could only appear in the lives of pupils who had gone away. He wanted to see and gather them himself. Perhaps this manhood, this precious un-boylike moral independence could be hastened. If it could be, he would have the joy of seeing the fruition of his labours in his own institution, and he would have a trained cadre of moral warriors to watch over, guide and discipline the intractable boyish elements. In this hope lies the origin of the Rugby praepostor, the precocious Arnoldian sixth-former.

Opinions are sharply divided still over the merits of Arnold's practice here. Was he being realistic at the same time as he was nobly trusting in the moral fibre of his precocious young men?

The fact that his system has been so widely copied suggests that it cannot have been wholly impractical.[1]

On the other side there are weighty complaints from those who maintain that Arnold attempted to frustrate the natural order by expediting the rate of growth, and that the most talented and sensitive boys suffered most from the forcing process.

III

It was shrewd of Arnold to see that he was naturally ambitious, and candid of Stanley to record this judgment on himself.[2] But it is a slightly misleading truth. Arnold was ambitious of achievement, *judged by his own standards*, and not as the world judges. The world would have taken it for granted in 1827 that it was a greater thing to be Dean of a great cathedral than to be headmaster of Rugby; but Arnold's ambition would not have led him to make the change. He wanted influence, not fame – and influence over men's consciences more than over public policies. Ambition of this type does not make a man pushing, or

[1] Some features of the system had a very long run, especially the idea that senior and responsible boys were more concerned in running the school than assistant masters. At Winchester in my time an assistant master who thought there should be a half-holiday had to persuade the head boy to ask the headmaster. A direct request would have been considered the height of bad taste, and, probably, would have been refused.

[2] Stanley, p. 31.

avid for honours, but it does make him egoistical. It was characteristic of Arnold to give as a reason why he might accept a bishopric in the Antipodes that this would ensure that at least one diocese was run on the principles he approved. Perhaps it was characteristic of Stanley not to see (or not to reveal that he saw?) that this was amusing.

This egoism may not have been the cause of Arnold's preference for delegating his authority to the sixth form rather than to his colleagues. No doubt he was sincerely convinced that he was doing the right thing; but it was also convenient. The praepostor owed his position entirely to Arnold, was at an age to be most strongly influenced by Arnold's magnetism, and would depart for ever in a year or two, to be replaced by another admiring boy. The assistant master is less impressionable, more permanent, and altogether more likely to raise objections.

We have seen that Arnold was a moralist rather than a theologian. One of the most striking impressions left by Stanley's book is of Arnold's immense power of feeling on moral questions. The idea of ethics as a rational system made little appeal to him. He would perhaps have claimed, if challenged, that his morality depended on his religious belief; but the statement would not have meant much, since moral ideas had so much greater prominence in his heart. Arnold's morality was a passion, not a code. It requires to be sketched rather than analysed. Its most striking feature was devotion to truth. Lying was the most terrible of all vices to him,[1] and he seemed to admit of no exceptions whatever. This, according to traditional ethical wisdom, is eccentric. Is it really a moral duty to answer truthfully if asked by a murderer which way his intended victim has gone? But it was a kind of eccentricity peculiarly characteristic of nineteenth-century Protestant England, and especially of the Broad Church school. But the *cause célèbre* involving the public clash of this view with its opposite, Kingsley's attack on Newman, was as yet many years in the future.

---

[1] For a revealing incident, showing Arnold's view of lying, see T. W. Bamford: *Thomas Arnold*, pp. 49–53. In this instance Arnold's passionate morality led him into trouble, since the boy to whom he gave eighteen strokes of the cane had been telling the truth after all.

Apart from this one imposing feature, Arnold's moral system lacks clear landmarks, and this is not surprising, since it is the tone of feeling that counts. Stanley, as a clever sixth former, sitting day by day under Arnold's eye, was wonderfully well-placed to catch the nuances of the ethos, and he developed later the literary power to convey what he had felt. The subject has an importance wider than the biographical, and wider than Arnold's (admittedly great) influence on the future of education. While we read Stanley's account in his third chapter, we get an inkling of an answer to that extremely complex question, 'What was the nature of the change from the romantic to the Victorian, or what are the underlying differences between the age of Byron and Shelley and the age of Tennyson and Browning?'

The prevailing impression left on a reader of the lives of Byron and Shelley is of the overriding power of impulse. Byron may have regretted being the creature of impulse; Shelley certainly gloried in it. For many young men growing up in the shadow of these short-lived giants, unpredictable impulses, and thus irresponsible actions, must have seemed like a proof of being really alive, since the most alive were those who felt the most. Untidy lives, and socially 'impossible' young men were the natural consequence.

We are apt, no doubt, to exaggerate the respectability of the early Victorians; and Thackeray, for one, is there to remind us that hints of disreputable ways of living lie under the surface of books considered perfectly proper for a young lady's table. But making full allowance for this, every impartial observer must be struck by the emotional power and the practical influence of the idea of duty in the years 1840–70. These were the years when Arnold's pupils flourished, and when many who had not been his pupils had adopted his ethos.

Arnold did not go counter to the ethics of impulse; he transformed them while maintaining their essential insights. He was at one with Shelley in despising dull routines and in believing that every significant act must have the quality of a deeply-felt experience. But the startling change he introduced was this: the deeply-felt experience could also be the everyday thing. Instead of a castle in Italy or a battle in Greece, Arnold put morning prayers or the first lesson on Cicero's style. To feel something ordinarily considered humdrum as exciting, to experience in the repeated acts of everyday, inspiration, mystery, terror as of the unknown and the unique – this is a kind of genius. Arnold had it; and it is a recognisable descendant of the original ecstasy of the romantic poets. Arnold, probably without conscious intent, but just through the prompting of his heart, and the extraordinary force of his personality, disciplined the ecstasy. He tamed it, but he did not weaken it. Rather he gave it staying-power. One of the most obvious advantages of the Arnold over the Shelley ethos lies in its power of facing the discouragements of life. Courage, endurance, hope take the place of lassitude, self-pity and despair.

Here, above all, we see the curious combination of the typical and the influential with which this chapter began. The characteristic tone of the mid-Victorian élite upright, passionate, dutiful, intensely emotional and immensely energetic – the tone, say, of Gladstone in his middle years around 1860 – is recognisably the Arnold tone. But Arnold had been dead since 1842.

The weak point of men of this type – on the whole a very strong and effective type – lies in hasty judgment and an unconscious tendency to self-righteousness. It was these qualities in Arnold that caused Stanley the most uneasiness, for, though he was a disciple, he was not a blindly admiring disciple; and, temperamentally, he was very unlike Arnold. He liked to be dispassionate, though there were times when the intensity of his feeling about Arnold decreed that he should not be. Arnold, like the romantic poets, thought that if you could not get excited about an issue, either it was negligible, or you were at fault for not feeling more. Thus it was extremely characteristic of Arnold to despise and dislike the subtle charm of rural Warwickshire, about which George Eliot was later to write with such eloquent admiration. His feelings required the drama and surprise of mountain scenery, and he never spent an unnecessary day in Rugby, if he could be in the Lake District.

Arnold's most recklessly unfair moments were those when he was influenced by *odium theologicum*; and this was directed mainly at Newman. Stanley was unhappy about this, both

because he hated to see Arnold being uncharitable, and because
he himself, as an undergraduate at Oxford in the early years of
the Oxford Movement, had felt something of Newman's intellectual authority and emotional sway. His personal difficulty in
reconciling his worship of Arnold with his deep respect for
the man Arnold hated can be seen in a letter of 1833, when he
says:

> He [Newman] does appear to be a man of the most self-
> denying goodness that can well be conceived, and to do
> good to a very great extent . . . I dread more and more a
> collision between Arnold and the High Church. At present
> he and Newman seem to be almost antagonist powers,
> whereas really they are of the very same essence, so to
> speak.[1]

'The very same essence' – how he would have liked to believe
that; but no one else believed it, least of all Arnold. Less than
three years later, in the *Edinburgh Review* for April 1836, Arnold
published a most intemperate and self-righteous attack on
Newman under the title (chosen by the editor) *The Oxford
Malignants*. The word *malignant* had strong seventeenth-century
associations, being a Roundhead word for High Churchmen and
royalists. Though Arnold did not choose the title himself, it
cannot be called misleading as a foretaste of what the article
contained.

The following is a typical passage:

> . . . the fanaticism of the English High Churchmen has been
> the fanaticism of mere foolery. A dress, a ritual, a ceremony,
> a technical phraseology; the superstition of a priesthood
> without its power . . . objects so pitiful that if gained ever
> so completely they would lead to no effect, except to the
> changing of sense into silliness, and holiness of heart and life
> into formality and hypocrisy.

Even as rumbustious party attack, this was extraordinarily
wide of the mark. Newman cared very little about ceremonies,
and every sensitive person who heard him preach, including
unsympathetic witnesses, like J. A. Froude, and rather detached
ones, like Arnold's son, testified to the strength and sincerity of

[1] Prothero, I, p. 134.

his thirst for personal holiness, and the searching examination of conscience that he stimulated in his hearers.

All this Stanley understood; and so, he was confronted as a biographer with a vexing dilemma. He tried to cope with it in the following passage:

> Though only a temporary production, it forms a feature in his life too strongly marked to be passed over without notice. On the one hand it completely represents his own deep feeling at the time, and in impassioned earnestness, force of expression, and power of narrative, is perhaps equal to anything he ever wrote; on the other hand it contains the most startling and vehement, because the most personal, language which he ever allowed himself deliberately to use. The offence caused by it, even amongst his friends, was very great; and whatever feeling, political or theological, existed against him was for the time considerably aggravated by it.[1]

The measured, judicial tone here should not conceal from us the pain, even humiliation that Stanley felt in making damaging admissions. He was telling the truth as he saw it, as Arnold would have wished; and he was expressing a balanced view, which requires little revision to-day. This is creditable, yet there is something lacking. He does not permit his own judgment here enough leverage on the general view of Arnold's character offered by the book as a whole. It is not enough to say that Arnold did this; we want to know why he did it, or at least to speculate what kind of man he must have been if he did it. Too truthful to conceal Arnold's weaknesses, he was still too warm an admirer to allow that they could be fundamental. But against this partial failure on Stanley's part must be set his splendid moments of insight as when he says 'He governed the school precisely on the same principles as he would have governed a great empire.'[2] This is most strikingly and suggestively true; it raises in our minds all sorts of parallels with the high imperialist phase in English history that was forty years or more in the future when Stanley wrote. Only a very perspicacious man could have written it in 1844.

[1] Stanley, p. 382.   [2] Stanley, p. 87.

Despite the admiring tone of the book as a whole, the *Oxford Malignants* is by no means the only topic on which Stanley feels able to criticise Arnold. The criticisms are there; they are intelligent and telling. But they are very unobtrusive. Anyone reading casually, 'for the story' might miss them altogether. At one point he does even generalise the complaint about the *Oxford Malignants* article; and this must be set against the criticism of Stanley made in my last paragraph. He says:

> He had a tendency to judge individuals, with whom he had no personal acquaintance, from his conception of the party to which they belonged.[1]

But even this does not fully cover the case, since the party's principles, as well as Newman's personal character, were misjudged by Arnold.

Sometimes the tone of the criticism, as well as its unobtrusive brevity, is a little misleading. For instance:

> The unwillingness which he had, even in common life, to act in any individual case without some general law to which he might refer it, ran through everything, and at times it would almost seem as if he invented universal rules with the express object of meeting particular cases.[2]

This is very shrewd, and could easily have made the keynote of an essay hostile to Arnold. It really means that Arnold exalted his accidental prejudices and personal tastes into eternal laws. This can lead to Pharisaism of the most deadly kind. Yet how emollient this damaging analysis sounds in Stanley's own words. Even when he is most critical, Stanley is an honest defence counsel making admissions. He is never a prosecutor.

Since he did not allow the blemishes he perceived in Arnold to affect the general tone of his panegyric, Stanley's fine, original and very influential book lacks one of the notes of the greatest biographies. Both Boswell on *Johnson* and Froude on *Carlyle* attain to a tragic grandeur, because the terrible Pascalian paradox on the greatness and littleness of man is clothed in the details and contradictions of a single memorable person. Johnson's secret terrors and his overbearing roughness are seen to rise from the same unfathomable mystery as his intellectual

[1] p. 171.   [2] p. 89.

brilliance and his touching generosity; and similarly with the greatness and littleness of Carlyle.[1] 'It is private life that governs the world.' So said one of the greatest public figures of Stanley's time.[2] It is private life that makes the greatest biographies. Stanley's cast of mind, as his theological and historical writings show, was notable for an abundance of 'negative capability' – the quality for which Keats praised Shakespeare. But he was insensitive to mystery, and impatient of paradox. Impressively equipped in many respects, he lacked part of the armoury of the very greatest biographers.

IV

But it is time to test this last assertion by turning to the finest and best-remembered scene in Stanley's book – the death scene. Its power, which is considerable, is a restrained power. Though writing so near the event, Stanley avoided strong expressions of grief and loss. Indeed, it is very surprising to turn from the finely structured closing pages to the actual record of what Stanley felt about the living and the dead Arnold. In May 1834, shortly before leaving Rugby, he wrote to a friend:

> Most sincerely must I thank God for His goodness in placing me here to live with Arnold. Yet I always feel that the happiness is a dangerous one, and that loving him and admiring him as I do to the very verge of all love and admiration that can be paid to man, I fear I have passed the limit and made him an idol . . .[3]

On hearing of the death on 12 June 1842, he took to his bed for some hours and then went at once to Rugby.[4] For the rest of her long life he always wrote to Mrs Arnold on the death-anniversary.

As a biographer Stanley was fortunate that he was not at Rugby himself at the time of the death, and that one of his closest friends, who was also one of Arnold's favourite pupils, was present. He was able to give a very full account of Arnold's last hours and the sequel, without having to rely on agonised

[1] See chapter 9.   [2] Benjamin Disraeli.
[3] Prothero, op. cit., p. 102.   [4] Ibid., p. 311.

perceptions of his own or bringing his own deep feelings directly into the narrative. He maintained thus what Prothero in one of his few memorable phrases calls the 'glow of repressed enthusiasm'[1] of the book as a whole. As a result, the book's last pages have a mingled quality of art and spontaneity. From the very start, in which he had unobtrusively mentioned the hereditary illness which led to the early death of Arnold's father and brothers, the whole book had been moving to this climax. The climax is presented by means of a sharp antithesis. On the one hand, this was an untimely death of a man of forty-six, who had still immense unfulfilled energies and capacities, and it was sudden and shocking, because he appeared to be in perfect health the day before. On the other hand, it was a destined fulfilment which must occur then and at no other time. Thus his last entry in his diary, written before any sign of disease was noticed, began:

> The day after to-morrow is my birthday, if I am permitted
> to live to see it – my forty-seventh birthday since my birth.
> How large a portion of my life on earth is already passed . . .
> how nearly I can now say, 'Vixi'.[2]

He died right at the end of the summer term, when the older boys were leaving for good, and when Arnold was thinking eagerly of the Lake District, where several of his children, though not his wife, had already gone on ahead. The news was brought to them 'just as the early summer dawn – the dawn of his forty-seventh birthday – was breaking over that beautiful valley'. This unobtrusive phrase, with its deliberately odd wording (for you do not usually speak of birthdays of the dead), subtly suggests eternal life, a stroke of fate that is also a decree of mercy.

All this is like a harmonious landscape painting, with all tones carefully matched. But at the same time Stanley is able to give some intimate touches, the touchingly useless curiosity of the dying Arnold about *angina pectoris*. How like him to want to know at such a moment why this disease was especially common in large towns. And how vivid is the reader's awareness of the shocked, dreary public-school Sunday, with nothing to do, and

[1] Prothero, I, 320.   [2] Stanley, p. 655.

thoughts of holidays suddenly unreal in the shadow of the catastrophe.

All sensitively-written death scenes are a product of tension between fact and interpretation. The most trivial remark or gesture can be endowed in the minds of onlookers with symbolic significance because it is the last. And death is at once a great mystery and a plain mundane fact with practical consequences. Stanley is one of the most successful of all English biographers in making this paradox fruitful for his art.

7

SMILES AS BIOGRAPHER

❀

For every man who has a strong influence on his contemporaries there develops a simplified impression of his personality and his thought. If he is one of those who later seem to have spoken only to their own time and not to all the ages, this simple version soon becomes an easy substitute for reading him. Of this there is no reason to complain. Life is short, and greater writers than Smiles are many. But the fortunate ones among this group are those whose public reputation either does them approximate justice, or does them wild injustice. Smiles's case is different from either of these. The simple intellectual sketch which the mention of his name suggests to an educated person, not deeply versed in his career, is subtly wrong, but not wildly wrong. A close look at him is needed to correct it; and in these circumstances honest misrepresentation is apt to perpetuate itself.

It must be admitted at once that the importance of Smiles is more historical than literary. Unlike the other biographers selected for detailed treatment in this book, he would be absent if literary merit or pure psychological interest had been my sole criterion. Smiles is important because of the general view of human life that he proposed, because millions were influenced by it,[1] and because the theme of his work, the adjustment of the human spirit to technical progress, is perennially important. Smiles's reputation as a rather unimaginative, literal-minded man does not, on the whole, belie him. A more penetrating mind than his would be needed to meditate profitably on the general and philosophical aspects of culture modified by new techniques. If he had written only books like *Character* and *Duty*, it would be possible to dismiss him as a second-rate purveyor of cheap uplift.

[1] In his popularity and influence in many countries, see Asa Briggs: *Victorian People*, 1954.

But his historical importance, as it happens, is the same as his importance for us; it lies in the fact that he was a biographer. And so we see, as we read him, this great issue of the consequences of technical progress in particular cases. And here, perhaps, we notice the first point at which the generally-accepted picture is subtly wrong. He is supposed, and with reason, to have possessed a simplifying, theoretical mind. Whatever we may think of the economic theory of the Manchester school, it is an undoubted historical fact that it appealed to able, practical men, to intellectual simplifiers, to what Bagehot, in speaking of Macaulay, so finely called 'inexperiencing natures'. It was more often rejected by subtle men, by men with a sense of the strange paradoxes and deep tragedies of life, like Disraeli, like Dickens, like Ruskin. But the usual impression of Smiles is inaccurate because the value of his work springs out of its mass of biographical detail, which enables the theoretical side of his work to be tested (by us, if not always by him); and moreover, because his work is full of concealed intellectual and moral tensions. No doubt he was a much less clever man than Macaulay, and no doubt his total literary achievement is less notable than Macaulay's. But he is less of a pure simplifier. The idea of progress, in Smiles's version, is more chequered with exceptions and regrets. There is a stronger sense than Macaulay ever shows of the effect of machinery on the rural scene; there is a deeper feeling for venerable ways of thinking and acting, and of possible impoverishments of civilisation when they are discarded.

Perhaps his *Autobiography* is the best place to begin in the hope of reaching the centre of a man who can easily appear, on a cursory view, to be all surface. It is very far from being a great autobiography. Smiles was not sensitive enough, or analytical enough, for that; and, in any case, he wrote it too late, and left it unfinished. We are not encouraged when we find that, though he professes to have had a happy marriage, he only devotes a paragraph to it, and does not mention his wife's name. But we soon find that some of the doctrines pervading his other works, which we had probably taken for slabs of arid theory, had their real source in experience. Thus he tells us that 'Active work is always attended with happiness. So, at least, I have found. . . .'[1] Many people have found otherwise; but Smiles has not a strong enough sense of his own personality to put this fact of his experience down to a special characteristic of his own. It becomes one of his general assumptions as a biographer; he finds it hard to imagine, and impossible to respect, a man so constituted that work was not a pleasure to him. It is revealing, too, and rather charming, to find this ruthless preacher of the value of every minute, whose biographies are full of the glories of learning Latin while running messages in the streets of Manchester, writing this, when he went in search of evidence about the Stephensons: 'Although my expedition was fruitless, I enjoyed the beautiful evening. . . .'[2] It is attractive to find this historian of the Huguenots praising the virtues of a Catholic community he visited. Above all, he wins our assent when he rebuts the charge of having written only of successful men, by pointing to the comparative failure with the public of his book on the lonely Scottish naturalist Robert Dick, whose career was a series of failures and miseries. 'Perhaps,' he says with some dignity, 'if I had written about millionaires I might have been more successful myself.'[3] The qualities that Smiles admired most, courage, endurance, industry and self-denial did often bring success, but not always, and Smiles cannot be accused of forgetting cases where they did not.

A further corrective to the stock view of him is required when we come to see that in some respects he is not theoretical enough. Thus he always writes of what he considers true Christianity with a patently sincere respect. If asked what it is, he seems to say that it is simply the opposite of the harsh, post-Calvinist ethos imposed on him in childhood. It is natural to him to assume that moral questions are the fundamental ones in religion, and that theology is obscurely threatening and narrowing. In fact, on these points, he says, with far less verve and talent, essentially what Charles Dickens said. This is undeniable; yet, what a strange collocation it makes, the hero-worshipper of the Manchester school and the author of *Hard Times*, the celebrator of the machine and the great despiser of

[1] Autobiography, p. 209.   [2] p. 180–1.   [3] Autobiography, p. 327.

all systems, the most prosaic and the most poetical of all Victorian writers on industrial society.

More striking still is his assumption that this simplified moral religious fervour is thoroughly compatible with the Manchester ethos; and this supposed harmony exists because it is assumed that rugged individualism and unselfish co-operation are in the last resort the same thing.

Here a fashionable line of criticism, which may well be appropriate in certain other cases, must be sternly resisted. Smiles's insistence on 'true Christianity', and his assertion of the social benefits of personal ambition are not hypocritical. There is no trace in his mind of the idea of 'dope for the masses'. It is characteristic of nearly all the tensions in his work that they are unfelt tensions. We may decide that his precious harmonies are unreal, but, if we do, we must make our criticism on intellectual grounds. Smiles did not always understand, but he never cheated. Sometimes the ease with which he slides over awkward cracks in his argument is breathtaking; and the following example may serve as an emblem of his method at its strangest. He is warm in the praise of the Barberini vase, of which he says:

> Some think it is a satire upon the vices of Heliogabalus; others consider it a eulogium on the virtues of his immediate successor Alexander Severus.[1]

The contrast between these two emperors allows Gibbon's love of antithesis one of its strongest triumphs. Elagabalus (Gibbon's more correct form of the name):

> dishonoured the principal dignities of the empire by bestowing them among his numerous lovers; one of whom was publicly invested with the title and authority of the emperor's, or, as he more properly styled himself, of the empress's husband ... Confining ourselves to the public scenes displayed before the Roman people, and attested by grave and contemporary historians, their inexpressible infamy surpasses that of any other age or country.[2]

Alexander is praised for his 'natural mildness and moderation of temper'.

[1] Josiah Wedgwood: *His Personal History*, 1894, pp. 261–2.
[2] Gibbon: *Decline and Fall*, chapter vi.

Almost anyone except Smiles might have thought it odd that there could be a doubt whether a painted scene castigated unnatural vices or lauded unusual virtues. Almost anyone but Smiles would have wondered whether the doubt should not create further doubts, either about the strange explanations or about the quality of the work so strangely explained. There is no vested interest, no concealed motive behind Smiles's incomprehension here. Nor is there any when the topic is religion, or industry or the profit-motive. Easy acceptances may have helped him towards that sympathy with his subject that is one of the biographer's most precious gifts. Thus in the same volume we hear that Wedgwood wrote to a friend:

> Have you forgotten how our hearts burned within us, when
> we conversed upon this subject on our way from Liverpool
> to Prescot? We were then persuaded that this *open, generous*
> plan would not only be most congenial to our hearts and
> best feelings, but in all probability might best answer our
> wishes in pecuniary advantages. . . .'[1]

The topic is simply the quality of pottery. A cleverer biographer than Smiles might have pointed to the incongruity of the language (with its clear reminiscence of the Journey to Emmaus) for a business conversation. But the sense of sympathy would have been lost, and with it, perhaps, part of the reader's sense of the real heroism and originality of men like Wedgwood.

II

The first and most obvious tension in Smiles's biographical work, is, we may freely admit, only a reflection of a real contradiction existing in the world. His secular saints, dedicated to the glories of mechanical progress, are at times both martyrs and public benefactors. And this needs stressing because the idea of the martyr is naturally absent from his best-known book, *Self-Help*. But *The Lives of the Engineers* contains many cases like that of Sir Cornelius Vermuyden who tried to drain the fens, while the rest of the nation was thinking of the Civil War. He died a poor, broken down old man, the lands he had reclaimed having been

[1] Op. cit., p. 160.

conveyed to strangers.[1] While the public is seen as the chief beneficiary even of the work of men who became famous and wealthy, there is a constant harping on an ignorant and opinionated public opposition to improvement.

If we admit, then, that Smiles is justified in showing public opposition to new ideas as frequently ignorant and unfair, why is his procession of martyrs for the cause of technical improvement a faintly unsatisfying one? There are two main reasons, one of which springs out of the nature of the subject and one from the author's own nature. In the *Lives of the Engineers* especially, his greatest work, Smiles is the historian of technical progress. In technical matters it is especially true that the right solution to any problem comes to seem obvious when the new device is successfully in use, and false starts and failures are soon forgotten. No doubt a diligent historian could gather any number of instances of fatuous and unworkable schemes being rejected by the sturdy insensibility of the public. But Smiles was writing on those engineers who could be seen in retrospect to have made a notable contribution. He forgets the others; perhaps he even sometimes forgets useless ideas that his heroes may have had in between their good ones. If we did not make comparisons with the rest of our experience, and remind ourselves how many misleading and plausible schemes actually are mooted, we could be bemused into supposing that every bright idea is a winner, and that it was invariably crass stupidity alone that opposed any innovation. Perhaps, indeed, after a session with Smiles's engineers, one should turn for refreshment to the history of more general ideas, and consider some case like the pantisocracy of Coleridge and Southey, where men endowed with great talents and deep sincerity concocted a scheme that would not work at all.

This tendency inherent in the study of technical history is intensified by a strange characteristic of Smiles himself. He always tends to present new inventions as simple and obvious because he is determined to praise industry at the expense of talent. It is not difficult to see why. The great theme of *Self-Help*, and of his innumerable lectures to working-class audiences,

[1] *Lives of the Engineers*, Murray, 1862, I, 64–5.

was that anyone can succeed in Victorian England. This is a thesis to which it is a little difficult to be fair to to-day; and it was strongly denied, often by men of greater talent and insight than Smiles, when he was young in the 1830's and '40's right through to his old age in the 1890's. We may think that Disraeli and Dickens, William Morris and General Booth were right and Smiles was wrong. But, if we take that view, we should first dismiss from our minds all idea of Smiles as a figure like Bounderby in *Hard Times*, whose assertion that anybody can get on really conceals a cynical sneer at those less fortunate than himself. Smiles was naturally an optimist, and a kindly man. He must not be too severely blamed for addressing his working-class audiences in words of hope; and the tributes he received prove that some of them at least found his words inspiring and true.

Great talents are rare. Smiles's natural optimism, coupled perhaps with an awareness of his own limitations, made him therefore eager to insist that talent could not be the real cause of achievement. One of his favourite themes is that industry will make good deficiencies of talent. Rennie, the designer of the Plymouth breakwater, is typical of many Smiles heroes in his attitude to holidays. In 1816 he was persuaded by a friend to go on a trip to Paris.

> This journey was the first relaxation he had taken for a period of thirty years; yet it was not a mere holiday trip, but partly one of business, for it was his object to inspect with his own eyes the great dock and harbour works executed by Napoleon during the continental war, of which he had heard so much, and to gather from the inspection such experience as might be of use to him in the improvement of the English dockyards. . . .[1]

When, as in this case, Herculean labours led to a premature ageing and death, Smiles stolidly records the fact, but draws no conclusions. A man like Smiles, perfectly candid, but limited in his vision, gives evidence of many things that do not fully come home to himself. It hardly occurs to him that incessant labour can be narrowing. Perhaps the saddest case of this he records is

[1] *Lives of the Engineers*, II, 274–5.

that of Telford, the great bridge-builder, clearly by nature a man of wide intellectual curiosity.

> In the midst of his plans of docks, canals and bridges, he writes letters about the peculiarities of Goethe's poems and Kotzebue's plays, Buonaparte's campaign in Egypt, and the merits of sundry new books recently published. He confesses, however, that he has now purchased the 'Encyclopedia Britannica', which he finds 'a perfect treasure containing everything, and being always at hand'.[1]

So it is that many of the accounts of inventions resemble this of Rennie's scheme for draining the fens:

> Any boy, they [Rennie's opponents] said, who played at dirt pies in a gutter, knows that if you make an opening sufficiently low to let the water escape, it will flow away. Very true; yet the thing had never been done until Mr Rennie proposed it, and, simple though the method was, it cost him many years of arguing, illustration, and enforcement, before he could induce intelligent men in other districts to adopt the simple but thoroughly scientific method. . . .[2]

Smiles almost seems to want us to think that one of the boys playing at mud-pies could have conquered the technical problems unaided. So it is that the opposition to his heroes comes to remind us of 'they' in Edward Lear's poems, rank upon rank of highhanded, complacent sneerers.

Of course, Smiles may sometimes have been right in asserting that hard work and not talent proved the key to success. But there can be no question that he turned the idea into a generalisation that becomes ludicrous in extreme cases. In the first chapter of *Self-Help* he blandly chooses two of the most unfavourable examples for his thesis that the political history of his time could show – Peel and Disraeli. When we are told that Peel, one of the most capacious intellects that ever turned his attention to public affairs in this country, was a man of 'comparatively moderate' powers, we are startled. But we may possibly try to excuse Smiles by saying that perhaps, compared with men of the greatest originality, Peel could be called,

[1] *LE*, ii, 372.   [2] *LE*, ii, 160–1.

though only by a very severe critic, in a sense mediocre.[1] But while we are resolving this question, the matter is put entirely out of doubt a page or two later, when we find that Smiles accounts for Disraeli's success mainly by his 'power of industry and application', and that, after his early failures, *Coningsby*, *Sybil* and *Tancred* (had Smiles read the latter part of *Tancred*?) proved the 'sterling stuff' of which he was made. Clearly, if you can turn Disraeli into a dull, painstaking burgher, you can perform the trick upon anyone whatsoever.

But it is more important to notice that once again Smiles's view bristles with paradoxes of which he seems oblivious. If spectacular achievement depends upon qualities that are very common, and habits that are easy to develop, what distinguishes the few who succeed in scaling the heights from the many who fail? Pure luck, or birth and influence? Or is the actual wish to succeed such a very rare thing? Smiles rejects all such suggestions. He seems to come near at times to saying along with a later commercial man, 'There's no such thing as luck'. As for birth and influence, social mobility is one of his great themes. He is fond of telling how an office-boy or a poor peasant boy became the great inventor, but he is almost equally fond of telling how the descendant of dukes now sweep the streets. These remarks sometimes read like a warning from the spokes-man of powerful commercial classes that the aristocracy, which still wielded so much political power, held it on sufferance and subject to reports of good behaviour.

But if Smiles shows so little sense of what genius really is that Shakespeare becomes merely 'a close student and a hard worker',[2] he shows even less awareness that a man's rise in the world may be assisted by his evil qualities, or even by his crimes. His Napoleon[3] is equally devoid of genius and wickedness. He becomes mainly, like the Duke of Wellington, a first-rate man of business.

---

[1] Even this will hardly wash. See for instance the account of Peel's viva vice examination at Oxford in G. M. Young: *Portrait of an Age*, 1953, p. 92n.
[2] *Self-Help*, chapter I.
[3] *Self-Help*, chapter IX.

III

But the tension in Smiles's work which seems to us the most obvious of all seems to be the one of which he is most oblivious. It is the tension between his individualism and his strong and sincere sense of social responsibility. At first sight his variety of attitudes here is bewildering. The *Self-Help* theme in its pure form seems to require the existence of a great mass of men who are not following his advice, and are therefore not rising in the world. These weaklings give the disciple of Smiles his opportunity. If everyone worked eighteen hours a day, no one would secure a personal advantage by doing so. At times, Smiles faces this harsh logical difficulty boldly. Thus, when Telford began his work as a mason in London, with his mallet and chisels, and his leather apron as his sole property, Smiles comments:

> In London the weak man is simply a unit added to a vast floating crowd, and may be driven hither and thither, if he do not sink altogether; whilst the strong man will strike out, keep his head above water, and make a course for himself, as Telford did.[1]

But at other times, when his hero-worship is not engaged, he seems to say that the interests of individuals do not matter very much, provided their misfortunes and deprivations forward the general interest. Thus he can also say, in the best collectivist style:

> Individuals may suffer from the cost of the experiments, but the nation, which is an aggregate of individuals, gains, and so does the world at large.[2]

The contradiction here is more apparent than real. The second quotation refers to the practical consequences of some of Brunel's innovations. The individuals who are said to suffer are anonymous, and soon forgotten both by author and reader. What is asserted is an identity of interest between the exceptional individual, Brunel, and society as a whole. Rugged individualism can thus take on the character of high social duty.

[1] *LE*, II, 308.   [2] *LE*, III, 399.

Self-love and social are the same, as Pope had said long before. It would not be long before socialists would invert Smiles's argument, and say that what was good for society must in the end be good for the individual. Smiles naturally disliked socialism, and socialists have often disliked Smiles. But the similarity of their optimism forms a concealed bond. And, no doubt, Smiles, if pressed, would have applied a similar argument to the first passage about Telford. He would have asserted that even the 'vast, floating crowd' would in the end be benefited by Telford's success in rising above them, and so making inventions that would increase the nation's wealth.

We see now, perhaps, why Smiles needed to be blind to the vicious egoism of Napoleon. His general view remained plausible as long as it seemed to him that there was a kind of selflessness in the sternest ambition. He maintains this in some cases where the impartial reader will not follow him; but being essentially honest, even he finds it incredible in certain cases. Hudson, the great railway swindler is one; of him and a few like him, Smiles speaks with the greatest severity, as men devoted to a cause speak of traitors.

When pressed, then, Smiles is prepared to admit that success may occasionally be due to bad qualities, and result in no social benefit. He is also prepared to admit a narrow class of exceptions to the thesis that only upright self-denying men can really benefit the public. Here, for instance, is his account of the railway navvies:

> Their powers of endurance were extraordinary. In times of emergency they could work for twelve and even sixteen hours, with only short intervals for meals ... They displayed great pluck, and seemed to disregard peril ...

> Reckless alike of their lives as of their earnings, the navvies worked hard and lived hard. For their lodging, a hut of turf would content them; and in their hours of leisure, the meanest public-house would serve for their parlour. Unburdened, as they usually were, by domestic ties, unsoftened by family affection, and without much moral or religious training, the navvies came to be distinguished by a sort of savage manner, which contrasted strangely with

those of the surrounding population ... Their pay-nights
were often a saturnalia of riot and disorder, dreaded by the
inhabitants of the villages along the line of the works.[1]

Smiles was secretary of the South Eastern railway at the time
of writing the *Lives of the Engineers*. The general strategy of his
work naturally makes the railways the grand climax of a long
process of improvement beginning with the canals and drainage
schemes of the eighteenth century. Indeed, one did not need to
be professionally concerned with railways to see the matter in
this way. Whether one regretted the loss of the old rural and
feudal England, like Wordsworth, or triumphed over its fall,
like Thomas Arnold,[2] it was natural in the forty years or so
after 1830, to see the railways as the arch-creators of social
change.

How candid of Smiles to present the navvies in this light; for
few could have disapproved more strongly of a way of life clean
contrary to the message he was always preaching. But how
strange is the absence of embarrassment, of explanation or
apology. Macaulay, one feels, would have undercut objections in
advance with some clever debating argument. But Smiles's
impressive grasp of facts, and his admirable candour are
unaccompanied by any imaginative sense of context. He does
not ask himself where the navvies came from, or what became
of them in old age, or how their children fared in the world. His
sense of social benefit is curiously limited. It is not callousness;
it is the unimaginativeness of the inexperiencing mind.

Nor did he ask himself why navvies should behave in this way.
Every feature of his mind combined to make him almost
oblivious of cultural influences upon the growth of the
personality. The men he admired most, the men he loved to
write about, were the men of strength and persistence, who
seemed not to need education, or a stable family background.
He knew so many cases of men triumphing over difficulties that
he almost came to think that difficulties made no difference.

[1] *LE*, III, 322–8.
[2] Smiles quotes, with warm approval, Arnold's remark at the opening of the
Birmingham line 'I rejoice to see it, and to think that feudality is gone
for ever.' (*LE*, III, 355).

One notes, in all his biographical accounts, a strange absence of context. The family background and early years receive perfunctory treatment or none at all. Smiles's heroes are literally self-made, not merely in the current sense of finding their own money. They love themselves, nurture themselves, educate and discipline themselves. And so Smiles's idea of the social good becomes mainly a matter of wealth. But this is emphatically not because he was in any crude sense a materialist. It is because the cultural and moral influences of society are barely recognised as having a corporate reality. Every man makes his own, and Smiles is very strong on the importance of making his own. Every good man is an enactor of the myth of Robinson Crusoe – an outward-looking, public-spirited solitary.

But, of course, the navvies did not have to initiate new engineering works; they only had to work hard and do as they were told. Is Smiles perhaps then telling us that their moral condition did not matter because they were only tools in the hands of the great inventive minds, who are the subject of his book? In a man so full of contradictions we shall not be surprised to find contradictions about class flourishing strongly. But on one point at least, he is ever consistent. Work is the great purpose of life, and life without work is morally null. He may sound sententious, but he is surely sincere when he says of the parents of George Stephenson:

> They belonged to the ancient and honourable family of Workers – that extensive family which constitutes the backbone of our country's greatness, the common working people of England.[1]

Such respect as he has for the aristocracy (and it is not very strong) is explained, or perhaps rationalised, by saying that they often work hard.[2] But the aristocracy (except in the very special case of the Duke of Bridgewater, to which I return later) generally concerns him little. Questions much more important for him, and much more confused, lurk in the relation between the working-class and commercial or professional people, especially when, as is often the case among his heroes, the latter have risen from the ranks of the former. In this connection he

[1] *LE*, III, 14.   [2] See *Self-Help*, chapter I.

has a most revealing anecdote about the bridge-builder John Rennie, who was born in 1761. While travelling to visit the Earl of Eglinton in his Scots castle, Rennie found that the axle-tree of the coach had broken on the bad roads. Rennie and the coachman carried the broken axle to a nearby forge, but the blacksmith was absent. So Rennie lit the forge fire, welded the axle and helped to carry it back to the coach. The other passengers 'who had been communicative and friendly during the earlier part of the journey, now became very reserved.' The journey over, Rennie proceeded to Eglinton Castle, and was sitting at breakfast with the earl next morning when one of the other passengers was shown into the room. 'Great indeed was his surprise and confusion at finding the identical "blacksmith" of the preceding day breakfasting with my Lord! The Earl was much amused.'[1]

Perhaps Smiles is not very clear what he is saying here. One element, of course, is the Cinderella myth, with the proper practical slant appropriate to the mechanical age. Rennie was not *really* a blacksmith; he only appeared to be one. By his patient acceptance of contempt he gave fate a chance to right him; and his exaltation was all the more majestic when it came. The earl neatly represents the prince, and reminds us that, however rich and powerful members of the commercial classes might become, they still measured their rise against the magnificence of an aristocracy imagined to be beyond the reach of change and decay. But the story has an opposite and balancing element. Rennie did not merely appear to be a blacksmith; he actually performed a blacksmith's work, and very capably. Had he not done so, the whole party would have been subject to delay. The moral seems to be that the skills of the engineer only cannot bring all his schemes to fruition unaided because he has not an unlimited number of hands. The engineer is all that the artisan is, and much more. Now this idea of a society divided into grades in which each group possesses the skills of the ones below stops short with the engineers. It certainly never occurred to Smiles to suggest that the earl could have done Rennie's work as Rennie did the blacksmith's.

[1] *LE*, II, 282.

We are left to think that the superiority of the engineers over the artisans is a superiority of merit, while the inferiority of engineers to earls is a matter of accident and convention only. So we have a neat little parable of the power of merit in a small class of energetic and inventive men to triumph within the existing order, while leaving the traditional privileges of the aristocracy untouched. At moments like this Smiles is, without any conscious design, the perfect laureate of the industrial revolution. And so the moral inferiority of navvies to engineers, however regrettable, has its place in Smiles's pattern.

It is disappointing, after this, to find that Smiles is still not free from the characteristic worry of his time about the meaning of the word 'gentleman'. Here the internal contradictions of the man's inexperiencing mind are at their most obvious. In his account of George Stephenson he gives a stirring quotation from Robert Nicoll on Burns:

> Like us, thou wast a toiling man –
> And we are noble now!

On the very same page he gives this prim little caveat against considering Stephenson too much in terms of his plebeian origins:

> He dressed neatly in black, wearing a white neckcloth; and
> his face, his person, and his deportment at once arrested
> attention and marked the Gentleman.[1]

Perhaps it would be impossible to say what the word 'gentleman' means here, since it is unlikely that Smiles thought at all clearly about his own meaning. But perhaps the nearest we can come is to say that a gentleman in this sense is a man who, without obvious incongruity, could sit down to dinner in the company of people of gentle birth. It is in effect a middle-class plea for widening the ruling class, but not for widening it too much, and certainly not for abolishing it. At moments like this, it does not matter that Smiles is not a great literary artist. He reveals almost as much as if he was.

But nothing could show more clearly the tensions engendered by this rather simple view of class questions than the contrast

[1] *LE*, III, 460.

(in Smiles's presentation) between Rennie's Earl of Eglinton, and the Duke of Bridgewater. The earl, as we have seen, exists in the story simply to be an earl, living as he ought in a castle, and making manifest, by the mere light of his countenance, hidden truths about the status of others. But the Duke of Bridgewater, the 'canal duke' and associate of Brindley, was, of course, one of the chief figures in the early part of Smiles's story. As soon as he makes his appearance, a certain uneasiness is apparent in the narrative. The reason is that Smiles is set upon making him at one and the same time the industrious apprentice and the far-sighted patron. At first we might be reading another account of a boy born in a labourer's cottage. 'He was a weak and sickly child', 'his mental capacity was thought defective', 'his mother neglected him'.[1] Apparently his survival until the age of seventeen was greeted with surprise and some annoyance by his relatives and guardians. At an early age he had a disappointment in love which prevented his ever speaking of love to a woman again. But 'like a wise man' (or rather like Smiles's other and more plebeian heroes) he buried his sorrow in work.

A little later,

> He was only thirty years of age – the owner of several fine mansions in different parts of the country, surrounded by noble domains – he had a fortune sufficiently ample to enable him to command the pleasures and luxuries of life, so far as money can secure them; yet all these he voluntarily denied himself, and chose to devote his time to consultations with an unlettered engineer, and his whole resources to the cutting of a canal to unite Liverpool and Manchester.[2]

The duke's financial affairs, as Smiles presents them, are hard to understand. We hear of his wealth and self-denial, of his inexcusable meanness to Brindley, and later to his needy widow, of the near-failure of the whole project through lack of capital, and of an extraordinary personal contribution of £100,000 to the Loyalty Loan. All these contrasting facts exist for Smiles in separate compartments of the mind; they do not react upon each other, and the final summary is a lame one:

[1] *LE*, I, 335–6.   [2] *LE*, I, 395.

His enforced habits of economy during the construction of
the canal had fully impressed upon his mind the value of
money. Yet, though 'near', he was not penurious, but was
usually liberal, and sometimes munificent.[1]

There is throughout, as this passage well shows, a total
failure to focus the man as a human being. Habitually Smiles
simplifies, and misses finer points, but all his other characters
are intelligible. Perhaps we should put this down to a conflict
between theory and custom. Society had very strong expectations about the way in which a duke should behave,[2] and Smiles
could not be impervious to their influence. But at the same time
he believed that the way of life of his self-made engineers was
the best and worthy of universal imitation, even by dukes. How
can he assert that dukes ought to 'know their place' when the
whole theme of his work is that no one ought to know their
place, but that everyone should strive against the misfortunes
of birth or poverty for the highest station he can attain? Once
again we can see that a cleverer man than Smiles might really
have told us less.

There is a similar, though less inhibiting, ambivalence in his
attitude to military things. He points out, most reasonably, that
some of his engineering heroes endured dangers and hardships
comparable to those that win soldiers a reputation for high
courage. He is critical of the scale on which public opinion rates
military and inventive achievement. He says:

> The victory of Wolfe on the heights of Abraham occurred in
> the same year that Smeaton completed his lighthouse on the
> Eddystone, and doubtless excited a far more general
> interest.[3]

[1] *LE*, I, 406.
[2] Cf. Trollope: *Phineas Redux*, chapter 24. When the old Duke of Omnium
dies and is succeeded by his industrious, and able nephew, it is said in the
clubs 'The nephew may be very good at figures, but he isn't fit to fill his
uncle's shoes'. Trollope adds: 'It was acknowledged everywhere that he
had played his part in a noble and even in a princely manner . . . And yet,
perhaps no man who had lived during the same period . . . had done
less, or had devoted himself more entirely to the consumption of good
things.' Trollope's passage is some ten years later than *The Lives of the
Engineers*.
[3] *LE*, II, 49.

Yet he is really happier in contemplating the wealthy young peer (mentioned in the first chapter of *Self-Help*) who chooses to join the army than the enigmatic Duke of Bridgwater. And he is fond of metaphors of military glory to describe the feats of his engineering heroes. His preference for peace rather than war is thoroughly genuine and honourable. But there is also a characteristic mid-Victorian resentment against an aristocratic military caste,[1] and a characteristic middle-class claim to equality. The constant implication is; 'We are not only more public-spirited than you upper-classes are, we are also your equals in the traditional aristocratic virtues of courage and manly independence.'

I have already contrasted Smiles with Macaulay, as being less of a doctrinaire about progress. Smiles does not think out his first principles; and thus he is more flexible than Macaulay in the face of unwelcome facts. Progress, as he sees it remains linked to specific improvements; he does not attempt to convince by a great flow of rhetoric that every kind of improvement is inseparable from every other so that a better method of stoking must make the stoker more likely to be sober and faithful to his wife. It does not worry him, dealing as he does in the current counters of economic theory and of proverbial wisdom, that some of his aphorisms seem to point in opposite directions. There is a rhetoric of inevitable progress and a rhetoric of inevitable decline. One moment he is quoting with approval Telford's claim that a particular improvement has advanced the country at least a century.[2] (Actually, this has no meaning at all, but how many readers were bothered by that?) At another, he is telling us that one of his heroes gave evidence 'in a modest, simple, straightforward manner' not in the 'glib and unscrupulous style which has since become the fashion'.[3] It would be a mistaken notion of Smiles's intellectual constitution, to suppose that he is preparing a detailed antithesis between

[1] The real existence of such an entity in England may be doubted, but memories of the Crimean War were recent and bitter; and the officers most in the news had all been great magnates, like Lucan and Cardigan, or members of the families of great magnates, like Raglan.

[2] *LE*, ii, 389.

[3] *LE*, ii, 79.

technical improvement and moral decline. Each idea exists comfortably in its own little pocket. Smiles is a great one for jumping to unexamined conclusions, but he is really very free from prejudice. His is a hospitable mind.

And, though he is not highly imaginative, he does have a sense of the dignity of past forms of civilisation, and of the ancient traditions of the land. It could not fairly be said of him, as Bagehot said of Macaulay, that he treated all existing men as only 'painful pre-requisites of great-grandchildren'. Rather to our surprise he begins his *Lives of the Engineers* by speaking with some feeling of the ancient earthworks of the British land. Later, speaking of the draining of the fens, he writes:

> The long rows of pollards, with an occasional windmill, stretching along the horizon as in a Dutch landscape – the wide extended flats of dark peaty soil, intersected by dykes and drains, with here and there a green tract covered with sleek cattle – have an air of vastness, and even grandeur . . . the churches of the district, built on sites which were formerly so many oases in the watery desert, loom up in the distance like landmarks, and are often of remarkable beauty of outline.[1]

That, for Smiles, is an eloquent passage; and it shows that he regarded his improvers as also, in part, conservators. Smiles is a fitting laureate of a nation, that in making the greatest social changes ever seen, remained in many respects conservative.

The *Lives of the Engineers* is one of those books that leave behind an impression both strong and vague. It is strong because the technical developments of two or three generations have been forcefully presented, because the reader is aware of an endless succession of men toiling against difficulties apparently insuperable. It is vague because no one member of this line of toiling men stands out much more clearly than the rest, because their inner hopes and fears are absent from the record. The figures remain immensely solid and impressive as a group that changed the face of England, and indirectly of the world. Each member is shadowy, and appears more like his neighbour than

[1] *LE*, II, 169.

he can really have been. Like a military historian, Smiles is more interested in what people did than in what they were. The paradox of this great ritual celebration of the high individualist creed is that his long line of great industrial commanders appear to us more like a long line of brave, dutiful, dedicated private soldiers.

8

TREVELYAN'S MACAULAY

❊

Macaulay is a great figure, and we should want his biography in any case. But we are fortunate in having just the book we have. For the peculiar combination of qualities and shortcomings in the author enables us to make certain discriminations in an unusually exact form. Macaulay was the product of two very different social sets. He was born into the Clapham Sect and he became a Whig, in the high élitist sense of that term. (Indeed, it has been suggested that Macaulay was the *only* Whig who was ever made and not born.)

The Clapham Sect and the particular impulse it gave to talented youth have already been discussed. But the peculiarity of Macaulay's nephew and biographer was that he was entirely untouched by this side of the tradition. The biographer's son, G. M. Trevelyan, in his life of his father records that, though he occasionally, as became the squire of broad acres, read the lesson in the parish church, he generally ignored Christianity as a thing he did not understand. On the other hand, George Otto was, as much as Macaulay himself, a natural Whig. When he repeats Whig phrases, it is idle to ask whether he is quoting. The whole point about Whig phrases and Whig arguments and Whig sophistries is that they come so naturally that they seem never to have been learned. When a man says 'Good morning', you do not ask whether he is quoting someone else who said 'Good morning' before. It is simply the right, the natural thing to say in certain circumstances; and so it is that George Otto adopts his uncle's tone and sometimes his very words without noticing it. So we have a biographer who has no sympathy with the tradition which formed his subject's childhood, and a complete, instinctive sympathy with the tradition which formed his early manhood, and remained dominant throughout his life.

In another way, too, G. O. Trevelyan's position as a biographer was unusual. There have been many biographies by close relatives, some of them, like Gwendolen Cecil's life of her father, among the best. But Trevelyan was the child of that sister in whom Macaulay enshrined his deepest affections. For an active, successful and very prosperous public man to be so devoted to his sister that he cannot marry, and that the prospect of her departure fills him with despair is most unusual. Indeed, one may fairly call it unnatural. But this unnatural bond is the link, as it were, between two very normal and happy families, in which Macaulay and Trevelyan grew up. It must be an odd experience for a little boy to come to realise that his affectionate, playful uncle is a writer famous throughout the world. But it must be much odder still to sense gradually, as adult understanding comes, that his mother is the focus of a brotherly affection which seems in a real sense to challenge his father's exclusive claim. And all this is more interesting still because Trevelyan is a reticent man, who speaks little of his own feelings, and yet an honest man who does not wish to falsify what many, in his place, might have felt was better concealed.

Trevelyan's treatment of Macaulay's early religious training is tantalising. He gives us several anecdotes to show how Biblical ideas were imbibed in the nursery. He tells us how the infant Macaulay, seeing a cloud of smoke pouring out of a tall chimney asked if that was hell,[1] how, when a maid disturbed his row of oyster-shells in the garden, he went into the drawing-room among his mother's visitors and said 'Cursed be Sally; for it is written, Cursed is he that removeth his neighbour's landmark',[2] and how at the age of six or seven he stood on a chair and preached sermons.[3] But he evades the question of the lasting effect of religious teaching on his uncle's personality. He gives full weight, indeed, to the moral side of the training. The public causes in which the men of the Clapham Sect were engaged, of which opposition to slavery was the chief, he approved and valued. But his final verdict on this education is as follows:

It would be ungrateful to forget in how large a measure it

[1] *Life and Letters of Lord Macaulay by his nephew*, Longmans, 1909, p. 19.
[2] Op. cit., p. 21.   [3] Op. cit., p. 25n.

is due to them [Zachary Macaulay and his Clapham contemporaries] that one, whose judgments upon the statesmen of many ages and countries have been delivered to an audience vast beyond all precedent, should have framed his decisions in accordance with the dictates of honour and humanity, of ardent public spirit and lofty public virtue.[1]

In fact, Trevelyan believes that the moral aspect of the Clapham education is totally separable from the religious. In the case of such a devout household it is hard to believe that.

But the great advantage for the reader of the school of biography to which Trevelyan belonged is this: he is provided with material for his own judgment when the author seems to judge wrongly or, perhaps, does not judge at all. What are we to say about the lasting effects of the faith of the Clapham Sect on Macaulay? Most certainly they were not obvious. Macaulay did not become an ardent Evangelical, nor did he react in any of the classic Victorian ways, by developing Clapham principles in a High Church or Roman Catholic direction, as the Wilberforces did, or by rejecting them altogether as Leslie Stephen did. In his early letters to his father on religious topics we find a curious cunning. He seems to write more like a lawyer than a son, eagerly agreeing when he can, and rebutting criticism by soothing, self-justifying parallels. At the age of thirteen, Macaulay was exhorted by his father to join with his school-friends in setting up a Sunday school, and in the same letter[2] the father expresses anxiety about a report that the son is distinguished in the school for 'the loudness and vehemence' of his voice. Macaulay's reply would enable one to predict a considerable success for him in the world. After carefully introducing a biblical quotation as comment on the peace of 1814, he undertakes to speak in a moderate key except for such special occasions as praising the *Christian Observer*. Omitting all reference to the proposed Sunday School, he concludes with an unfriendly description of a clerical foe of the Bible Society. It is a masterly performance; but the worldly success which one would have predicted for the boy of thirteen who wrote it would not have

[1] Op. cit., p. 52.   [2] Op. cit., p. 35.

been that which he attained. Macaulay's great talents were effective in the world largely because he was supremely confident and because of his wonderful ability to simplify. On all the great public issues, whether as politician, administrator or historian, Macaulay was able to present a clear, coherent, simple view, supported by a vast array of facts, but lacking nuances and oblivious of fine distinctions. This is what he did in 1832 over the Reform Bill; he did the same in the most momentous and influential of all his writings, the minute on Indian education;[1] he did the same when he came to instruct the public in the proper Whig view of the Exclusion Crisis and the Revolution of 1688. But this is just what he did not do in answer to his father. A man whose cleverness takes the form of subtle worldly wisdom and cunning persuasion when he is thirteen, and of bold assertion of a party line when he is middle-aged is a strange portent.

But it would also be a mistake to suppose that the religion of Clapham meant nothing to Macaulay, and that he only, for the sake of a quiet life, pretended to his father that it did. Trevelyan

---

[1] If Macaulay had never written a line for publication, he might not have been famous; but he would still have played an important part in world history. It would be hard to think of a more momentous official document composed by any Englishman than Macaulay's Minute on Indian Higher Education of January 1835. At a time when opinion was equally divided between encouraging Oriental or English teaching Macaulay came down with decisive eloquence on the side of English. The great Hindu classics which T. S. Eliot thought so subtle that they made the finest European thinkers look like schoolboys seemed to Macaulay puerile trifles. He complained of 'astronomy that would move laughter in the girls at an English boarding-school – history abounding with kings thirty feet high, and reigns thirty thousand years long – and geography made up of seas of treacle and seas of butter' (see *Life*, 291). The 'inexperiencing nature' again. But Macaulay, though imperceptive about oriental culture, was not here being narrowly insular. The superiority he thought he saw in the West, was more Greek than English. He believed that the intellectual heritage of Homer, Thucydides and Aristotle was the rightful possession of the whole world, and that it would be cruel to refuse it to the educated classes in India. Macaulay's minute was decisive. Some of the 'Orientalists' on the Committee of Public Instruction resigned. In March 1835 it was authoritatively stated that 'the great object of the British Government ought to be the promotion of European literature and science among the natives of India'. The effects of this decision are still felt; and its merits are still a matter of debate among Indians.

gives us a revealing sketch of Macaulay electioneering in 1832.[1]
Macaulay was challenged to state his religious allegiance:

'Let that man stand up!' he cried. 'Let him stand on a form,
where I can see him.' The offender, who proved to be a
Methodist preacher, was hoisted on to a bench by his
indignant neighbours; nerving himself in that terrible
moment by a lingering hope that he might yet be able to
hold his own. But the unhappy man had not a chance
against Macaulay, who harangued him as if he were the
living embodiment of religious intolerance and illegitimate
curiosity. 'I have heard with the greatest shame and sorrow
the question that has been proposed to me; and with
peculiar pain do I learn that this question was proposed by
a minister of religion. I do most deeply regret that any
person should think it necessary to make a meeting like this
an arena for theological discussion. I will not be a party to
turning this assembly to such a purpose. My answer is short,
and in one word. Gentlemen, I am a Christian.' At this
declaration the delighted audience began to cheer; but
Macaulay would have none of their applause. 'This is no
subject,' he said, 'for acclamation. I will say no more. No
man shall speak of me as the person who, when this
disgraceful inquisition was entered upon in an assembly of
Englishmen, brought forward the most sacred subjects to be
canvassed here, and to be turned into a matter for hissing or
for cheering. If on any future occasion it should happen that
Mr Carlyle should favour any large meeting with his infidel
attacks upon the Gospel, he shall not have it to say that I
set the example. Gentlemen, I have done; I tell you, I will
say no more; and if the person who has thought fit to ask
this question has the feelings worthy of a teacher of religion,
he will not, I think, rejoice that he has called me forth.'

The crushing superiority, the terrifying sense of personal
rightness shown here was so characteristic of Macaulay at all
times that it is perhaps idle to inquire whether it was a Clapham
superiority, or a Whig superiority, or merely a personal
superiority. But the *tone* surely derives from Clapham and not

[1] Op. cit., pp. 204–5.

from Whiggery; at first sight one might say that it was the
Clapham tone turned to opposite purposes, turned against
the Clapham view that religion is always the guiding star of
politics. But this would not be quite true. Macaulay is rebuking
the man for not being religious enough. The man (in Macaulay's
highly-coloured and exaggerated version) is dragging the taber-
nacle down into the market-place. He is being assimilated not to
fanatics and sectarians, but to sabbath-breakers and worldlings.
The tone of grand moral denunciation about what was, at worst,
only an error of taste is almost Pecksniffian, and is characteristic,
not so much of Clapham itself, as of Clapham's feebler successors
in Macaulay's own generation. One of the saddest features of the
years 1830–70 is the intellectual and moral decline of the high
Evangelical ethos into the kind of canting, snivelling, petty
people whom Dickens and Trollope would later satirise as
representative Evangelicals. The entire lack of any sense of tact
or proportion in Macaulay's outburst here suggests that he is
helping to prepare the way for this melancholy decline.

Occasionally, though, Macaulay parodies the Clapham style
deliberately. In a letter to his beloved sisters of 16 August 1832,[1]
he writes:

> But I have thought it my duty to set before you the evil
> consequence of making vows rashly, and adhering to them
> superstitiously; for in truth, my Christian brethren, or
> rather my Christian sisters, let us consider &c. &c. &c. But
> I reserve the sermon on promises, which I had intended to
> preach, for another occasion.

The context is political, and the tone of the whole letter
lighthearted. One can imagine the frisson that went through the
minds of the admiring younger sisters at the dreadful daring of
their wonderful, clever brother. But they may have thought, and
been right in thinking, that such casual bits of fun implied no
serious disrespect.

The fact is that all uses of the Bible and the Evangelical
tradition came equally natural to Macaulay. It is natural to him
to say in his private diary when preparing to review Gladstone's
book on Church and State: 'The Lord hath delivered him into

[1] Op. cit., p. 196.

130

our hand';[1] and it comes natural to him to complain that the beer was 'in exactly the state of the Church of Laodicea'.[2] He used the Bible as he used the facts of English history. His capacious memory found in both a treasure-house of allusion and comparison. Each was part of his mental world, but there was no sense of a spiritual pre-eminence in the Biblical.

So it is that the usual pattern of the spiritual history of the early Victorian intellectual is conspicuously absent. There is no period of doubt and darkness, no crisis, no conversion. How strongly the Clapham ethos tended to favour this pattern needs no demonstrating.[3] Macaulay is here a strange exception; to react to Clapham neither positively nor negatively, to take its religious ethos as most people take their parents' table-manners, is strange indeed. For a clever man of forceful and dominant temper it is stranger still. Does Trevelyan provide us with any clue to the understanding of the strangeness?

Formally, of course, Trevelyan gives no answer because he sees no question. Being devoid of the faculty by which men understand religious discourse, he tended to divide all religious statements into sound moral doctrine and unmeaning cant. Good taste and a genuine respect for his great-uncle Zachary caused the latter judgment to be almost entirely muffled in the *Life of Macaulay*. But it was characteristic of him in less guarded moments to express astonishment that any intelligent man should take an interest in matters ecclesiastical. Thus his son records his disappointment on going to see Gladstone and finding him 'reading nothing but a silly little Church goody book'.[4] Nevertheless, his narrative does suggest an answer; and it does so by means of the most paradoxical aspect of the whole portrait of Macaulay that the book presents. Trevelyan sees Macaulay as a great man, a man of lofty abilities and majestic attainment in the world who was at heart a child. This is particularly striking when we remember that Macaulay died in the year in which Trevelyan came of age, so that he had only childish and boyish

---

[1] p. 373.   [2] p. 441.
[3] See, for instance, the case of the Wilberforce brothers in David Newsome: *The Parting of Friends*, 1966.
[4] G. M. Trevelyan: *George Otto Trevelyan*, p. 69.

memories of his uncle. In general, one might say that the adult
eye alone perceives immaturity in adults. Thirty-eight years
separated the two men, and Macaulay was middle-aged and
celebrated before Trevelyan was old enough to be aware of him
at all. Yet the impression of Macaulay as a child remains very
strong. Macaulay's great aim seems to have been to recapture
the ancient joys of the Clapham nursery, which his sister, the
mother of the biographer, described thus:

> He hated strangers; and his notion of perfect happiness was
> to see us all working round him while he read a novel, and
> then to walk all together on the Common, or, if it rained, to
> have a frightfully noisy game of hide-and-seek. I have often
> wondered how our mother could ever have endured our
> noise in her little house.[1]

Macaulay attempted (successfully, on the whole) to recreate
these scenes with the beloved sister's children. Trevelyan also
stresses his intense love of favourite old books, especially if they
had no merit, his love of producing endless doggerel verses, his
immense enthusiasm for any task or pastime that engaged his
attention and his corresponding obstinate refusal to do anything
that went against the grain or failed to suit his mood. Thus, it
was characteristic of him (Trevelyan thought), that when he was
supposed to be training to be an advocate he failed to learn any
law, but when he was on his voyage to India, he mastered it with
extraordinary ease because he was 'fired by the prospect of the
responsibility of a law-giver'.[2] There was, too, as Trevelyan saw,
a boyish romanticism in Macaulay's character as a historian.[3]
The sage Whig doctrine is applied on the top of a simple love of
the relics and records of the past.

But, of course, there is nothing inherently childish in the
enjoyment of children's company or in antiquarian zeal. These

---

[1] Trevelyan, p. 43.   [2] Op. cit., p. 80.

[3] For instance, Margaret Macaulay wrote in her journal for March 30, 1831:
'My accuracy as to facts,' he said, 'I owe to a cause which many men
would not confess. It is die to my love of castle-building . . . I am no sooner
in the streets than I am in Greece, in Rome, in the midst of the French
Revolution . . . The conversations which I compose are long, and
sufficiently animated; in the style, if not with the merits of Sir Walter
Scott's.' (Quoted Trevelyan, p. 133.)

things have to be interpreted, and might justly receive very
different interpretations according to the rest of the evidence.
The crux of the matter lies in Macaulay's feelings for his sisters.
This is both a difficult and delicate question; and we can be
grateful for the solid, documented, unemphatic biographical
tradition to which Trevelyan belongs. He allows Macaulay, in
the main, to speak for himself in this matter, and we can try,
as far as possible, to imitate him in that. And, indeed, no
commentary could well add to the poignancy of Macaulay's
simple statement of heartbreak at the death of his sister Jane,
his avowal that he did not dare, for a whole year after the death
of his sister Margaret, 'to remain alone a moment without a book
in his hand'.[1] But Trevelyan saw, too, that Macaulay was able,
to a surprising extent, to analyse and understand the state of his
affections. And he came to realise that while his grief at the
death of sisters might be within normal limits, his feeling about
Hannah's marriage to Sir Charles Trevelyan – a marriage, which
with characteristic stoicism he outwardly approved as most
suitable – was far beyond any normal limits.

His letter to his other sister, Margaret, of 7 December 1834,
is extraordinary and revealing. Written from Calcutta to
England, it runs (in part):

She is going to be married, and with my fullest and warmest
approbation. I can truly say that, if I had to search India
for a husband for her, I could have found no man to whom
I could with equal confidence have entrusted her happiness ... I would as soon have locked my dear Nancy
[Hannah] up in a nunnery as have put the smallest obstacle
in the way of her having a good husband, I therefore gave
every facility and encouragement to both of them. What
I have myself felt it is unnecessary to say. My parting from
you almost broke my heart. But when I parted from you I
had Nancy: I had all my other relations: I had my friends:
I had my country. Now I have nothing except the resources
of my own mind, and the consciousness of having acted not
ungenerously.[2] But I do not repine. Whatever I suffer I
have brought on myself. I have neglected the plainest

[1] Op. cit., p. 319.   [2] Macaulay was entitled to say that.

lessons of reason and experience. I have staked my happiness without calculating the chances of the dice. I have hewn out broken cisterns; I have leant on a reed; I have built on the sand; and I have fared accordingly. I must bear my punishment as I can; and, above all, I must take care that my punishment does not extend beyond myself.

Nothing can be kinder than Nancy's conduct has been. She proposes that we should form one family; and Trevelyan (though, like most lovers, he would, I imagine, prefer having his goddess to himself), consented with strong expressions of pleasure.[1]

This letter is crucial; and its almost unbearable sadness is only increased by the fact that the other sister to whom it was addressed never saw it. She was dead before it arrived.

It is at moments like this in Trevelyan's work that one is most struck by the sparing nature of his comment. He cannot be accused of a feeble attempt at respectability, for he does print the letter. But there are all kinds of ideas that rush into the mind of the reader of it, and of these he gives no hint. How strange that a man as eminent as Macaulay, who could command the best English society in India, as he had in London, should be willing to live in the house of a man whom he knew to be unwilling to have him; how strange for a proud man to take advantage of Trevelyan's dutiful but unfelt generosity. Above all, how very strange that, having swallowed his pride and yielded to his overmastering affection enough to agree to sharing the proposed ménage, he should still feel he had lost his sister. Why should he feel that? Only one explanation seems possible. He felt it because he knew in some obscure way that he wished his sister to have for him the feelings of a wife, and knew that she never could again.

Throughout the chapters that follow Trevelyan often quotes from Macaulay's diary to show that he realised his own folly in setting his affections on those who could not return them in the only way that would have satisfied him. In this way an added appeal and poignancy are given to Trevelyan's own childhood memories of wonderful games with the wonderful uncle. For

[1] Op. cit., pp. 277–80.

here was a mitigating factor that softened much of the bitterness of Macaulay's emotional life. The absolute difference between a sister and a wife is not repeated in an absolute difference between a nephew and a son. The children were able without any unnatural twisting of their emotional lives to give Macaulay the return he needed in gratitude, admiration and love.

I have said that Trevelyan does not effectively comment on Macaulay's revealing letter, but it would be wrong to suggest that having done his duty by quoting it he hastily moves to safer ground. He rightly sees the whole issue as one of the most important in Macaulay's life. He shows him in 1856 still passionately grieving over the death of one of his sisters in 1835.[1] And he gives full weight to the tragic misunderstandings of his last days. At the end of 1859 Macaulay knew that Hannah and her husband must soon go back to India, and that he could not go with them. Trevelyan writes:

> The trial which now at no distant date awaited Macaulay was one of the heaviest that could by any possibility have been allotted to him, and he summoned all his resources in order to meet it with firmness and resignation.[2]

Sound, sombre and truthful words; everyone supposed that his unwonted silence (he had been talking continuously since the age of four, when he said 'Thank you, madam, the agony is abated')[3] was due to dejection at his sister's approaching departure. So the rapid onset of death passed unnoticed by this affectionate family; the only time in his life the support of the family failed him was the time he most needed it.

We are left, then, with two intertwined but separate questions, both of them difficult. Is it right to link Macaulay's lack of reaction to the intense religious life of his parents with the arrest of his affections, his desolation at Hannah's marriage, and his own inability to marry?[4] And does Trevelyan understand the full measure of abnormality in Macaulay's feelings as a brother? First, was Macaulay a child all his life? The faintly irritated

[1] Op. cit., 642n.   [2] p. 683.   [3] p. 20.
[4] *Inability* may be over-strong. As a young man, he believed that he was sacrificing any wish to marry to the financial welfare of the family. But as he became rich this explanation gradually ceased to be plausible to himself – or to us.

fascination which is a common reaction of readers of his history could well be ascribed to the feeling that Macaulay's mind is an elephantine version of the clever, knowing little boy. His encyclopaedic knowledge is not like that of other great scholars, because it is constantly marred by crudity of interpretation.[1] It is apt to remind us, instead, of the knowledge of juvenile cricket-watchers, who keep the bowling analysis, point out that even Test Match umpires sometimes allow seven balls to an over, and never fail to provide a parallel from the *Wisden* of 1903. Some of Macaulay's most memorable epigrammatic judgments have just this touch of hollow juvenile cleverness. To say of Boswell 'If he had not been a great fool he would never have been a great writer' is clever. It is also manifestly seen, on a moment's reflection, to be untrue; and that is only one of a long line of similar cases. On this view we shall also say that Macaulay's most childish characteristic is his extraordinary inability, for such a brilliant and well-informed man, really to question anything. Once he had invented (or more often adopted) a thesis, he was incapable of seeing the evidence either for or against it. He incorporates it into a kind of high schoolboy code. His feeling for the Whig tradition is more like the 'honour of the house' and the lump in the throat at the old school song than it is like any intelligible resultant of thought and argument. Such a line of thought is, or could be made, very persuasive. But certain objections to it occur. One function of the mind that one must concede as genuinely adult is the power of detached analysis of the emotions. And does not Macaulay sometimes attain to this when he writes with understanding of his own folly in storing all his affections in the keeping of his sisters? Is there not an adult tragedy rather than a childish pathos in the words quoted above: 'I must bear my punishment as I can; and, above all, I must take care that the punishment does not extend beyond myself?'

On this view, another interpretation is possible of the strange failure to react to the Clapham experience. Was it not so much a childlike failure to compare his family with any other family,

---

[1] E.g., his letter of 18 Dec. 1837 (Trevelyan, p. 337): 'I have read Augustine's *Confessions*. The book is not without interest; but he expresses himself in the style of a field-preacher.

as a deep-seated reticence, which is a common characteristic
in overwhelming talkers? Perhaps he did react, consider,
compare; perhaps he did arrive at a settled adult view of his
parents and of Evangelicalism, only – we shall never know for
certain what it was.

How well did Trevelyan understand? Like all biographers of
his time, he had his reticences, but we need to distinguish
several different kinds of reticence. One kind is simply
deferential to the current public view of decency:

> One repartee survives, thrown off in the heat of discussion,
> but exquisitely perfect in all its parts. Acknowledged with-
> out dissent to be the best applied quotation that ever was
> made within five miles of the Fitzwilliam Museum, it is
> unfortunately too strictly classical for reproduction in these
> pages.[1]

'Classical', of course, here means indecorous. Macaulay's undergraduate days, to which this passage refers, were the days of the
Prince Regent; and very distant they seemed in 1876. There is
no serious suppression, still less distortion here of anything in
Macaulay's character. He may have relished a broad joke when
he was an undergraduate; but his adherence to mid-Victorian
standards of decency was entirely sincere, as can be seen, for
instance, in his sweeping condemnation of the moral tone of the
seventeenth century, and in private comments in his journal,
expressing strong distaste for licentious passages in Plato's
Phaedrus and in Virgil.[2]

Sometimes, though, we can only be surprised by the things
Trevelyan leaves uninterpreted. In part, this is a common
feature of the biographical writing of his time. Working in the
shadow of Boswell and Lockhart, mid-Victorian biographers
believed above all in documentary evidence. This book is one of
many significantly entitled *Life and Letters*. If the low Victorian
reticence is just a fear of being improper, the high Victorian
reticence is a worthy belief in the supremacy of original sources
over secondary comment. In all this Trevelyan – a distinguished
historian – shares.

Yet there is still another and more personal kind of reticence

[1] p. 57.   [2] Cf. Trevelyan, p. 601n.

at work in Trevelyan's book. Its characteristic feature is a failure of connection, and it is very hard to be sure whether it is deliberate. Thus he quotes Macaulay as writing to his sisters: 'I dined yesterday at Holland House: all Lords except myself.'[1] For the interpretation of this everything depends on the tone. Is it snobbish, or merely playful? Were his sisters meant to read it with pride or with amusement? The most watchful reader needs some help here and he gets none. Within a year Trevelyan has Macaulay writing to Hannah 'the institution of the Peerage is evidently dying a natural death'.[2] It is interesting that Macaulay was so completely mistaken here, interesting that he showed no regret at having hitched his political car to an order he supposed to be dying, interesting that he did not seem to notice any connection himself. Failure to comment here may fairly be put down either to lack of genuine curiosity or to a wish to shield his hero from awkward inquiry. And when in 1845, Macaulay writes to Hannah that he will have 'two thousand a year for the trouble of signing my name'[3] it is hard to know whether Trevelyan fails to comment because he is ashamed for his uncle or because he is such a true Whig that it does not occur to him that anyone could possibly object to sinecures provided the right people held them.[4]

These are small matters, but occasionally we find cases where Trevelyan is less candid than he seems on points of real importance. Thus he quotes a stirring patriotic passage in Macaulay's speech of April 1840 on the Chinese question.[5] Trevelyan says, accurately enough, that this kind of thing goes

[1] p. 187. [2] p. 216. [3] p. 459.
[4] That the latter alternative is the correct one is suggested by a letter Trevelyan wrote more than thirty years later, on 15 April 1908. Asquith had just been forming his government and Trevelyan wrote:

'Since our party came in, full recognition has been given to the past services of those who in old days served the country and the cause, by the employment of their sons and relatives . . . Now that several younger men have been placed in office, while my son is left out, I must protest, once for all, that I feel the exception made in our case very deeply.' (See Roy Jenkins, *Asquith*, 1964, p. 183.)

That 'our' in the last phrase is the perfect essence of Whiggery. A Tory or Radical father, writing to complain in similar circumstances, would have written 'his case'.
[5] p. 391.

straight to the heart of the House of Commons. But he does not say that in the opinion of some, including Gladstone, Macaulay's speech appeared as a dangerous piece of rabble-rousing chauvinism, and that in their eyes, the Chinese, not the English, were the injured party.[1]

It is not true to say that Trevelyan was so much under Macaulay's spell, in the way Stanley was under Arnold's, that he could not see any faults. But it is true that he sometimes preferred to let his uncle off lightly, because, of course, the Whigs, whatever their peccadilloes, were always fundamentally right, and it is foolish to present too wide a target to the enemy. And there are times when this last sentiment, instead of causing undue reticence, produces a comment that one can only wish away.

The strangest of these relates to Macaulay's defence of Lord Cardigan when he was Secretary at War in 1841. Cardigan, afterwards celebrated as the leader (and unlikely survivor) of the Charge of the Light Brigade, was the most notoriously violent and unreasonable of all overgrown aristocratic puppies of the nineteenth century. With characteristic honesty, Trevelyan accepts this. He writes:

> Within the space of a single twelvemonth one of his captains was cashiered for writing him a challenge; he sent a coarse and insulting verbal[2] message to another, and then punished him with prolonged arrest, because he respectfully refused to shake hands with the officer who had been employed to convey the affront; he fought a duel with a lieutenant who had left the corps, and shot him through the body; and he flogged a soldier on Sunday between the services, on the very spot where, half an hour before, the man's comrades had been mustered for public worship.[3]

Having given us this highly-coloured, though perfectly accurate, account of Cardigan's conduct, Trevelyan takes our breath away with the following:

> The Secretary at War *had to put the best face he could* on these ugly stories. When it was proposed to remove Lord

---

[1] Cf. Morley: *Gladstone*, I, 226.
[2] Presumably Trevelyan meant *oral*.   [3] p. 399.

Cardigan from the command of his regiment, Macaulay took refuge in a position which he *justly regarded as impregnable*. 'Honourable gentlemen should beware how they take advantage of the unpopularity of an individual to introduce a precedent which, if once established, would lead to the most fatal effects to the whole of our military system, and work great injustice to all officers in Her Majesty's service. What is the case with officers in the army? They buy their commissions at a high price, the interest of which would be very nearly equal to the pay they receive ... Is it to be expected that men of spirit and honour will consent to enter this service, if they have not, at least, some degree of security for the permanence of their situations?[1]

In 1876, when these words were published, Army purchase had been abolished, and Gladstone's long premiership of 1868 was over; Trevelyan himself was still under forty, and had over fifty years still to live. One cannot refuse a grudging admiration at the persistence of Whiggery in an increasingly unfriendly world. A man who can actually say that it is better to have the worst imaginable officers than to have to pay for good ones is worthy of the respect we always give to brazen, unblushing honesty.

I have said that Trevelyan was in every fibre of his being a true Whig, and in the end, given his honesty, his lucidity, his shrewdness and his unobtrusive narrative skill, this is the strength and the weakness of this fascinating book. It is the strength because it allows a coherent, well-shaped narrative, such as can only be written long after the event, to be informed with the very feelings of the moment as they pass. Trevelyan, because of his Whiggery, and because of his close personal knowledge and affection for his uncle, did not need to exercise historical imagination. The great heroic Whig days, like the days of the Reform Bill debates of 1832, were immediately present to Trevelyan's consciousness. The excitement, the hopes and fears, the wonderful double vision of being at the same time the most powerful and exclusive clique in the world, and radical tribunes of the people, the deep, unquestioning assurance that history

[1] My italics.

140

was on the side of the Whigs, all these stirring ideals and magnificent illusions were there ready-made in the mind of the biographer who was not born in 1832. Bagehot, in what is still on the whole, the most intelligent and the wittiest short appreciation of Macaulay,[1] said of him in the '50's, 'He is still the man of '32', and went on:

> The events of twenty years have been full of rich instruction on the events of twenty years ago; but they have not instructed him. His creed is a fixture.

He could have expanded his twenty years into forty and said the same about Trevelyan, and his grandson, if he had one, could have said the same of Trevelyan in his old age.

Bagehot also complained in a pregnant phrase of Macaulay's 'inexperiencing nature'. Bagehot was very fair, and he gave Macaulay credit at the same time for many fine intellectual and moral qualities, but this inability to compare and question received opinions is equally characteristic of the uncle and the nephew. It is important to realise that the tendency to stick fast in 1832, which Bagehot noticed, is entirely unconscious. Mid-Victorian and later Whigs seemed old-fashioned to their contemporaries. They did not seem old-fashioned to themselves, for to them English history from the reign of Charles I to their own time was a seamless garment. The same issues were constantly recurring, the same high principles, which were recognisably Whig even in the seventeenth century before they acquired that name, were constantly guiding the best people, and enabling them to guide the nation in the paths of prudence and progress. Indeed, the 'progressive' character of the principles needs to be emphasised as much as their deep-rooted, unconscious conservatism. For instance, Trevelyan is not being satirical, as most people would be if they wrote his words to-day, when he describes:

> a pleasant nest of villas which lie in the southern suburb of Liverpool, on Dingle Bank: a spot whose natural beauty nothing can spoil, until in the fulness of time its inevitable destiny convert it into docks.[2]

---

[1] See his *Estimations in Criticism*, vol. II, ed. Cuthbert Lennox, 1909.
[2] p. 207.

666666

Whigs are in key with inevitable destiny; therefore its decrees must be right, even when the consequences are slightly disagreeable.

From this point of view, Trevelyan's other biography, his account of the early life of Fox (1880), is especially interesting. The Whigs are avowedly the party of change, so that it never worries them to find that their heroes in previous ages believed more in privilege than they do themselves. Rather the other way; the strategy of Whig dialectic is to exaggerate the amount of change that has already occurred in order to imply, but not to state, that not much more change is required. Hence the immense exaggeration by Whig writers of the popular character of the exceedingly aristocratical 'final' settlement of 1832. And so, writing of Fox, Trevelyan emphasises the smallness and compactness of the high political world of Fox's youth and he says:

> A few thousand people who thought that the world was made for them, and that all outside their own fraternity were unworthy of notice or criticism, bestowed upon each other an amount of attention quite inconceivable to us who count our equals by millions.[1]

The unconscious slide from the tiny charmed circle of Fox's day to those entitled to vote in 1880, is characteristic. Trevelyan forgets that he is not comparing like with like, and that many had votes in Fox's time without having political influence, while the charmed circle which would make a fair comparison, was somewhat more broadly-based indeed, but how much more really? It is the life of Fox, too, which provides us with the delightful phrase 'levanting for France'[2] which tells more than many speeches what Whigs really thought of foreigners. Exactly so, when Trevelyan was in his cradle, had Macaulay said of an Italian official: 'precious fellow; to think that a public functionary to whom a little silver is a bribe is fit society for an English gentleman.'[3]

In conclusion, then, we cannot call Trevelyan's book a

---

[1] G. O. Trevelyan: *The Early History of Charles James Fox*, new edition, 1881, p. 67.
[2] Fox: p. 72.   [3] Trevelyan: *Macaulay*, p. 367.

masterpiece of our great biographical tradition in the way that Froude's *Carlyle* is. Its interest is both intense and extraordinarily various. But it cannot be said that it sees its subject complete and in perfect proportion with his surroundings. And it is not difficult to say where it is lacking, though it would be more than difficult to supply the deficiencies. The ideal biography of Macaulay would show a man of exceptional energy, learning, lucidity and decisiveness, whose life was dominated by three strongly-contrasting facts. The three great facts of Macaulay's life are that he was born into the centre of the high Evangelical tradition, that he fixed all his affections on his sisters and nephews, and that he adopted the high, aristocratical Whig posture, and, surprisingly, was accepted by its hereditary representatives as their spokesman. The ideal biography would analyse these three influences in full, assess the importance of each for Macaulay, and show in detail the strains inflicted on him by their incompatibility. It would do this without failing to do what Trevelyan actually does so supremely well, to give the sense of Macaulay's daily life, and the stages of his career, as they were present to him at the time. For vividness, Trevelyan has only a few superiors, of whom Boswell and Froude are the most obvious. In intelligent, analytical understanding, he has many superiors; and yet, by sharing so completely many of Macaulay's most questionable assumptions, he provides us with a unique opportunity to make an informed judgment on the Whig ethos in its most splendid form. In dealing with what was sexually abnormal, Trevelyan is admirable in his honesty, his tact, and his genuine respect for a temperament so different, in this respect, from his own. In his easy, civilised control of vast masses of material, he is again admirable. In the end it is the perfect honesty that I wish to stress – a quality so easy to praise and so difficult to achieve. But it would be misleading to praise it without adding that, in some ways, Bagehot's phrase about Macaulay is true of his nephew, too – an 'inexperiencing nature'.

9

FROUDE'S CARLYLE

❋

1. *General*

To understand what Froude really did with Carlyle's life[1] as a sage, it is helpful to consider what he did not do. There was a model in existence, known to everybody and approved by most, which fitted the case well. It was the model of the industrious apprentice. As we have seen, it issued in a type of biography that fulfilled several mid-Victorian emotional needs. Its most obvious features were that merit triumphed despite discouragement and handicaps, and that private life was subordinated to public usefulness. (Thus Smiles tells us that Brindley only went to the play once, and the Richard III so excited him that it hindered his work for several days, and so he vowed never to go again.)[2] How neatly, how appropriately Carlyle could have been fitted to this pattern. He was a poor boy sternly brought up in poverty; he was by nature ambitious, determined and incorruptible; he was free of the vices of the flesh; his industry was stupefying; in the face of long discouragement and sudden disaster (the destruction of the *French Revolution* manuscript) he attained a stoic calm. When prosperity finally came to him he lived simply.

Froude's conception is the opposite of all this. Where Smiles aims to interpret a mass of detail through a simple, linear,

---

[1] Froude's work was published in two parts, each of which contained two volumes. The first part *Thomas Carlyle, the history of the first forty years of his life, 1795–1835* appeared in 1882. It is represented in notes by E.L.=Early Life. The second part, *A History of his Life in London, 1834–1881*, appeared in 1884. It is represented in notes by L.L.

Letters and Memories of Jane Welsh Carlyle (1883), prepared by Carlyle and edited by Froude, is represented by L.M.

[2] *Lives of Engineers*, I, 370–1.

progressive formula, Froude is dialectical, and, by implication at least, tragic. Take for instance his comment on the profession of literature, and its effect on Carlyle's personality. We remember that everything significant that Carlyle achieved, he achieved through literature. In other occupations, like teaching, in so far as he attempted them at all, he failed. Froude quotes from Carlyle's journal for 19 February, 1838, the year after the publication of *The French Revolution*, and the first year, therefore, of assured literary success: 'It often strikes me as a question whether there ought to be any such thing as a literary man at all. He is surely the wretchedest of all sorts of men.'[1] And Froude goes on:

> Let young men who are dreaming of literary eminence as the laurel wreath of their existence reflect on these words. Let them win a place for themselves as high as Carlyle won, they will find that he was speaking no more than the truth, and will wish, when it is too late, that they had been wise in time. Literature – were it even poetry – is but the shadow of action; the action the reality the poetry an echo. The 'Odyssey' is but the ghost of Ulysses – immortal, but a ghost still.

And he goes on to speculate whether Homer himself might not have echoed the words of Achilles, when he said that he would rather be the servant of a landless man than be a king among the dead.

Here we have an exact mirror image of Smiles, who would at this point have been telling his young readers to imitate Carlyle in order that, one day, they might become great and famous like him. This is a simple case. A much more complex effect is achieved by the placing of events at the end of the two parts of the biography. *Carlyle's Early Life* ends in 1834 at the moment of greatest uncertainty in Carlyle's career. He was approaching forty; he had very little money and no regular source of income. London seemed vast, unfamiliar and unsympathetic; his literary reputation had hardly begun to grow.

It is at this point, with all the emphasis that naturally falls to the last paragraph of a book, that Froude chose to write:

L.L. I., 138. All quotations are taken from Longman Edition of 1896.

'They call me a great man now,' Carlyle said to me a few days before he died, 'but not one believes what I have told them.' But if they did not believe the prophet, they could worship the new star which was about to rise. The Annandale peasant boy was to be the wonder of the London world.[1]

Respice finem, the constant cry of the biographers of the industrious apprentice school has here a reversed, ironical effect. The hardships and dangers of the early struggle would dissolve more quickly and easily than seemed possible in 1834. Of course, talent like Carlyle's will make its mark in the world. But the final goal of serious ambition, the desire to speak with the voice of a prophet, and to influence mankind for good – this is the chimera.

The first readers of this passage had over two years to wait before they could study Froude's account of the next stage in Carlyle's career. The more reflective of them may perhaps have wondered how Froude would deal with this death when he came to it. One must admit that circumstances favoured the pattern of Froude's presentation. For Carlyle died old and lonely, in the month of February, in one of the hardest winters of the nineteenth century.[2] He died in London, but he was buried in Annandale. The small band of mourners, of whom Froude himself was the chief, travelled by the mail train.

The hearse, with the coffin, stood solitary in the stationyard, as some waggon might stand, waiting to be unloaded. They do not study form in Scotland . . . A crowd had gathered at the churchyard, not disorderly, but seemingly with no feeling but curiosity.[3]

In another way, too, Froude presented a pattern opposite to that of Smiles. Instead of unifying public and private life, he set them from first to last in manifest contrast. For him, all Carlyle's vices were domestic, all his virtues effectively operative in the great world. Now Carlyle's great private vice, in Froude's

[1] E.L., II, 495.
[2] Readers may remember the winter of 1963, which had a strong similarity to that of 1881.
[3] L.L., II, 503–5.

opinion, which most of us will share, was a repulsive egoism issuing in an insane irritability. Carlyle never grasped imaginatively that any experience of his own was comparable to that of anyone else. If he was awakened by a crowing cock, this was an event different in kind from the sleeplessness of others. No one can doubt that Froude did full justice to this aspect of his subject. But he confined it almost exclusively to private life. Was he right?

His considered judgment on Carlyle as a writer is this:

I have found no sentence of his own which he could have wished unwritten, or, through all those trying years of incipient manhood, a single action alluded to by others which those most jealous of his memory need regret to read, or his biographer need desire to conceal.[1]

This is surely impossible to accept. It may be a hard question whether the force operative upon Froude here to make him (with entire honesty) misrepresent the truth is the prevailing moral ethos, or his own feelings as a disciple. But it can hardly be denied that Carlyle's writings, both public and private, are disfigured from first to last, and more horribly as he grew older, with signs of the two of the worst of all vices, pride and hatred. Moreover, we may well suppose that the same weaknesses of character were at work all through. The same reckless egoism, the same callous disregard of others which made his wife's whole married life a torment was at work when he so absurdly said that Newman had not the brain of a rabbit. His contempt was strongest against the greatest and worthiest men. Gladstone, in a letter of 23 March, 1873,[2] he called 'One of the contemptiblest men I ever looked on'. He had once admired Mill and been grateful to him, but after reading his autobiography he wrote: 'I have never read a more uninteresting book, nor I should say a sillier, by a man of sense, integrity and seriousness of mind.'[3] More than twenty years earlier, before old age could begin to be regarded as an excuse, he had applied a similar, though a more witty, contempt to Coleridge.[4] He enjoyed reading Dickens, but he patronised and despised him. Wordsworth was a 'small

[1] E.L., II, 490. [2] L.L., II, 452. [3] L.L., II, 449.
[4] In chapter VIII of the *Life of Sterling*, 1851 (see chapter IV above).

diluted man'.[1] If we ask ourselves what is the common factor in
the immense human variety of Wordsworth, Coleridge, Newman,
Mill, Gladstone and Dickens, we shall almost be forced to reply
that there is only one, they were all great men. Carlyle despised
almost everything and everybody, except his parents and Oliver
Cromwell. (Rather to our surprise he makes a partial exception
for Tennyson.) He despised the small because they were small
and the great because he envied and feared them. A similar
argument could be used to explain the crazy violence of almost
all his references to the Catholic Church. He respected it, he
feared it; he wrote, therefore, as if he despised it.

Of course the reason for Froude's failure of vision here is that
he wrote as a disciple. He says so himself:

> I had, however, from the time when I became acquainted
> with his writings, looked on him as my own guide and
> master – so absolutely that I could have said: 'Malim errare
> cum Platone quam cum aliis bene sentire'; or in Goethe's
> words which I often did repeat to myself: 'Mit deinem
> Meister zu irren ist dein Gewinn.' The practice of submission
> to the authority of one whom one recognises as greater than
> oneself outweighs the chance of occasional mistake. If I
> wrote anything, I fancied myself writing it to him . . .[2]

This sense of Carlyle's overriding authority affected every
part of Froude's intellectual life, and not least it affected his
thoughts about biographical method. In his Preface he quoted
what Carlyle had written long before when he reviewed
Lockhart's *Scott*:

> How delicate, decent, is English biography, bless its mealy
> mouth! A Damocles' sword of *Respectability* hangs for ever
> over the poor English life-writer (as it does over poor English
> life in general), and reduces him to the verge of paralysis . . .
> The English biographer has long felt that if in writing his
> biography he wrote down anything that could by possibility
> offend any man, he had written wrong. The plain con-
> sequence was that, properly speaking, no biography
> whatever could be produced.[3]

Froude had accepted the argument, as he had accepted so

[1] L.L., I, 47.   [2] L.L., II, 195.   [3] Quoted E.L., I, viii–ix.

many other more dubious ones, and, except on the most difficult question of impotence, had accepted its implications. He followed Carlyle's theory so closely, indeed, that he was widely, though absurdly, thought to be his enemy. There is no doubt of the sincerity of Froude's desire for a true balance in his account. But he remained convinced that the eventual triumph of Carlyle's ideas would be the saving of England. It was natural, then, that he should, without knowing it himself, try to detach the man from the doctrine. To the ordinary reader, now as in his own time, Carlyle appears incapable of abstract thought. His whole brilliant, tortured personality is present in every idea, in every sentence. Froude's vivid accounts of the torment Carlyle experienced in composing his books show that in one way he was aware of this. Nevertheless, he tried to separate the man and the work. He wanted to believe that there was some invisible inner temple in Carlyle's mind uncontaminated by the poisons of egoism. He wanted to show us the man as tragic, but the thinker as inevitably triumphant in the eyes of posterity. He may have pushed too far the idea of opposing the man against the work, the suffering mortal and the prophet of immortal truth. If so, the mistake was venial, since he was able to convey so memorably the essential point – the greatness and the littleness of Carlyle. This contrast of greatness and littleness is more than a diffused presence through the book. He proceeds everywhere by opposites, by careful collocations of light and shade. Insanely irritable about trifles, he was heroic when chance threatened to destroy his career as a writer. On the 6th of March 1835, Mill staggered, deadly pale, and supported by Carlyle's arm, into the house in Cheyne Row. He explained that the borrowed manuscript of *The French Revolution* had been destroyed by a servant.

Froude continues:

Carlyle wrote always in a highly-wrought quasi-automatic condition both of mind and nerves. He read till he was full of his subject. His notes, when they were done with, were thrown aside and destroyed; and of this unfortunate volume, which he had produced as if 'possessed' while he was about it, he could remember nothing. Not only were 'the fruits of

five months of steadfast, occasionally excessive, and always
sickly and painful toil' gone irretrievably, but the spirit in
which he had worked seemed to have fled too, not to be
recalled; worse than all, his work had been measured
carefully against his resources, and the household purse
might now be empty before the loss could be made good.
The carriage and its occupant drove off – and it would have
been better had Mill gone too after he had told his tale, for
the forlorn pair wished to be alone together in the face of
such a calamity. But Carlyle, whose first thought was of
what Mill was suffering, made light of it, and talked of
indifferent things, and Mill stayed and talked too – stayed,
I believe, two hours. Mrs Carlyle told me that the first words
her husband uttered as the door closed were: 'Well, Mill,
poor fellow, is terribly cut up; we must endeavour to hide
from him how very serious this business is to us.'[1]

Froude could rely here on his readers to feel, as he did, that
Carlyle could be heroic at terrible moments, and all the more
impressive because his calm, offhand tone, which his wife
remembered so well, and reported long after, suggested that he
was unaware of his own heroism.

But Froude is just as ready to tell us of times when Carlyle
eagerly seized on a heroic role. Thus he quotes a letter to Jane
of 2 July, 1862:

Last night, in getting to bed, I said to myself at last,
'Impossible, sir, that you have no friend in the big Eternities
and Immensities. . . .'[2]

Froude goes on:

. . . if his little finger ached he imagined no mortal had ever
suffered so before. If his liver was amiss he was a chained
Prometheus with the vulture at his breast, and earth, sea
and sky were invoked to witness his injuries.

Sometimes he quotes a long passage from the journal, and
then punctures it with a cool footnote. When Carlyle writes of
Mrs Buller:

Adieu, therefore, to ancient dames of quality, that flaunting,

[1] L.L., I, 28–9.   [2] L.L., II, 269.

painting, patching, nervous, vapourish, jigging, skimming, scolding race of mortals. . . .[1]

Froude comments:

Poor Mrs Buller! A year back 'one of the most fascinating women he had ever met'. She was about forty, and had probably never flaunted, painted, or patched in her life.

At other times, the contrasts between Carlyle's greatness and littleness are neither heroic, nor comic, but pathetic. Perhaps the most moving comes in the account of the year 1832.[2] In the sadness, perhaps bitterness of her feelings about their hard and lonely life at Craigenputtock, Jane wrote a poem addressed to a swallow that built in the eaves of their cottage. Identifying it with herself, she asks what brought it to this sad place:

> What was it then? some mystic turn of thought,
> Caught under German eaves, and hither brought,
> Marring thine eye
> For the world's loveliness, till thou art grown
> A sober thing that dost but mope and moan
> Not knowing why?

She gave these verses to Jeffrey of the *Edinburgh Review,* and Froude pictures him reading them with foreboding about her future. Then he goes on: 'The fact was not as Jeffrey saw it. Carlyle was a knight errant on the noblest quest that can animate a man.'

His own personal sympathy for Jane was very strong; and the temptation to expand upon her miseries here must have been strong too. But he remains true to his dialectical method. He will never allow the greatness or the littleness of Carlyle to hold exclusive attention for long. He sees them as inseparable.

Froude found his way of interpreting Carlyle to be a great help in dealing with the flow of time. Since Carlyle was never contented or easy, but only excited or dejected, he needs to give us both the intensity of the moment and the dreariness of the passing years. So whenever he wishes to convey the passing of a long tract of barren time, he has recourse to the journal. The sadness, the regret, the impotent yearning, the absence of

[1] E.L., I, 234.   [2] E.L., II, 301–3.

regular occupation, the loneliness, the spleen all are there. The reader receives an oppressive sense of the sheer weight of days without variety, without gaiety, without a sense of purpose. But he knows that the time will come again in his reading when the intense moment, the piercing vision, the overwhelming sense of destiny will return to the narrative. Carlyle is shown as a man grand in the moment, in the point of time which touches eternity, miserable, dejected in the years. The book conveys the sadness of time by showing us a man ill-adapted to the time process itself.

Distinguished and versatile writer though he was, Froude would not have been equally successful with another subject. Indeed, his other biographical works, such as his life of Disraeli, are slight and lack memorable features. The greatness of this biography springs from a perfect aptness of author and subject that is almost, if not quite, unique. Froude's sincere discipleship, his sense of drama and destiny, his cool, ironic detachment, his rough humour, his lucidity, his powerful sense of order – all play their part. Both Carlyle and Froude, in slightly different ways, were prejudiced and insular men. It would have gone against the grain with both to find in Pascal the true source of the book's wisdom. Yet it is of Pascal's analysis of the greatness and littleness of human nature that we are driven to think. At the end of four volumes, we see Carlyle as a deposed king. To Froude alone among English biographers belongs the distinction of having incarnated this view of man in a great mass of biographical material about a man. For one reader, at least, this makes him the greatest of all our biographers.

2. *Background and Religion*

To give a general impression of the milieu in which Carlyle grew up was one of Froude's easier tasks. The word 'Cameronian', which he introduces on the very first page of his work, is the operative one; and Carlyle's own *Reminiscences* could be regarded as a definitive source for the understanding of his parents and of the social setting. Carlyle's great respect for the integrity and courage of both his parents, and for the vigorous, though somewhat undeveloped, intellectual gifts of his father were important points about his character to which Froude gave full weight.

So much was clear and simple, but a very difficult issue lurked behind – the issue of Carlyle's religious belief and of its precise relation to the belief of his parents. And Froude well saw that this was an issue that had several different kinds of importance. Its biographical importance was obvious; we can never understand a man until we know his real attitude to the ultimate questions. Less obvious, but just as real, was the general historical importance of Carlyle's type of religion. For Carlyle was a precursor of the great Victorian enterprise, the attempt to separate the soul of Christianity from its body. In considering Carlyle's religion, Froude was called upon to judge this enterprise. Of course, it took many forms. Matthew Arnold's version of the essential spiritual message of religion is not the same as Carlyle's. But the same unavoidable primary questions lie in the path of anyone attempting to judge either version. Are dogma, miracle and history essential or inessential parts of the Christian tradition? Is the importance of religion primarily, or only secondarily, in its moral statements and influence? Froude summarises Carlyle's religious situation in about 1819 as follows:

There had come upon him the trial which in these days awaits every man of high intellectual gifts and noble nature on their first actual acquaintance with human things – the question, far deeper than any mere political one, What is this world then, what is this human life, over which a just God is said to preside, but of whose presence or whose providence so few signs are visible? In happier ages religion silences scepticism if it cannot reply to its difficulties, and postpones the solution of the mystery to another stage of existence. Brought up in a pious family where religion was not talked about or emotionalised, but was accepted as the rule of thought and conduct, himself too instinctively upright, pure of heart, and reverent, Carlyle, like his parents, had accepted the Bible as a direct communication from Heaven. It made known the will of God, and the relation in which man stood to his Maker, as present facts like a law of nature, the truth of it, like the truth of gravitation, which man must act upon or immediately suffer the consequences. But religion, as revealed in the Bible, passes beyond present conduct, penetrates all forms of thought, and takes possession wherever it goes. It claims to control the intellect, to explain the past, and foretell the future. It has entered into poetry and art and been the interpreter of history. And thus there had grown round it a body of opinion, on all varieties of subjects, assumed to be authoritative; dogmas which science was contradicting; a history of events which it called infallible, yet which the canons of evidence, by which other histories are tried and tested successfully, declared not to be infallible at all. To the Mainhill household the Westminster Confession was a full and complete account of the position of mankind and the Being to whom they owed their existence, The Old and New Testament not only contained all spiritual truth necessary for guidance in word and deed, but every fact related in them was literally true. To doubt was not to mistake, but was to commit a sin of the deepest dye, and was a sure sign of a corrupted heart.[1]

Froude goes on to give an able account of the nature of the doubts that afflicted Carlyle, which were based mainly upon the objections made by the eighteenth-century philosophers and historians, especially Hume and Gibbon. Many chapters later he quotes from Carlyle's Journal for 1 February 1833:

Oh for faith! Truly the great 'God announcing miracle' always is faith, and now more than ever. I often look on my mother (nearly the only genuine Believer I know of) with a kind of sacred admiration.[2]

These words were written only a few months before the Oxford Movement began, and only a few months before the death of William Wilberforce – an event which was almost simultaneous with the greatest practical triumph of the Clapham Sect, the passage through Parliament of the Bill to abolish slavery. Here were two religious traditions, perhaps (as Gladstone was so persuasively to suggest much later) much more closely

[1] E.L., I, 66–7.   [2] E.L., II, 342.

connected than they appeared to be. What had Carlyle to say to *their* claims to share with his mother the honour of a genuine belief?

The answer is simple. Carlyle in a variety of intemperate and often scurrilous references to 'Jesuitry', Puseyism, breeches pretending to be men, etc. etc., denied all sincerity to the religious parties of his day. And Froude, in several passages, which are unlike Carlyle's in being calm and not hysterical, and in being free from personal vituperation, solemnly endorsed this judgment.[1] Now this is very strange; and, paradoxically, one has more sympathy for the wild misjudgments of Carlyle than for Froude in his cool support of them. To deny that Newman really believed in and cared about Christianity is to move into the realm of madness; and madness is more sympathetic when it is violent and tortured than when it is bland and cool. Moreover, Froude had better means than Carlyle of understanding the magnitude and the absurdity of the mistake. His brother was Newman's early and influential associate; he himself knew Newman well and, for a time before his decisive shift away from orthodoxy, collaborated with him. His own celebrated essay on the Oxford Movement, entitled *The Oxford Counter-reformation*[2] is indeed misleading in certain respects, but it is based on a good deal of personal information, and its tone, though critical, is worlds away from Carlyle's hysterical abuse. Here he gives Newman credit for 'a clearness of intellectual perception, a disdain for conventionalities, a temper imperious and wilful, but along with it a most attaching gentleness, sweetness, singleness of heart and purpose'.[3] The last phrase is, of course, particularly important as showing his acceptance of Newman's sincerity, which, one would imagine, no one who knew anything of men and the world could doubt. 1881, the year of the appearance of this article, was also the year of Carlyle's death, and the year before the appearance of the first part of the *Early Life*. We can hardly suppose that a few months brought a radical change of mind about events so far in the past. We are forced to admit that

[1] E.g. E.L., II, 6.
[2] In *Good Words*, 1881, reprinted in *Short Studies of Great Subjects*, vol. IV.
[3] *Short Studies*, IV, p. 273.

Froude's detachment in judging Carlyle was curiously patchy. Even while his faults were clearly perceived, his opinions exercised a hypnotic power – so great a hypnotic power that Froude, a very clever man after all, was completely unaware of the inconsistency between the two views of Newman found in his own writings. There can be no doubt that this is a blemish in Froude's work. But we should not condemn it too sternly. For it is precisely this strange magnetic power in Carlyle's thinking that gives Carlyle much of his importance and the biography much of its fascination. The man who bemused Froude into forgetting and denying what he really knew quite well about Newman was the same man who even after his long, lonely and ineffective old age and his death could still be venerated as a master by a great man like Ruskin.

We must now turn to a more important question. How correct was Froude's interpretation of the positive aspects of Carlyle's religion? Carlyle had written in the *Reminiscences*, and Froude quotes him:[1]

> The sound of the kirk-bell once or twice on Sunday mornings (from Hoddam kirk, about a mile on the plains below me) was strangely touching, like the departing voice of eighteen hundred years.

In one sense, and with one part of his mind, Carlyle believed that Christianity was dead. In another it was eternally true, containing the most necessary affirmations about the moral nature of the universe and the meaning of the historical process. Carlyle used, and Froude accepted, the analogy of the Copernican revolution in astronomy to account for his conviction that everything could change in theology and yet everything really remain the same. We still guide our ships by the stars even though we no longer believe that all the stars exist to serve the purposes of earth. We are still just as dependent on the sun for all our physical life as our ancestors were. We can correct their Ptolemaic errors without questioning that dependence. So can we do away with Incarnation, Redemption and miracle, and still hold to the essential truths that lie behind them. 'The theories,

[1] E.L., I, 318.

Froude wrote, 'which dispensed with God and the soul Carlyle utterly abhorred.'[1] This, taken *au pied de la lettre*, would seem to be true. But taken with its normal implication that he actively believed in God and the soul, and therefore in immortality, it becomes more doubtful. Froude did not, for instance, quote the following from the *Life of Sterling*: 'There follow now [in one of Sterling's letters] several pages on "Personal God", and other abstruse or indeed properly unspeakable matters.'[2] This is ambiguous. Does it only mean that the highest matters are beyond the reach of discussion; or does it mean that the very ideas were shadowy and unreal? But Froude does quote Carlyle's cry of despair in old age:

> He himself never doubted; yet he was perplexed by the indifference with which the Supreme Power was allowing its existence to be obscured. I once said to him, not long before his death, that I could only believe in a God which *did* something. With a cry of pain which I shall never forget, he said, 'He does nothing.'[3]

Froude's interpretation of this, as a cry of pain within a structure of faith, rather than a denial of faith, may be correct. It is very hard to be sure. But Froude is more certainly open to criticism in his account of the content of Carlyle's religion. It is strange how he, the son of an archdeacon in Devonshire, allows Carlyle to pre-empt for Calvin and the Scottish Lowlands the entire Christian tradition. He hardly comments, and never adversely, upon one of the most obvious features of Carlyle's habitual religious language, that it derives from the Old Testament rather than from the New, that it speaks much of justice and little of mercy, that the idea of *caritas* is absent. Admittedly, Froude faced a difficult problem here. He could claim that he had done full justice to Carlyle's practical failure in charity and forbearance. Was it not enough to deal honestly with that and pass on? The answer must be that, difficult as it is to distinguish, it is not enough. An orthodox Christian who was as harsh, as unforgiving, as self-righteous as Carlyle was, might yet be in a totally different theoretical position. It was Froude's duty to discover, if he could, Carlyle's belief as well as his conduct. Here

[1] E.L., ii, 5.   [2] *Life of John Sterling*, Part II, chapter 2.   [3] L.L., iv, 280.

the following, which Froude very honestly quotes, seems to me entirely characteristic:

> All mortals are tumbling about in a state of drunken saturnalia, delirium, or quasi-delirium . . . a very strange method of thanking God for sending them a Redeemer; a set singularly worth 'redeeming', too, you would say.[1]

It would be unfair to make much of this if it were only an expression of irritation. But its exact expression of Carlyle's lifelong attitude makes it more significant. The idea of mercy to ordinary erring human nature was not only incredible to Carlyle. It was also repellent, weak, enervating. How, in view of that, can one conclude that Carlyle retains the moral essence of the Christian Faith? Surely it must be clear, even to those who can accept that dubious set of analogies called the Clothes-Philosophy, that when the clothes of dogma were stripped away, the naked flesh of Carlyle's belief was something other than Christianity. If Froude understood this, he never said so, and he is excessively tender, too, to the most unfortunate feature of Carlyle's secularisation of dogma. By putting history in the place of scripture, as Carlyle habitually did,[2] he transposed the idea of Divine Judgment into a process completely visible in time. This tended to mean in practice that Carlyle's own particular views about current political events were endowed with a charisma of Divine and infallible judgment. Thus Froude, for once, is simply inept when he says of the war of 1870:

> The finer forces of nature were not sleeping everywhere, and Europe witnessed this summer, in the French and German war, an exhibition of Divine judgment which was after Carlyle's own heart.[3]

Here Carlyle's magnificent, unspeakable Power, who must not be limited by terms like 'Personal God' seems more like a ventriloquist's dummy. If Froude, so conspicuously honest in his account of his hero's failings of temper, could have brought himself to say so, the biography would have been an even greater book than it is; and that is saying a good deal.

[1] L.L., II, 213.
[2] See, for instance, the essay *On History Again*, 1838.
[3] L.L., II, 427.

3. *Politics*

Anybody who has ever read much of Carlyle's work may well have been puzzled about his political attitudes. Here is a man who was always forthright – not to say violent – in expressing his opinions. Yet his political ideas wear an ambiguous look. Was he the arch-radical or the arch-reactionary, or was he both in turn? How can the man who saw the justice of heaven in the fate of the French aristocracy in the Revolution have written *The Nigger Question* with its frightening scorn for weakness and ignorance? Or how could he have so misjudged the Reform Bill of 1867 as to speak of 'shooting Niagara'? The picture of Lord Derby and Benjamin Disraeli as reckless adventurers gambling with the future of their country seems a chimera only likely to present itself to a timid and ultra-conservative mind.

Carlyle wrote in his *Reminiscences*:

I had plenty of Radicalism, and have, and to all appearance shall have; but the opposite hemisphere (which never was wanting either, nor will be, as it miserably is in Mill and Co.) had not yet found itself summoned by the trumpet of time and his events (1848; study of Oliver etc.) into practical emergence, and emphasis and prominence as now.[1]

Written in his old age, after his wife's death, this passage refers generally to the late 1830's and early '40's. Carlyle was, in effect, though not in intention, giving Froude a clear outline for one of his largest biographical tasks. In its acceptance of the dialectical nature of his own thinking, it is obviously in key with Froude's whole method of presenting Carlyle's character and opinions. Its stress on a break after 1848, rather than on a steady development, was taken by Froude in a rather special, personal sense, though it might well have secured Carlyle's agreement, had it been put to him. Froude chose to think that it was more the practical bearing than the actual proportions of Carlyle's political thinking that changed after 1848. Briefly, we may say that Froude maintained that Carlyle's increasing pessimism after 1848 was due mainly to the badness of the times, not to personal factors.

[1] *Reminiscences*, vol. II, p. 186.

'Radicalism,' Froude wrote, 'lay in the blood of the Scotch Calvinists, a bitter inheritance from the Covenanters.'[1] And he quotes freely and fairly from the numerous passages in which Carlyle speaks of killing partridges as the whole aim of aristocratic life, or asserts that a wealthy man consumes the wages of several thousand workers, and asks (with the French Revolution, of course, in mind) whether this can possibly last. The key question, for Froude and for us, is the precise relation between this 'radicalism' and the Carlyle who wrote *The Nigger Question* in 1849, and *Shooting Niagara* in 1867. Froude boldly asserts a continuity, indeed an identity, between the two attitudes. After quoting one of the radical tirades, he goes on:

> When Carlyle published his views on 'the Nigger Question', his friends on both sides of the Atlantic were astonished and outraged. Yet the thought in that pamphlet and the thought in 'Sartor' is precisely the same. When a man can be taught to work, he had a distinct value in the world appreciable in money like the value of a horse . . . Slavery might be a bad system, but under it a child was worth at least as much as a foal, and the master was interested in rearing it. Abolish slavery and substitute anarchy in the place of it, and the parents, themselves hardly able to keep body and soul together, will bless God when a timely fever relieves them of a troublesome charge.[2]

In fact, Froude maintains, Carlyle's attitude to the West Indian negroes was an instance of his whole complex of radical-authoritarian-paternalist views, and of a piece with his hatred of Manchester economics and upper-class irresponsibility. But was it?

> If precisely the Wisest Man were at the top of society, and the next-wisest next, and so on till we reached the Demerara Nigger (from whom downward, through the horse, etc., there is no question hitherto), then were this a perfect world, the extreme *maximum* of wisdom produced in it.'[3]

So Carlyle: and this quotation is fair to him. It would be easy

[1] L.L., I, 14.   [2] E.L., II, 140.
[3] 'The Nigger Question' in *English and Other Critical Essays*, Everyman, p. 314.

to quote some violent hyperbole, product of his violent temper
more than of his thinking mind. But this is what he really meant
to say; and it has indeed, as Froude maintained it had, elements
of paternalism, elements of *care*. It is a waste of time to reproach
Carlyle for not being a democrat; and Froude is perfectly correct
in distinguishing sharply between radicalism and democracy.
But there is nevertheless a vital point which Froude misses.
Whether consciously or not, Carlyle is sliding from the idea of a
right inherent in a wise man to govern a fool, and the idea of
a wise race governing a foolish race. And where, we may well
ask, in the wide world is there to be found such a thing as a wise
race? No one knew better than Carlyle that there was no such
thing in nature. And where is the ground for the other
assumption that an individual negro could not be or become
wise? Was it for the poor boy from Ecclefechan who came for a
time almost to dominate the English intellectual world to deny
that possibility? On these crucial points Froude is altogether
silent, and so allows to Carlyle a consistency of view to which he
is not entitled.

Of the general nature of Carlyle's paternalist theory, Froude
says:

> Majorities, as such, had no more right to rule than kings, or
> nobles, or any other persons or groups of persons, to whom
> circumstances might have given temporary power. The
> right to rule lay with those who were right in mind and
> heart, whenever they chose to assert themselves. If they
> tried and failed, it proved only that they were not right
> *enough* at that particular time.[1]

This is an admirable statement of the real nature of Carlyle's
'Right is Might' doctrine. It is just in denying the accusation so
often made against Carlyle, in his time and since, that he
worshipped power for its own sake. But again, Froude is being
too kind, because he strongly implies, both here and throughout,
that Carlyle consistently judged all political events according to
the doctrine. But how can it be made to fit his account of
Cromwell, the Commonwealth and the Restoration? If history
really reveals Divine Purpose, why must the Restoration,

[1] L.L., I, 389.

obviously a notable event of some sort, be the solitary exception? And how does Carlyle face the idea that Cromwell was not 'right enough' at the time? He simply does not face it all in his *Cromwell*;[1] and Froude allows this serious inconsistency to pass. Now there is nothing accidental about these lapses on Froude's part. Indeed, the whole book seems to be remarkably free from accidental lapses, a few of which would be venial, in view of the mass of material, and the haste of composition. I should be very ill-employed, if I were doing something analogous to the passage in a review that draws attention to misprints. It is Froude's whole strategy that commits him to errors of this sort; they are due to his determination to build a wall between Carlyle's public and private life, and to chalk up all his errors and failings to the latter.

On the other hand, Froude is admirably clear-sighted in distinguishing Carlyle's authoritarianism from conservatism. As he most truly says Carlyle was 'never a conservative', for he believed that 'unless there was a change, impossible except by miracle, in the habits of and character of the wealthy classes the gods themselves could not save them'.[2] And his statement of the links between Carlyle's radical, revolutionary and authoritarian views is succinct and convincing:

> The will of the people, shifting and uncertain as the wealth, would make an end of authoritative action. And yet such a government as he desired to see could be the product only of revolution of another kind. He said often that the Roman Republic was allowed so long a day because in emergencies the constitution was suspended by a dictatorship. Dictatorships might end as they ended at Rome, in becoming perpetual – and to this he would not have objected, if the right man could be found; but he was alone in his opinion . . . [3]

Nor does Froude allow all this to become too abstract. He did not forget that a biography is only in the second place a study of a man's thought. And he has almost at the very end of his long book a characteristic anecdote of Carlyle inciting the famous soldier, Sir Garnet Wolseley, to imitate Cromwell by

[1] Cf. chapter 4 above.   [2] L.L., I, 390.   [3] L.L., 471.

locking up the House of Commons and sending all the members home.[1]

But, though Froude insists too strongly on Carlyle's intellectual consistency in politics, he was well aware that the faults of temper, that dominated his private life, adversely affected his effectiveness as a political persuader; and he sees, plausibly enough, a decisive increase in anger and prejudice, about the time of *Latter-Day Pamphlets* in 1850. The following is admirable alike in its vivid portraiture and in its just judgment of Carlyle's state of mind:

> ... the fierce acid had accumulated again and had been discharged in the *Latter-Day Pamphlets* – discharged, however, still imperfectly, for his soul was loaded with bilious indignation. Many an evening about this time, I heard him flinging off the matter intended for the rest of the series which had been left unwritten, pouring out, for hours together, a torrent of sulphurous denunciation. No one could check him. If anyone tried contradiction, the cataract rose against the obstacle till it rushed over it and drowned it. But, in general, his listeners sate silent. The imagery, the wild play of humour, the immense knowledge always evident in the grotesque forms which it assumed, were in themselves so dazzling and so entertaining, that we lost the use of our own faculties till it was over. He did not like making these displays, and avoided them when he could; but he was easily provoked, and when excited could not restrain himself.[2]

The last point, that Carlyle did not really want to behave as he did is particularly striking; and it is a tribute to Froude's objectivity here that he could perceive this amid the frustrations experienced by a captive and battered audience.

But we are still left with the most important aspect of Carlyle's political and economic influence – his attack on the doctrine of *laissez-faire*. Froude was right to attach the highest importance to this; and it is easy for present readers, living in a time when the sacred cows of the 1840's have a harmless historical air, to underrate the courage and originality

[1] L.L., II, 478. [2] L.L., II, 48.

of Carlyle's attack. Froude scarcely exaggerates when he says:

> *Past and Present* appeared at the beginning of April 1843, and created at once admiration and a storm of anger. It was the first public protest against the 'Sacred Science', which its chief professors have since discovered to be no science, yet which then was accepted, even by the clergy, whose teaching it made ridiculous, as being irrefragable as Euclid. The idol is dead now, and maybe laughed at with impunity.[1]

Writing in the '80's, Froude (we may be inclined to feel) was one-sided in giving all the credit to Carlyle, and none to Ruskin, whose attack on political economy is more profound. But here Froude might reasonably say that Carlyle has the privileges of a pioneer, that it was a different thing to attack the 'dismal science' in the '40's and in the '60's, that Ruskin always admitted freely that he had learnt from Carlyle, and that anyway, it was Carlyle's life that he was supposed to be writing.

4. *Marriage*

That the Carlyle marriage was a very unusual one is a commonplace. Men of genius are few; few of those few marry women of exceptional intellectual gifts and vivid powers of literary expression. One may hope that marital discord on the scale endured by these two is rare; but at any rate lively, minute accounts of it, written by one partner and read and commented upon by the other, where both combine extreme emotional intensity with facility for detached and witty comment – these, one can be sure, are very rare indeed. Herein, of course, lies the great importance of the publication by Froude in 1883, between the appearance of the first and second parts of the Carlyle biography, of Jane's *Letters and Memorials*, with her husband's notes, written after her death. Yet another striking feature is the strong sexual attractiveness possessed, and perhaps one may add, wielded by both the man and the woman, as they maintained a permanent union, as affectionate as it was miserable, while at the same time it was the considered opinion of those who knew them best that the marriage had never been consummated.

[1] L.L., I, 306.

But the strangeness, perhaps the uniqueness, of the facts thus baldly catalogued is still less striking than the uniqueness in the tradition of biography of Froude's treatment. Recalling that Johnson was a widower when Boswell first met him, we may say that Froude's intimate knowledge of the feelings of both partners, his determination to break decisively with long-established traditions of reticence and his great literary gifts make his treatment of this marriage without peer or rival in the whole of English biography. He was fortunate, no doubt, in his moment. If Carlyle had died with his wife in 1866, Froude, bold man as he was, might not have dared to write as he did in the '80's. And, of course, his material would have been poorer by an item of the first importance – Carlyle's own sad retrospective view of the record of his wife's miseries. It is true, certainly, that in the '80's Froude's work aroused severe criticism and dislike; but the opposition was beginning to wear an old-fashioned look, and support and encouragement were not altogether wanting.

If so much is accepted, it still leaves out of account a key point. Froude's break with the tradition of reticence was not as decisive as it seemed. The concluding volumes of the biography were published in October 1884. Some two and a half years later, in March 1887, Froude wrote without any thought of publication[1] an intimate account of the evidence on the question of Carlyle's impotence. It is the work of a man approaching seventy who feels the burden of years heavily. The very rapid writing of the biography had affected his health, and he had been exposed to a prolonged persecution from those of Carlyle's relatives who believed not only that he had defamed the master, but that he had acted improperly in claiming possession of the documents and in using them for his book. Though he was writing without an immediate audience, he wrote defensively. Fatigue and discouragement show through. It is not surprising, perhaps, that he fails to be wholly consistent in his attitude to Miss Jewsbury's revelation that Jane had told her of Carlyle's impotence. At one moment he speaks of:

> something which I would infinitely rather have remained in ignorance of, because I could not forget it, because it must

[1] *My Relations with Carlyle* was published posthumously in 1903.

necessarily influence me in all that I might say, while I
considered I must endeavour if possible to conceal it.[1]
But later he says:

I was keeping back the essential part of the story which had
governed my own action, and the world, not knowing the
full truth, considered that I had made too much of trifles . . .

In fact, his biographer's instinct warned him that Carlyle's
sexual constitution must be an indispensable datum for the
interpretation of his character, while his sense of respect for his
subject's agony, as well as delicacy, and a real, though limited,
respect for public opinion drove him in an opposite direction.

We must now consider two problems which a reading of
My Relations with Carlyle as a supplement to the biography
itself makes insistent. First, did Froude have good reason for his
belief that Carlyle was impotent? Second, could the attentive
reader of the biography alone have inferred that such was
Froude's belief?

To the first question I have little hesitation in answering, yes.
In the first place, the general antecedent probabilities favour the
hypothesis. Carlyle's violence, anger and frustration, Jane's ill-
health, the general opinion of those who frequented the house,[2]
and the separate bedrooms, together with other less tangible
impressions, mean that the issue does not turn solely on Miss
Jewsbury's credibility as a witness. But her obvious admiration
for Carlyle, whom she described to Froude as 'the nobler of the
two',[3] and the solemn circumstances in which the revelation was
made, when she knew she was dying, make the passionate malice
required for a deliberate lie somewhat improbable. But if this
passionate malice had indeed existed, it seems still more
improbable that Froude, possessed of a much subtler mind than
Miss Jewsbury, would have completely failed to detect it.
Perhaps most cogent of all, Froude knew Carlyle intimately for
many years both during and after the marriage; the quality of
his work as a biographer proves that he understood him as one
man seldom understands another. Miss Jewsbury's revelation
came to him as the missing key to many mysteries; it seemed to
harmonise with all the mass of evidence that he already

[1] Op. Cit., p. 20. [2] Ibid., p. 37. [3] Ibid., p. 23.

possessed; the difficulties it raised were moral and practical only, and not in the least intellectual. It seems more than rash to suppose him utterly mistaken, while the suggestion that Froude himself was actuated by malice in the matter cannot be taken seriously. It is contradicted not only by Froude's known character and by his veneration for Carlyle, but also by the important fact that he never published or caused to be published his own conclusions on the subject.

The second question, that of the impression given in the biography itself, is more difficult. It is not possible to settle it by an appeal to the comments of the first reviewers, since the reticence that prevented Froude from speaking clearly may also have prevented some of them from indicating that they had nevertheless understood him. It is important to remember, too, that in searching for clues in the biography itself, we know what we are looking for, while the first readers, unless they belonged to the inner ring of intimates at Cheyne Row who had already heard rumours, would probably not have known. There are many causes of marital discord, and of these, perhaps impotence may be one of the less common. It is obvious throughout that Froude is saying that the marriage was very unhappy. Does he appear to give adequate reason for this, if the whole question of impotence is left out of account? The answer would seem to be that he did. He says that Jane's early love for Irving was deep and strong, and that Carlyle never realised this. He says that the peasant life at Craigenputtock was a severe discipline for a woman used to gentler ways, and that Carlyle never understood this. After the move to London, he stresses the effect of financial anxiety. Above all, he constantly reminds us that Carlyle was an impossible man to live with on any terms, not merely in the marital relation. His mother found him difficult, his patron Jeffrey found him difficult, his friend and disciple Froude found him difficult. A man who cannot bear the slightest opposition, a man who insists on being alone almost all day, and then emerges to talk but not to listen, a man unable to distinguish clearly between having his liver out of order and being Prometheus chained upon a rock, what can he be but a very difficult husband? And if the wife is clever, spirited, and apt to

brood upon injuries, what can the marriage be but unhappy?
It would be hard indeed to say that, if we take the biography
alone on its merits, the misery of the marriage seems to lack
explanation.

There are a few passages, not very obtrusive, or perhaps very
likely to be dwelt upon by a casual reader, that repay closer
scrutiny. Chapter XIX is particularly important. Froude says:
'His life had been pure and without spot',[1] that after marriage
'he remained lonely and dyspeptic',[2] that 'the slightest noise or
movement at night shattered his nervous system; therefore he
required a bedroom to himself',[3] and he prefaces all this with a
declaration that he had learned from Carlyle himself the duty of
a biographer 'to keep back nothing and extenuate nothing'.[4]
Now the cumulative tendency of these remarks is surely not to
arouse thoughts in the reader about impotence, but rather to
remove them if he already had them. The separate bedrooms are
explained with a reason plausible enough in itself, but misleading.
The phrase 'pure and without spot', though vague, is likely to
suggest to most readers resistance to temptations to fornication,
which we must presume, at least in Froude's opinion, had no
real existence. (In the second part of the biography, he puts the
same point less evasively, and therefore with a greater tendency
to mislead, when he says: 'There are no "sins of youth" to be
apologised for.')[5] His summary at the end of Chapter XIX
remains to be considered. Froude says:

> Miss Welsh, it is probable, would have passed through life
> more pleasantly had she married someone in her own rank
> of life; Carlyle might have gone through it successfully with
> his mother or sister to look after him. But, after all is said,
> trials and sufferings are only to be regretted when they have
> proved too severe to be borne. Though the lives of the
> Carlyles were not happy, yet if we look at them from the
> beginning to the end they were grandly beautiful. Neither
> of them probably under other conditions would have risen
> to as high an excellence as in fact they achieved; and the
> main question is not how happy men and women have been

[1] E.L., I, 369.   [2] E.L., I, 379.   [3] E.L., I, 381.   [4] E.L., I, 369.
[5] L.L., I, 5.

in this world, but what they have made of themselves. I well remember the bright assenting laugh with which she once responded to some words of mine when the propriety was being discussed of relaxing the marriage laws. I had said that the true way to look at marriage was as a discipline of character.[1]

It is just possible, I suppose, that an exceptionally watchful reader might pick up a hint from that remark about 'mother or sister'. But there cannot be much doubt that the general effect of the whole discussion will usually not have been to excite suspicions of impotence, but rather to lull them if they already existed. Given Froude's definite conviction in the matter, the phrase about keeping back nothing comes to have an ironical look. Almost, Froude stands self-condemned. We need not, we should not, be very hard on him for this. His position was a very difficult one, and in biography the difficulties and temptations of one age are not those of another. But it seems to me that we must acknowledge a blemish in this great biography. The blemish is not the reticence itself, but the prevarication involved in pretending that reticence had not been required.

In dealing with the rhythm of the marriage, Froude's interpretation rests upon a simple and effective contrast. Carlyle and Jane were very affectionate when separated by distance; when they were together the affection was forgotten, overwhelmed by a torrent of inconveniences, reproaches and incompatibilities. As a point of biographical technique this is admirable; for the inescapable problem of biography, where the material is very voluminous and the treatment very full, is that the plain lines of interpretation may be lost in a mass of insignificant facts. An interpretation of this kind does not need to be true in any absolute sense, since exceptions can always be noted when they occur. Moreover, in this case, exceptions are surprisingly rare; the interpretation is about as flawless as any simple statement about the intangible webs of personal life can ever be. Tactically then, Froude made the right choice here, but more than tactics was involved. Strategically, the value of Froude's conception lies in the facts that Carlyle outlived his wife by nearly fifteen

[1] E.L., I, 881.

years, that he felt deep remorse for his marital conduct and said so in commenting on Jane's *Memorials*. The long and affectionate absences intervening between the quarrels and discord were a foretaste of that unending separation, which was to plunge Carlyle into a permanent condition of sadness, tenderness, remorse and regret. All this is most effective, because it is simple and moving and true. But even this does not exhaust the value of Froude's basic interpretation of the marriage.

His interpretation also enabled him to make a most important link between Carlyle's private and public life. Carlyle's greatest period as a writer and his greatest period of influence upon his more gifted contemporaries may be dated roughly from 1835 to 1845. In these years he was fighting a hard battle with the world, he was only gradually becoming known to a wider public, and he was frequently short of money, and even in apparent danger of destitution. In the long years after 1850 he was on the one hand a venerable sage, on the other a reckless, disregarded railer against everything new, whether good or bad, while his financial and social position was assured. Froude was justified by the facts in his desire to present a strong contrast here. The young or middle-aged Carlyle, the bold and inspiring thinker, to whom the best minds of a new generation paid homage, was in domestic matters savage and unappreciative. The lonely, disappointed, angry old prophet, respected but ignored, as he threatened the world with doom after the Reform Bill of 1867, was a tender, disconsolate widower, ever remembering his dead wife and giving lavishly to beggars.

Froude most certainly did not minimise the marital discord, nor exaggerate the force and sincerity of Carlyle's remorse. On one point only does his interpretation seem open to a slight question. A careful reading of Jane's letters suggests that he somewhat underrated the working of humorous sympathy between the two which may have moderated Jane's sense of the bitterness of their daily disharmony. There is a significant assimilation of her literary style and point of view to his. Of many passages that could be quoted this may serve:

> ... on our return from a visit to Captain Sterling, she
> [Helen, the maid] first would not open the door; and at last

did open it, like a stage ghost very ill got up: blood spurting from her lips, her face whitened with chalk from the kitchen floor, her dark gown ditto, and wearing a smile of idiotic self-complacency. I thought Mr C. was going to kick his foot through her, when she tumbled down at his touch. If she had been his wife he certainly would have killed her on the spot.[1]

The strange mixture of callousness, comedy and violence is very Carlylean, as are little points of detail, like the mannered use of 'ditto'. The last sentence should give us pause. However much she suffered under her husband's temper, passages like this suggest that sometimes, perhaps often, she saw the comic side of it even at the time. Thus, when she had to go in his place after a sleepless night in November 1855 to a difficult interview with the tax inspector, she wrote: 'It was with feeling like the ghost of a dead dog, that I rose and dressed and drank my coffee and then started for Kensington. Mr C. said "the voice of honour seemed to call on him to go himself". But either it did not call loud enough, or he would not listen to that charmer.'[2] Surely she enjoyed the humour of this. It is noticeable too how many shared jokes there are in the letters, and how many of these depend upon traditions in Carlyle's own family before they were married. One supposes that she listened eagerly to his accounts of his dead relatives and early acquaintances. However, the correction suggested by these points is a small one – more a matter of catching a tone than of changing an interpretation. It is perhaps asking too much even of a bold Victorian biographer that having presented an unhappy marriage in its dismal details, he should then admit that from one point of view the matter could be seen as comic. Moreover, there is one notable passage, coming rather too late to alter the reader's general impression, where Froude does do full justice to Jane's humour, and Carlyle's response to it. He quotes at length the amusing 'parliamentary document' by means of which Jane secured, without the usual explosion of ill-temper, an increase of £30 in the housekeeping allowance.[3]

But we have still to consider what must have been, with the

[1] L.M., ii, 87, dated May 1849.   [2] L.M., ii, 263.   [3] L.L., ii, 176–86.

single exception of the question of impotence, Froude's most difficult task in describing Carlyle's marriage. What was he to say about his relations with Lady Ashburton, and about Jane's jealousy? There were difficulties here of a more fundamental kind than those that hampered the account of Carlyle's ill-temper. The difficulties in that case had only been difficulties of delicacy, not of interpretation. Froude's whole assessment of his subject's character required the idea that he was strong in great things and weak in little, that his far-ranging vision and majestic genius made him impossible on the cramped domestic stage. But Lady Ashburton was a different matter. There was something trivial and vain in Carlyle's conduct here. The figure of the incorruptible man of the people, the man who combined the high intellectual culture of his time with faithful adherence to the tradition of Covenanting simplicity – this attractive conception could only be tarnished.

Once again Froude must have felt the theme of impotence as a subterranean obstacle in his path. How did it alter Jane's jealous feelings? Did it actually supply part of the motive for Carlyle's desire for a flirtation? Did Lady Ashburton know about it, or did she guess, and, if so, how was her attitude affected? All difficult questions, but yet questions demanding to be answered if a full and balanced judgment was to be reached. In saying that there were no actual grounds of the ordinary kind for wifely jealousy, Froude was no doubt correct. But clearly, such a statement has a different flavour if a husband has not the power to provide these grounds. Granted the original, and here rather damaging, decision to conceal, Froude handles the matter with both honesty and tact. He catches the essence of the situation very well by a literary allusion:

> She became Gloriana, Queen of Fairyland, and he, with a true vein of chivalry in him, became her rustic Red Cross Knight, who, if he could would have gladly led his own Una into the same enchanting service. The 'Una', unfortunately, had no inclination for such a distinguished bondage.[1]

This may be accepted as a substantially accurate picture. The word 'rustic' is a cunning addition, which the later course of the

[1] L.L., I, 368.

narrative develops and explains. For essentially, there are two
charges made by Froude against Carlyle in the matter, or
perhaps it would convey the flavour of the writing better to say
that Froude on Carlyle's behalf pleads guilty on two counts.
First, he was inept, unimaginative, uncomprehending of the
niceties of feminine feeling. Here the spirit of comedy has a
legitimate moment of supremacy. After quoting one of Carlyle's
more wild and windy denunciations of the world and its public
men, he says:

> He had reasons for uneasiness besides the state of the
> universe. His wife had been ill again. Lady Harriet Baring,
> hearing she was alone in Cheyne Row, had carried her off to
> Addiscombe, and little guessing the state of her mind, and
> under the impression that she was hypochondriacal, had
> put her under a course of bracing. She wanted wine when
> she was exhausted; Lady Harriet thought wine unwhole-
> some. She was not allowed to bed when tortured with
> headache. She suffered from cold, and lighted a fire in her
> bedroom. Fires were not allowed at Addiscombe so early in
> the autumn, and the housemaid removed the coals . . . one
> asks with wonder why he could not tell Lady Harriet plainly
> that, if she wished for his wife's friendship, she must treat
> her differently.[1]

But the other charge to which Froude pleads guilty is, for
him, though not necessarily for us, a graver one. It is the charge
of snobbery. Snobbery is a vice extremely common in the world,
which everybody is very quick to condemn in the abstract, but
which very few people perceive in themselves or in those they
love. Some of us may feel that it is really much more venial than
the callous treatment of a wife. But it is important to see why
Froude could not take this view at least in Carlyle's case. In the
whole strategy of his presentation of Carlyle as a flawed man of
supreme genius he had from the start conceded that he was an
almost impossible husband. But at the same time he had
stressed throughout his incorruptible fidelity to his covenanting ancestors, his hatred of cant and sham, his power to see
every mundane question *sub specie aeternitatis*. Harshness and

[1] L.L., I, 445.

anger are consistent with this interpretation; snobbery hardly is.

Carlyle was unusual in discerning snobbery in himself, though he claimed, perhaps with truth, that he had not much of it.[1] Certainly there was no other time in his life when its effect upon him was so obvious or its consequences so serious. Froude's conduct as a biographer here is exemplary. He feels that the main lines of his interpretation can withstand a few exceptions, and that these exceptions must be fairly and strongly stated. He dismisses the matter with a robust comment:

> But it is impossible not to ask 'What was Carlyle doing in such a galley?' Why was he there at all? It is with real relief that I approach the end of the half-enchanted state into which he had fallen after 'Cromwell'.[2]

A small point, perhaps. But I end with it because it shows something important. Froude succeeds as a biographer because he is firm in his strategy and flexible in his tactics. The main lines of interpretation are never obscured by the rush of facts; but exceptional and surprising facts are never suppressed or misrepresented because they might blur the picture's clear outline.

[1] Cf. Carlyle's *Reminiscences*, ii, 189.
[2] L.L., i, 449.

10

MORLEY'S GLADSTONE

❀

When Morley died in 1923, he could well be considered the last
survivor of the high Victorian agnostic tradition. The length,
variety and distinction of his political and literary career only
serve to enforce upon our minds its extraordinary inner
consistency. The Morley who published the *Recollections* in 1917
is very difficult to distinguish from the author of *Burke* (1879).
It is to some extent a matter of taste whether we lay stress on
fidelity to principles or rigidity of view. The student of political
history may well be astonished, and perhaps delighted, by the
spectacle of the lifelong exercise of a virtue so rare in politicians.
Morley resigned in 1914, but how many former radicals and near-
pacifists were not transformed overnight into militant patriots,
not to say militarists?

But for us, whose concern is with Morley as a writer, and
therefore also as a philosophical student of men and affairs, the
emphasis falls differently. There was in Morley, as the price of
this tenacious consistency, a certain rigidity, a certain obstinate
inner resistance to new thinking which may at times have
limited his practical understanding. It was a rigidity of a very
special kind that requires exact definition – a kind very
characteristic of that high mid-Victorian agnostic élite to which
he belonged. Morley was, of course, an intelligent man, a wide
and perceptive reader, and in some ways a receptive spirit. It
goes without saying that in such a man rigidity will not be
another name for crude prejudice or a refusal to learn new facts.
If the paradox may be allowed, the high agnostic rigidity is a
flexible rigidity. It leaves room for change, for development,
even for surprise. What do we mean then by calling it rigid? Its
rigidity lies mainly in the unqualified acceptance in every
context, appropriate and inappropriate, of the idea of process,

development, evolution. A classic instance of the misunder-standing, indeed the blindness, induced by such assumptions is to be found in Leslie Stephen's *History of English Thought in the Eighteenth Century* (1876), the reader of which is aware of a prolonged conjuring trick, whereby the Augustan merges gradually into the Victorian agnostic, and the torments and ecstasies of Burke and Coleridge, the French Revolution and the Hungry Forties become unimportant deviations, or exceptions only apparent to the general tendency of gradual intellectual enlightenment. Though he lived much longer, Morley was almost a contemporary of Stephen; he belonged to the same evolutionary school, and, though less robust and less opinionated, he was markedly similar in his general mental approach.

The kind of 'flexible rigidity' I mean is like a stratum of rock on which the whole landscape rests, but which has only occa-sional outcrops. One has to learn to watch for small indications. Thus we find Morley in Chapter VIII of his *Burke* dropping a phrase like this: 'When our grandchildren have made up their minds, *once for all*,[1] as to the merits of the social transformation which dawned on Europe in 1789 . . .' In another, less lucid, less exact author, the phrase italicised might pass as a negligible rhetorical flourish. But it is what Morley really means; and the implications are large and a bit frightening. What is envisaged is a kind of secular, evolutionary Day of Judgment, in which events of the past will be judged by their ultimate consequences. From this judgment there will be no appeal because the general spread of liberal principles and the progressive improvement of human society, upon the lines envisaged by the nineteenth-century reformers, are apparent, self-validating principles. Just as for a religious thinker, to determine the relation of an event to the Will of God would be to determine its ultimate value and position, so here. But there is this important difference; the Will of God may be conceived as mysterious, comprehensible only in part. But the only uncertainties in Morley's system are uncertainties about facts. We cannot judge yet, he is saying, because some of the wider effects of the French Revolution are still to be observed.

[1] My italics.

Thinkers of Morley's school looked, of course, to Mill as their saint and guide. But Mill's mind was not only a more powerful intellectual instrument than those of Stephen and Morley, it also possessed types of awareness of which theirs were oblivious. Very significant is Morley's discussion[1] of Mill's crucial late *Essay on Theism*:

> In 1874 Mill's posthumous essay on Theism appeared – a piece that dismayed his disciples not merely as an infelicitous compromise with orthodoxy but, what was far more formidable, as actually involving a fatal relaxation of his own rules and methods of reasoning. It made a sort of intellectual scandal, like the faith of Pascal, that most intrepid of reasoners, in the unspeakable miracle of the Holy Thorn. It seemed a duty to keep the agnostic lamps well trimmed. I made no attempt to argue with the mystic or the transcendentalist, but only with the rationalist master of those who know, on rationalistic ground expressly chosen and profoundly impressed by himself . . . Without irreverence be it said, the essay that wrought so surprisingly upon us was in substance a laboured evasion of plain answers to plain questions. Of these the central one was vividly put by Man Friday to Robinson Crusoe – Why did not God kill the Devil? – one of the master interrogatories of human speculation.

Morley then proceeds to devote several pages to a respectful, indeed reverential, pained and intellectually quite inadequate, reply to perhaps the most interesting speculative piece that Mill ever wrote.

One does not wish to be too severe on the weaknesses of the passage just quoted, for if Morley had not been very much more impressive as a biographer than as a philosopher, we should not be thinking about him now. Nevertheless, in biography as in other major literary forms, it is the whole man who writes, with all his instincts, ideas and prejudices. The salient point is that Morley does not perceive that in writing as he does, he himself is actually engaging in theological speculation. Had he perceived this, it is almost certain that a host of considerations

[1] *Recollections*, I, 106ff.

would at once have occurred to him, intelligent, well read, honest and fair as he was, urging him to tear the passage up. He would have realised that a study which has engaged the attention of minds of the calibre of St Augustine, of Pascal, of Newman, is inadequately represented by the mediocre mind of Daniel Defoe. He would have reflected, perhaps, that the Book of Job had something to say about those who measured the mind of the Almighty as Morley is doing here, which is just in the way that a shop assistant measures a length of cloth. But such thoughts never crossed Morley's mind because he imagined himself to be talking in plain commonsense terms about a plain, practical problem. In this, of course, he is extremely character-istic of the mid-Victorian agnostic generation. Parallels could be found in the work of T. H. Huxley and others. And it is one of the most important merits of Mill's later works that they point away from this bad tradition. But Morley was writing more than forty years after Mill's death; Morley was old-fashioned.

Like most agnostics of his generation, Morley had a positive as well as a critical side to his theological speculation. The obverse of the neat little syllogisms designed to overthrow the Christian tradition in a paragraph is to be found in high, cloudy, resonant invocations of unknowable mystery, like this:

> The narrowness of the cribbed deck that we are doomed
> to tread, amid the vast space of an eternal sea with fair
> shores dimly seen and never reached, oppresses the soul
> with a burden that sorely tries its strength.[1]

Yet this habitual quasi-religious feeling about the unknow-able and the unfathomable is always used as a foil to definite practical certainties about secular knowledge, about politics, about the progress of society. Religious doubt for Morley was not like a shaken foundation that makes all the building insecure; it was more like hard winter weather that makes one's familiar fireside all the more attractive and com-fortable. There were areas of his mind that were simply im-pervious to new impressions. Thus in his very natural and

---

[1] *Voltaire*, p. 44. Quoted by D. A. Hamer: J.M: Liberal Intellectual in Politics, Oxford, 1968.

honourable dislike of the tone of public life at the turn of the century, he could write:

The moral and political atmosphere of my own country has become intolerably close and asphyxiating . . . the situation is really hellish.[1]

Yet neither this dislike nor the events of 1914 made any perceptible impact upon political assumptions of a markedly optimistic character. In reading his own account in *Recollections* of his tenure of the India Office, one begins to wonder whether he ever succeeded in making imaginatively real to himself the differences between the Indian and the English social scene. The courteously expressed exasperation of the Viceroy is not surprising.

Now it has often been said – and the charge has recently been authoritatively endorsed in an interesting article by the editor of Gladstone's diaries[2] – that Morley's great drawback as a biographer of Gladstone was that he did not understand Gladstone's religious commitment. In a general sense, I think this notion is both true and important; but I also think that the nature and limits of its truth require more exact definition than they have received. A few preliminary points are obvious. It is obvious that Morley profoundly admired Gladstone, and that any errors he thought he perceived in him seemed to him noble errors. It is obvious that Morley gave Gladstone unlimited credit for sincerity, even at times when not every reader of Morley's book has been able to give Gladstone the same credit. Morley stated very clearly that for Gladstone religion always came first. Right at the start of his long book he quoted with warm approval Lord Salisbury's dictum, in his tribute in the House of Lords after Gladstone's death, that the essential thing about him was that he was 'a great Christian'. He showed both dignity and good sense, while stressing that for Gladstone 'political life was only part of his religious life'[3] when he referred to his own inability to share Gladstone's faith, and said:

No amount of candour or good faith – and in these essentials

[1] Letter to Frederic Harrison, 23rd December 1900.
[2] M. R. D. Foot in *Bulletin of Rylands Library*, Spring 1969.
[3] John Morley: *Life of William Ewart Gladstone*, 1903, I, 200.

I believe that I have not fallen short – can be a substitute
for the confidence and ardour of an adherent, in the heart
of those to whom the church stands first.[1]
What, then, is the just complaint against Morley on this
score?

In the first place, Morley's third chapter, entitled *Oxford*,
clearly shows that Morley misconceived the nature of the Oxford
Movement. He misunderstood it in ways that follow naturally,
perhaps inevitably, from the adherence to the progressive,
evolutionary outlook sketched above; and since this outlook
was shared by so many of the most distinguished men of his
time, he was in good company in his misunderstanding. Morley
realised, in a vague and rather tentative way, that the 1820's
and 1830's were a time of intellectual renewal and spiritual
excitement in Oxford.[2] And he knew that the Oxford Movement
began in 1833. But his whole progressive, evolutionary cast of
thinking, his whole set of rather narrow certitudes made it
imperative for him to turn his back upon the obvious lines of
connection between these two facts. After speaking of the years
of Gladstone's residence (which began in 1828) as 'the eve of an
epoch of illumination',[3] Morley, as if suddenly becoming
nervous about the possibility that the logic of his own remarks
might soon be driving him to admit that this epoch and the
Oxford Movement were one and the same, hastily goes on:

As we shall soon see, both the revival of learning and the
reform of institutions at Oxford were sharply turned aside
from their expected course by the startling theological
movement that now proceeded from her venerable walls.

Morley gives not the slightest indication as to who had
actually entertained these erroneous expectations; and it is
doubtful whether, if challenged, he could have answered with a
single name. The real meaning of that word 'expected' is quite
different. It means 'the course they would have taken if the
progressive and liberal principles for the prediction of future

[1] *Life*, I, 3.
[2] The best modern account of this is to be found in David Newsome: *The
Parting of Friends* (Murray 1966, esp. chapter II).
[3] *Life*, I, 51.

events which I apply to current events in foreseeing the future had actually proved veridical in this case'. Morley's cardinal weakness as a thinker, and to a lesser extent as a biographer, is seen here. He evades the difficulty instead of taking it into account, and even perhaps using it to modify his principle. If Bagehot had lived long enough to comment upon Morley, he might have said of him, as he did of Macaulay, that he had an inexperiencing nature.

Bound to his simple categories of progressive and reactionary, Morley could only see the Oxford Movement as reactionary, and thus an odd, accidental bedfellow of the progressive intellectual movement, which gradually transformed the dull, formal, educational process of eighteenth-century Oxford into a system based on the Socratic tutorial. But for Gladstone, as for New-man, these two processes were alike, because each meant an arduous return to the origins and meanings of things that had become habitual, and therefore had lost their immediacy. People parroted Aristotle without realising the nature of the problems he was trying to solve; people took bishops for granted as part of the established order without thinking what they were, still less what theological ideas were implied by submission to them.

It is not true, then, that Morley failed to assess the influence of religion simply because he was an agnostic himself. (Indeed, some unguarded comments on this topic seem to involve the perilous conclusion that one can never understand a man unless one agrees with him, a doctrine which would inhibit the practice of biography as we know it altogether.) The passage from Morley's *Voltaire* quoted above, and many others that could be given, are enough to show that Morley – typical in this as in so much else of the high mid-Victorian agnostic tradition – was possessed of a strong religious sensibility. Gladstone's serious-ness about religion, his minuteness in judging points of con-science, his deep conviction that obligations apparently trivial are not really trivial because they are linked to the general web of things – all this Morley could understand, and to a large extent share. But he failed to distinguish between a quest for origins and meanings, involving a return to the primitive

sources of a tradition and a mere habitual conservatism. He
did not reflect, for instance, that Coleridge, the source of so
much high Anglican thinking, was a ruthless critic of the eighteenth-century High Church school. He did not see, in short,
that for a man of Gladstone's temperament the advance from
an Evangelical to an Anglo-Catholic form of faith could be
experienced as a liberation.

II

Throughout the life of Gladstone, Morley favoured simple
explanations. Before criticising him for this – and in the end I
think one must criticise him for it – one should pay tribute to
the merits which the book in its finished form owes to this fact.
The book as we have it is not only lucid and readable (and these
are great merits), it is also extraordinarily full and detailed.
Not deliberately perhaps, but in effect, Morley sacrificed
subtlety of motive for complexity of detail. If he gave up much,
he achieved much by the sacrifice. The first casualties of
Morley's simplifying were the characters and motives of other
statesmen. The relation of a great man to his contemporaries
is always a difficult topic for biography, and nowhere more than
in political biography, for politics is a battle, and the power of
the adversary must be felt if the whole nature of the battle is
not to be falsified. And yet, the purpose of biography itself is
frustrated if opponents, or allies, are given too much space and
detail.

Ideally, Palmerston, Disraeli, Salisbury and the rest should
have loomed up grandly but briefly, like gigantic Homeric
heroes in a mist. Gladstone was a great man, but he was not a
giant among pigmies; and the sense of his greatness is partly
lost when it is suggested that he was. The case of Disraeli is the
most crucial of all, because of his extraordinary talents, his
long rivalry with Gladstone and the strong mutual dislike
between the two men. Here Morley was required, as part of his
duty as a biographer, to consider the causes of Gladstone's
dislike of his opponent, and to adjudicate on the justice of his
censure. Instead, the following passage is typical. Commenting

182

on Disraeli's speech about the reform of Oxford in 1854, Morley says:

> High fantastic trifling of this sort, though it may divert a later generation to whose legislative bills it can do no harm, helps to explain the deep disfavour with which Disraeli was regarded by his severe and strenuous opponent.[1]

The reader, even though a warm admirer of Gladstone, may be reluctant to admit that the judgment of Gladstone in the heat of party conflict on a man naturally antipathetic to him was also history's last word . . . But Morley was always fair in intention. Twenty years later in Gladstone's career there comes a moment when Gladstone had to acknowledge magnanimity in Disraeli.[2] He duly records that Gladstone considered Disraeli's speech of 19 March, 1874, about the date of the dissolution 'generous'. But having noted this, Morley passes on. He does not allow himself to ask how this admission affected Gladstone's settled view of Disraeli's character, or whether, if it did not affect it at all, it ought to have done so. He does not seem to see that, though it is not his duty as a biographer of Gladstone to reach any final verdict on Disraeli, it is his duty to form a view on Gladstone's whole method of judging other politicians, and that the case of Disraeli is one of the most interesting and difficult. Two important components of biography are lacking here, a determination to probe motives, and a willingness to allow evidence from one part of his hero's life to be carried over to help in the interpretation of others. It seems that Morley was so secure about the validity of the plain lines of his interpretation that he allowed no resonance between one event and another. The incident that had once been described was closed.

This refusal to connect one event with another is more obvious still when Morley comes to the events of 1858 and 1859, when Gladstone refused office under Derby, replied coldly to Disraeli's overtures, and accepted office under Palmerston. Disraeli's letter and Gladstone's reply[3] are too long to quote, but they constitute some of the most fascinating and ambiguous of all Morley's voluminous material. We ask, 'Did Gladstone simply disbelieve Disraeli's letter? Was he determined not to be

[1] *Life,* I, 508.   [2] *Life,* II, 496.   [3] *Life,* I, 587ff.

hampered by being on the same side as the only man of his generation whose talents might be thought equal to his own? Did he regard the letter as an impertinence as obtruding upon a solemn personal decision?' These and many more questions might be asked, but Morley sweeps onwards without any substantial comment at all.

A little later Gladstone took office under Palmerston. Morley says:

> The appointment did not pass without considerable remark. 'The real scandal,' he wrote to his Oxford chairman, 'is among the extreme men on the liberal side; they naturally say, "This man has done all he could on behalf of Lord Derby; why is he here to keep out one of us?" ' Even some among Mr Gladstone's private friends wondered how he could bring himself to join a Minister of whom he had for three or four years used such unsparing language as had been common on his lips about Lord Palmerston. The plain man was puzzled by a vote in favour of keeping a Tory government in, followed by a junction with the men who had thrown that government out.[1]

Morley as biographer is in a difficult situation here. It is possible that Gladstone's real reasons cannot in the end be known; it is possible that they can be known and would prove to be discreditable. What is quite certain is that the problem is not one with an obvious solution, and that if Gladstone can be justified at all, the justification must be complex and contain elements of the unexpected. Further, since it is clear that Gladstone always had a higher personal opinion of Derby than he did of Palmerston, then the factor of personal animosity, if there was one at all, must relate to Disraeli.

In this difficult situation Morley fails – fails utterly and lamentably. First he quotes, as if it threw light on the question, Gladstone's very odd, and indeed irrelevant, defence that in a time of crisis, and European war, he 'could not have looked anyone in the face' if he had refused his aid. This evades altogether the question of his treatment of Derby. Then he quotes several longer letters of Gladstone, which by their constant

[1] *Life,* I, 626.

reiteration of the idea that his conscience is clear, leave no doubt
that Gladstone was worried by the whole question, and tend to
suggest that he felt guilty. Then, without inquiry into the inner
psychological meaning of these letters, which so urgently
demand a biographer's analysis, he sums up thus:

> The dilemma between joining Derby and joining Palmerston
> was no vital choice between two political creeds. The new
> Prime Minister and his Chancellor of the Exchequer had
> both of them started with Canning for their common
> master; but there was a generation between them, and
> Gladstone had travelled along a road of his own, perhaps
> not even now perceiving its goal. As we have seen, he told
> Mr Walpole in May 1858 (p. 584) that there were 'no
> broad and palpable questions of principle' that separated
> himself from the Derbyite Tories. Palmerston, on the other
> hand, was so much of a Derbyite Tory that his government,
> which Mr Gladstone was now entering, owed its long spell
> of office and power to the countenance of Derby and his
> men . . . the political identity of the two leaders was
> recognised. To join the new administration, then, marked
> a party severance but no changed principles. I am far from
> denying the enormous significance of the party wrench,
> but it was not a conversion . . .[1]

'I am far from denying the enormous significance of the party
wrench.' But that is exactly what Morley is implicitly denying
with every sentence that leads up to the surprising disclaimer.
He does not ask himself why, if Palmerston and Derby were so
similar in their politics, he should not have submitted to the
one who bore the same party label, who was, in Gladstone's
opinion, the better man and, above all, *who asked first*. Gladstone's conduct can only be defended, perhaps only understood,
on the assumption that Derby and Palmerston were politically
unlike in some important respect. Morley enunciates his paradox
that Gladstone was quite right to treat them in opposite ways
because they were really just the same, with the confident air
of a man repeating a truism. Morley speaks as if only personal
ill-will or party rancour could possibly have found fault with

[1] *Life*, i, 631.

Gladstone here. And he shows a sad lack of anticipation about his readers' likely impressions. Any attentive reader is likely to connect all this with Disraeli's letter, which comes only one year, and half an hour's reading-time before. If we were to assume that Gladstone desired office, but was determined not to be on the same side as Disraeli, the puzzle would become clear.[1] Morley did not believe this explanation, and he may have been right. But it was extremely injudicious, if he wanted the reader to reject it, not to take note of it and try to find some counter to it. And it was extremely incurious not to probe the strange logic of Gladstone's self-justifying passages. Morley's last shot on this topic is perhaps the oddest of all. He quotes a letter of Newman's, written no less than fourteen years before the events with which he has just been dealing. This letter has great intrinsic interest, but it has been omitted from its natural context, relating to the year 1845, and the Maynooth question, and is only an irrelevance here. Morley does not even attempt to suggest that there is an effective parallel. Moreover, Morley is hoist with his own petard, for his lack of understanding of the Oxford Movement, noticed above, led him to accept uncritically[2] the baseless attacks on the truthfulness of the patently sincere men of the Oxford Movement, which have their ultimate tainted source in the ravings of Kingsley and the half-truths of J. A. Froude. So Morley was here in the pitiful position of calling as the chief witness for the defence a great man indeed, but a great man who had given evidence on a different question, not on the one in dispute, and a witness whose reliability Morley himself had most unnecessarily brought into question.

This is an extreme case, but not an isolated one. Morley was seldom so confused as this, but he was often just as incurious. Take, for instance, the moment towards the end of 1867 when Russell finally decided, at the age of 75, to resign the leadership of the Liberal Party. Gladstone would have been more or less than human if the news had not excited some personal interest

---

[1] I am far too much an amateur in political history to assert that this, or any other, explanation is the correct one. I am considering the matter solely from the point of view of the art of biography.
[2] *Life*, I, 164–5.

in him. Palmerston, after all, had kept men waiting for his shoes until he was over eighty, and then had died in office. Morley only says: 'Mr Gladstone did not deny his claim to repose.'[1] Did it not occur to him, we ask, that this simply could not have been Gladstone's only thought on such a question? Or take the case of Gladstone's election statement in 1880,[2] replying to Disraeli's accusation that the return of a Liberal Government might threaten the union between England and Ireland. Gladstone called the accusations 'baseless insinuations'. At this point almost every reader's mind leaps forward to 1886. No doubt Gladstone was quite sincere in 1880, and perhaps Disraeli was only making a lucky shot in the dark. But how can Morley suppose that if he says nothing the anomaly will simply not be noticed?

Now there is more coherence and consistency in Morley's view of these things than such isolated passages taken alone will allow us to see. The key point about Morley's method of writing in this book is that it is retrospective. Morley saw Gladstone's career as a whole, as one glorious development, as a lengthy saga of power being unshackled. Morley's interpretation, in its simplest terms, is this. Gladstone was by nature a man of stupendous moral, intellectual and political gifts. These gifts were hampered in their exercise, and thwarted in their public usefulness, by inherited Tory opinions. Very gradually, this man of great gifts worked himself loose from his restrictions, discarding nothing of value that he had held, but developing all the time in the direction of liberty, liberty for himself in the use of his transcendent powers, and liberty for the people whom he led, in whose wisdom and trustworthiness Gladstone came more and more to believe. Thus, when Gladstone supports a cause of which Morley disapproves, like the retention in 1865 of the Anglican test for membership of Convocation at Oxford, it is always, in Morley's view, because he *had not yet developed far enough*.

It is obvious that both the essential features of Morley's way of thinking and the practical accidents of the situation told in the same direction here. Morley's whole way of thinking, as we

[1] *Life*, ii, 243.   [2] *Life*, ii, 606ff.

have seen, was evolutionary. At the same time, he was nearly thirty years younger than Gladstone, never met him till he was well past middle age, and eventually became his friend and close political associate when Gladstone was at a time of life when most men have ceased their active work in the world. Of course, then, Morley had no hesitation in seeing the 1880's and '90's as the crown and climax of Gladstone's career. Of course, he had a more vivid impression of things he remembered than of things he had only read about. But this had implications which he may hardly have considered.

The retrospective view is not a bad method of writing biography, but it is one that involves certain sacrifices in consideration of certain gains. Its gain is in coherence; properly used, the method ensures that the life as a whole becomes significant. The mass of detail does not produce a sense in the reader of chaos leading to insignificance. In a life so various and active as Gladstone's, for which the documentary material was so abundant, this was no small gain. But any biographer who adopts the method does well to consider the corresponding losses and to try to mitigate them. There is a loss of the actual texture of living, the sense, which every man has about his own life, of the uniqueness of the present moment, between the settled past and the unknown future. And there is a loss of the sense of choice and possibility. When Gladstone was a young Tory, he did not dream that he would ever be a Liberal. The other kind of biographer, the one who does not take the retrospective view, but attempts to recapture the living moment of his subject's life as it goes, would have had more opportunity to do justice to that.

In his treatment of the last two incidents mentioned, then, Morley was guided by his retrospective method. A long life like Gladstone's, full of distinction and solid achievement, takes on a unity, partly real and partly, perhaps, specious, when it is considered in retrospect. It would seem that in the first case, that of Russell's retirement, he forgot that no one could know in 1867 that Gladstone would be Prime Minister four times, and that his last premiership would stretch well into the '90's. Because it had happened, with momentous consequences for the country and for Morley himself, it came to seem inevitable, and Russell by now long since dead came to seem a negligible obstacle to Gladstone's triumphant progress. This is clear enough; the Irish case is a little more difficult. Morley, of all people, could be in no danger of underrating the significance of Gladstone's conversion to Home Rule. Why not say something about it then, when Disraeli's shrewd prediction of 1880 was first mentioned? At first sight, it might seem that the retrospective view would actually encourage Morley to make a comment.

First of all, of course, neither Gladstone nor Morley ever liked to admit that Disraeli was right. This is the obvious answer, but not, I believe, taken by itself, the true one. A deeper reason, and a much less petty one, lies in Morley's sense of process. For Morley, thinking of Gladstone in 1880, the time for Irish Home Rule was not yet. Gladstone could never be hurried. His solemn and majestic mental processes needed ample time; everything had its appointed hour in Gladstone's destiny. To talk of Home Rule in 1880 may have seemed to Morley almost like talking of marriage when writing of a boy of 15. No doubt he will marry, in fact we know that he afterwards did, but how can that be relevant here? This is speculative, but seems to me the nearest approach we can make to an explanation.

Now, of course, Morley was justified in thinking of Gladstone's development in this way; and this sense of slow ripening is one of the most memorable things that the reader derives from the biography as a whole. But a great public figure cannot reasonably expect to be judged solely by his inner life and development. His decisions affect other people; and his friends and his opponents have to guess what he will do, and take the results of their guesses into their practical calculations, before he has decided himself. Does not Disraeli deserve a little credit for guessing right?

But even when we restrict our view to Gladstone's inner development, Morley's sense of the man's gradual evolution into wisdom involves some misrepresentation. It leads him to underrate the force of conflict, the uncertainty of choice and, above all, the clash of principles when each principle is felt in its own way to be true. The issue of the religious test for membership of convocation at Oxford will serve here. It does not seem to me as it did to Morley that a just statement of the case is achieved by saying that Gladstone's gradually increasing Liberalism was just insufficient in 1865, but then just sufficient in 1871, to make him pronounce the test unfair. It is rather that a difficult synthesis was eventually achieved in Gladstone's mind. He was just as devoutly Anglican, just as strongly convinced of the need for a religious basis for society, for education, and for all thinking in 1871, or in 1891, as he had been in 1865. He was able in 1871, but not in 1865, to satisfy himself that all these truths could somehow be included in a synthesis which allowed also for freedom of conscience and a lessening of exclusiveness. Where Gladstone saw a subtle synthesis, Morley only saw a bad principle gradually yielding to a good one.

So it is that Morley makes far too little of Gladstone's permanent Conservative strain.[1] He does not suppress its existence – he is too fair-minded deliberately to suppress anything – but he does not see it, as it could and probably should be seen, as one of the master-keys to Gladstone's whole mystery. This appears most obviously in an odd way. Friends and hero-worshippers of great men normally and naturally tend to exaggerate the significance of their own personal relations with these men, and especially any informal private conversations they may have had. Morley's relations with Gladstone were, of course, important in any case on public grounds even when not exaggerated. But in his account of 1891, Morley records a fascinating private conversation with Gladstone without comment, obviously without foreseeing the deep interest and significance it would have for later readers. He records Gladstone as saying:[2] 'I once asked who beside myself in the party cares for the hereditary principle.' This in 1891. This after his Irish policy had done so much to alienate the aristocracy and the owners of landed property from himself and from the Liberal Party, Morley must have seen the paradox; but it did not fit his scheme of things to make it a key point. If the words had been spoken

[1] On this point, see M. R. D. Foot, loc. cit.   [2] *Life*, III, 470.

twenty years earlier, he would perhaps have explained them as
an issue of the gradually diminishing residue of Tory prejudice.
But Gladstone was over 80 in 1891, and knew well what he had
done in 1886. It was too late to change. Morley's gradualism
does not seem to fit the case. So what might have been a great
moment of truth in the biography remains only another detail
conscientiously recorded. Of the many other moments when the
reader may feel that Morley's refusal to comment is a tantalising
waste of opportunity, I will mention only one – a minor but, I
think, a significant one – and a happy one because it involves
the mention of one of Morley's best passages. Morley understood
very well what Dante meant to Gladstone. His account of
Gladstone's lifelong admiration[1] is excellent as biography, and
in small scope, shrewd and sensible as literary criticism. Morley
here compares well with Matthew Arnold, whose Dante is un-
recognisable to those who have read him. But then Morley
drops a phrase right at the end of his long book; 'he would not
read Dante in the Session'[2] [i.e. of Parliament]. How much
about Gladstone that suggests; but how unobtrusive it is; how
few readers perhaps notice it at all. And, if Morley were to
urge in his defence that he was writing for those few who did
notice, one might reply that even they want to know more,
they want to know if he ever said why, whether it was a matter
of time and concentration, or rather (as seems quite likely) a
setting apart of an experience held as quasi-sacred. Of course,
Morley's book was already very long. But one reader at least
would have given up one or two twists of the Turkish question
for the sake of knowing this.

This chapter may seem to the reader, and perhaps even to the
writer, to tend towards the hyper-critical. If so, I may plead
that it has been my aim to judge Morley's book as a work of
biographical art, and not just, as it is normally treated, as a
mine of political information. But perhaps the balance can be
redressed a little by quoting one of Morley's best passages. It
refers to 1885; Gladstone had not been Prime Minister since
1880; the new Prime Minister, Salisbury, was more than twenty
years his junior. He was 75, and his future was uncertain. It

[1] *Life*, I, 202ff.   [2] *Life*, III, 550.

might have seemed to some good judges that his career was over. Gladstone went on a visit to Norway:[1]

> He was touched by a visit from the son of an old farmer, who brought him as an offering from his father to Mr Gladstone a curiously carved Norwegian bowl three hundred years old, with horse-head handles. Strolling about Aalesund, he was astonished to find in the bookshop a Norse translation of Mill's *Logic*. He was closely observant of all religious services whenever he had the chance, and noticed that at Laurvig all the tombstones had prayers for the dead. He read perhaps a little less voraciously than usual, and on one or two days, being unable to read, he 'meditated and reviewed' – always, I think, from the same point of view – the point of view of Bunyan's *Grace Abounding*, or his own letters to his father half a century before. Not seldom a vision of the coming elections flitted before the mind's eye, and he made notes for what he calls an *abbozzo* or sketch of his address to Midlothian.

That is surely admirable. It shows the old man in all his restless energy, his devout solemnity, his piety towards the past, his ranging intellectual curiosity, his recreative calm before the ferocious storm of his renewed political attack, and his quirkish touch of pedantry in the word *abbozzo*. Judged by the highest standards, Morley's is not a great biography. But it could have been. A passage like that proves that any failure was more in execution than in understanding.

[1] *Life*, iii, 218.

11

WARD'S NEWMAN

❋

It would be hard to exaggerate the difficulties that faced Wilfrid Ward in writing Newman's life.[1] It was a life which combined in an extraordinary degree the passionate and the uneventful. The springs of feeling and the sources of thought are unusually obscure. The shy young man at Oriel, who walked round Christ Church meadow by himself and would not speak in common room, becomes the tongue-tied Cardinal of the '80's who stood in front of the fire after breakfast at the Oratory and did not speak to the admiring, overawed young men, and then, perhaps, went to his study and wrote a letter explaining his silence. All this is hard for a biographer, but harder still to grasp and convey is that strange charm, piercing the shyness, which affected all sensitive acquaintances, and the heart-breaking eloquence of his preaching and public speaking. Here, and in the progress of his intellectual and spiritual lfe, the essence seems too fine for analysis.

The problem of continuity and change, always difficult in biography, can seldom have been as difficult as here. There is a sense in which Newman felt himself to be, and was, consistent from first to last, and spent nearly three-quarters of a century developing all the implications of that first Calvinist conversion at the age of 15, just as the word development signalises his most original and characteristic contribution to theology. There is a sense in which he came to adore what he had burnt, and burn what he had adored. ('I do profess *ex animo* that the thought of the Anglican service makes me shiver.')

A more superficial kind of difficulty, and yet one which has been damaging to many writings on Newman, lay in the hero's solitary suffering. It is undeniable that throughout his long life

[1] Wilfrid Ward: *Life of John Henry, Cardinal Newman*, 2 vols., 1912.

Newman was often treated both by ecclesiastical authority and by private persons with all kinds of incomprehension ranging from petty misunderstanding to crass ineptitude, and with all kinds of impoliteness ranging from small slights to grotesque bad manners. It is undeniable that he was sensitive to all this. But the danger of it for the biographer is that it may lead him to remove Newman from his context, to allow him to become an *exemplum* of hagiography, not a living controversial figure who fought hard himself, who blandly asked whether Dr Arnold was a Christian, who said when he left Oxford that the Liberals had beaten him in fair field, and who once gave as his reason for not writing more books that 'Hannibal's elephants could never learn the goose-step'.

All these and other perplexities were intensified, in Ward's case, by factors affecting himself alone. He was the son of one of Newman's most distinguished followers, who became, on many disputed points, one of his bitterest opponents. When he came to consider a *Life of Newman*, he had already written at length on his father's life and on the life of another powerful friend-and-enemy of Newman, Cardinal Wiseman. He had inevitably anticipated some of Newman's history, so inextricably bound up as it was with the history of these others. And, as regards the years 1833–45, he was faced with the Chinese wall of Newman's own matchless *Apologia*.

Ward was Newman's junior by some fifty-five years. From boyhood, he will have been accustomed to hear his father speak of him as the great leader of the old days; and as he drew nearer to death, Ward *père* spoke more and more of those old days, long before his disagreements began. After his father's death in 1882, and when Newman was already over 80, Wilfrid Ward got to know the Cardinal fairly well himself, as the old man came more and more to value the few surviving links with his early years.[1]

It is obvious that Ward was presented with a strange set of problems. His first impressions will have been paternal accounts of momentous events many years before his own birth in 1856;

[1] For these and other details see his *William George Ward and the Catholic Revival*, esp. the later chapters.

his second a personal impression of the very gradual decline of a man whose work was done, whose memory was failing, and who in his ninth decade had been placed by the cardinalate for the first time in his adult life finally above the struggle. Then, after all this, he came to deal with a biographer's usual material, letters, diaries and documents of all kinds, which existed in this case in a variety and profusion quite unusually great.

The first decision that he made was a bold, even a strange one, and one not altogether easy to defend. After an introductory chapter of a general character, only one chapter of the remaining thirty-four is given to Newman's Anglican period, which was virtually half his life. For a large part of this period of more than forty-four years there was ample evidence and profuse documentation. It seems, then, that the decision can only be defended on the score of the definitive character of the *Apologia* as an account of these years. Now, outstandingly truthful, lucid and brilliant as the *Apologia* is, this cannot be called a fully satisfactory idea. The difference between biography and autobiography is fundamental; and it is seen in its chemically pure state when each is true and good in its own way and when most of the working materials are the same. It may be a matter of regret that Ward wrote no full account of those early years, even though he was no doubt right to feel that no work of his could have equalled the *Apologia* either in literary distinction or in historical interest. Without doing that, it could have been valuable, and it could have added weight to the interpretations offered of Newman's last forty-five years. However, right or wrong, the decision was made; and once he had made it, Ward was faced in aggravated form with the problem of continuity to which I have already referred as chief among all the general difficulties of biography. It seems to me that he solved it with wonderful success.

He had, of course, certain advantages here that were inherent in Newman's own nature. Until his very last years Newman had intensely vivid memories, a keen interest in dates and anniversaries, and the sense of a bond, physical almost in its intensity, with any place in which significant experience had come to him. Thus at times, Ward (one of whose best features as a biographer was that he knew when no comment at all was necessary) was able to achieve a strong effect of continuity and perspective by merely quoting something of this kind:[1]

> *To Dean Church*   *12 April, 1885*
> My dear Dean – Thank you for your impressive Easter Sermon. It is 63 years to-day since I was elected at Oriel; the turning day of my life.
> > Yrs affly
> > J. H. Card.   Newman

Or this, to the President of Trinity College, Oxford, of which he was by now an Honorary Fellow:

> *18 May, 1885*
> . . . May your yearly Festival ever be as happy a day to you, as in 1818 it was to me.
> > I am, my dear President,
> > Sincerely yours,
> > JOHN H. CARD.   NEWMAN
> P.S. Excuse my handwriting. I am now scarcely able to form any letters.[2]

But other cases are not so clear. The *Apologia*, certainly, had demonstrated once and for all the continuity of thought and feeling, the inner line of spiritual consistency. But continuity means other things beside this; and there were in Newman's career a number of false starts based on misleading analogies. Let us take the case of the founding of the Catholic University in Dublin. Ward shows that Newman saw from the first a good many discouraging features in this affair. He was induced to persevere by three motives, each strong in itself, but widely different in kind. There was the general, lifelong tendency to accept anything that appeared to be a *leading* towards the effective public use of the great intellectual gifts he knew himself to possess. There was a somewhat abstract historical conviction, later regretfully abandoned, and entirely distinct in its character from a loyal Catholic acceptance of Papal authority

[1] II, 524.   [2] II, 525.

– a conviction that projects on which the Holy See smiled were bound to prosper. And there was a much more intimate and personal sense of the recovery of Oxford, where he had once thought he would remain till death. Perhaps, he thought, a new Oxford could be recreated in Dublin, a new citadel of the disinterested intelligence, which would cure his yearning for the scenes of his youth.

Now these three different motives all need different handling by the biographer, and in each case a right handling must be very tactful. The first, lying in the intimate realm of responsibility to God, is, ultimately, beyond his power to judge. The second, Newman himself eventually came to see, is an illegitimate materialisation of the theological principle of Papal authority. The third is a strongly emotional cry of mingled loyalty and regret of a man in exile from the friendships and associations that had made him what he was. Ward's treatment of all this complex matter is exemplary in its intelligent comprehension and its unobtrusive brevity. He quotes just the passages in Newman's writings necessary to a clear understanding and no more, and he writes:

His own feelings were evidently, even before the succession of discouragements which followed, somewhat mixed. He saw at once that a scheme which was strongly opposed by the ablest ecclesiastic in Ireland, Archbishop Murray of Dublin, and which aimed nevertheless at founding a university in Dr Murray's own diocese, was a bold one . . . Still the work was entrusted to him by the hierarchy as a whole, and was undertaken in obedience to the Holy Father's wish. It came to him unsought. His antecedents fitted him for it. The thought could not but arise – was the hand of Providence leading him on to a repetition in new surroundings of the great battle of the Oxford Movement?[1]

Having said this, he refrains from pointing out at the time any weak point in these arguments and imaginings. He proceeds

[1] *Life*, i, 312–13. I may add, speaking generally, that while I cannot claim to have read all of Newman's published, and still less his unpublished letters, I have read a good many; and I have almost invariably found that Ward has chosen what seem to me the best, and, more important, has really made them carry weight in the story.

with his narrative until all the necessary evidence has been assembled about the actual state of Irish education, ecclesiastical opinion, and lay apathy. Taken together, this evidence showed not only that the project was likely to fail, but that its divergence from the Oxford model, had it been successful, would have been complete. His definitive judgment is expressed thus:

> Here, then, was the position gradually brought home to him. A Catholic university was wanted as a political and ecclesiastical weapon against mixed education. For this purpose his name was a valuable asset. In this sense all the Bishops favoured the university. But, as a practical project, in the interests of education, hardly anyone took it seriously.[1]

Ward gives his balanced judgment of this complex issue in his introductory chapter:

> There is no faltering in his loyalty to Rome. But in this, as in other feelings, buoyancy has left him. The thought that almost a miracle might come if he followed Peter's lead is sadly allowed to have been in this case a dream and not a vision. The authorities at Rome had not realised the conditions which prevailed in Ireland. They had relied on local information which proved to be inaccurate. It was a simple and not surprising fact. It impugned no dogma of his faith. But it meant that the years had passed, not in justifying for him an almost prophetic vision in the face of chilling criticism, but in finding by experience that the critics had been right and his work vain.[2]

A few sentences earlier he describes the effect of all this on Newman:

> He keeps writing to his friends of satisfaction and success – until suddenly he breaks down. He compares the founders of the university to Frankenstein. They were scared at their own monster. He resigns his office. But the long strain has been too much. Buoyancy has gone for ever. He finds himself an old man.

The difference in the flavour of these two passages (written

[1] *Life*, II, 336.   [2] I, 9.

198

on the same page about the same topic) is a guide to Ward's essential quality as a biographer. His power of empathy by which he enters into Newman's excessive temporary disappointment does not inhibit the judicious balance of his historical account. This ability to *vary the distance* from the subject is both rare and valuable.

If from one point of view Newman was simply mistaken about the possible likeness between Oxford and Dublin, others beside Newman had some right on their side or, at least, an intelligible motive for acting as they did. The Irish bishops were high-handed, and one or two of them were discourteous, but did they not have some reason to fear that Newman was unconsciously serving the old, hated policy of the Pale – the creation of a small Anglicised élite with every privilege to rule over a mass of Papist barbarians? They had duties to all their flock, not just to that tiny minority capable of appreciating the intellectual glories sketched in *The Idea of a University*. Ward is aware of all this too, and so here and throughout the book, Newman is always surrounded by living, breathing men, acting on principles of their own, often wrong as against Newman, but sometimes right. There are so many biographies in which, as in a bad novel, there is really only one character, who is the author's mask or his ideal, and all the others only exist in the way that stage properties do. Here and elsewhere Ward could be stern in showing how Newman was misled in his constant search for continuity in a life full of flux. He was stern because he wished to enforce the contrast with the inner consistency really present in Newman's life. Very near the beginning of his long book,[1] Ward quotes Newman's words in a letter of 6th January, 1877, in which he likened the irreligious tendencies of the age to a flood, which would continue to rise until 'only the tops of the mountains will be seen like islands in the waste of waters'. And he asserts, very cogently, that Newman was speaking then, at the age of 75, of matters that had preoccupied him for some fifty years. As Newman said himself, his struggle was against Liberalism; and it is perhaps the essential test of any serious writing on Newman that it should show the range of meaning

[1] *Life,* I, 5.

this word had for him, and the difference between his sense of the word and what later readers expect it to mean. Liberalism, for Newman, had little to do with the freedom which is permitted by authority. It meant, rather, the freedom a man illegitimately allows to himself, the freedom to ignore truth, to refuse to listen to properly constituted authority, to stifle his conscience with specious reasonings. Indeed, Newman's sense is actually opposite to some current uses of the word. Racialism is, in Newman's sense, a liberal idea, since it denies what both reason and revelation tell of the unity of human nature. Liberalism meant believing what your prejudices and interests made it convenient to believe.

But the matter is further complicated by Newman's positive and approving uses of the word 'liberal', especially of the phrase 'liberal knowledge', and by the various, mostly vague, political uses to which the word was put by the surrounding society. Many writers have been confused by all this; Ward stands out among critics of Newman in the exactness and the justice of the distinctions he makes between all these senses of a most difficult word, and a key word in Newman's thought.

An equally difficult task was to bring out the fiery independence of Newman's personality, which contrasts so strongly with his intellectual acceptance of authority. He had a strongly English sense of a man's responsibility for and to himself. Then there was a hidden, but at times influential, feeling about his own intellectual powers, that they were finer than those of his critics and detractors, and finer too than those of the men set in authority over him. Cardinal Manning, not an altogether impartial critic certainly, said that Newman's career had been spoilt by temper. Manning was not always right, least of all about Newman, but what he said never lacked plausibility or insight. All these points had to be given the due weight in counterpoise to the great theme of the war on liberalism. Finally, there was the intellectual boldness, the dialectical cast of mind which caused Newman at all times, but especially in later life, to state the contrary view to his own with all his eloquence and rational force.[1]

[1] For instance: 'If I looked into a mirror, and did not see my face, I should

Now some of these points, difficult as they are, might be adequately explained by a critic who was not a biographer. It was Ward's duty, as a biographer, to detect the moment of crystallisation – that is, the moment when events made Newman understand which way his whirls and eddies of feeling were really taking him. The case of the proposed return to Oxford in 1867, and of the instruction from Rome forbidding it, is illuminating. Newman's feelings about this were both contradictory and turbulent. He had never gone back to Oxford (though he was to do so later when Trinity made him an Honorary Fellow); and he had referred briefly and poignantly to his long absence in concluding the *Apologia* three years before. Ward shows by quotation that Newman on the whole supposed himself to be reluctant to return. ('The very seeing Oxford again, since I am not one with it, would be a cruel thing – it is like the dead coming to the dead.')[1]

But as the prospects appeared to grow brighter, and the time seemed to be drawing nearer, there is an undercurrent of joy in Newman's plans and comments, while the sentiments of dread become more feeble. Ward conducts us to the moment when, as Newman is happily talking to Father Neville about details of the Oxford project, 'the servant, who opened the door to admit them, at once gave Newman a long blue envelope'.[2]

A life of Newman, in the nature of the case, moves mainly in the realm of thoughts and feelings. But mundane physical detail was certainly not disdained by Ward. It was used rather as dialogue is used in the novels of Balzac, kept in reserve so as to be telling and memorable at special moments. So, in the Irish part of his narrative, the coarse mutton and suffocating feather beds of the Irish bishops became emblematic of Newman's deeper frustrations over the Dublin University.

In general historical terms, that long blue envelope, containing Rome's courteous but final refusal to entertain the scheme of Newman's residence at Oxford, was characteristic of a whole

have the sort of feeling which actually comes upon me, when I look into this living, busy world and see no reflection of its creator' (*Apologia*, chapter v).
[1] ii, 130.   [2] ii, 138.

phase of policy on educational matters – one that was not to
change until after Leo XIII became Pope in 1878. It was a
policy disliked both by Newman and Ward, and one which
Newman's old rival, Manning, now Archbishop of Westminster,
advocated in Rome with all his energies and diplomatic gifts.
Ward does not dwell on all this; he sees his duty as a biographer
to assess the effects of the contents of that envelope.

> Newman opened and read the letter, and turned to William
> Neville: 'All is over. I am not allowed to go.' No word
> more was spoken. The Father covered his face with his
> hands, and left his friends, who went to his room and
> unpacked his portmanteau.[1]

This bleak little scene, so much more effective for the absence
of rhetoric or comment, marks a moment of truth in Newman's
self-knowledge. When Oxford is forbidden him, he not only has
a deeper yearning for it, but also an indignant sense of the loss
he has suffered by submitting himself to the authority of the
Church. The biographer's duty here, well performed by Ward,
is to show when Newman suddenly discovered which, after all,
was the dominant emotion in a mass of conflicting sentiments.

But there is something deeper here than feeling about
Oxford, and it brings me to Ward's second great theme. It lies
in the difference between religious authority as a principle and
the same authority as a worldly fact. To Newman religion
meant dogma, and dogma meant authority; on that he never
wavered. But authority means people exercising authority, and
those people part of the foolish, wicked world we know. It is in
this tension, mainly, that Ward finds his essential link between
the inner and outer in Newman's life. I have already spoken of
his caution in the use of opportunities to turn Newman into a
martyr, so that the Newman of the biography remains of the
same essential clay as those who opposed him. But since Newman was so spiritual, so immersed in the effort to understand
the 'two and two only absolute and luminously self-evident
beings', some stronger link is artistically necessary for the
biographer between Newman and the life of his time. You can
avoid making Newman into a plaster saint, and Ward carefully

[1] ɪɪ, 139.

does so. But you cannot, without contravening truth, and frustrating the whole purpose of your writing, deny that he was a very exceptional man, not only in the degree but in the kind of his talents and aspirations.

This contrast between authority as a principle and authority as a practical fact was a fruitful organising principle, because it joined hands, so to speak, with the particular and the general. Complex ecclesiastical intrigues are a matter of nuances, of personalities, of petty disputes, important because of the principles underlying them. They cannot, in the nature of the case, be comprehended without the presentation of great masses of detail. So it is that Ward can present (say) a letter from Manning to Talbot in Rome without ever irritating us with the suspicion that he is being over-elaborate.

On the other hand this contrast between abstract and concrete authority is a special case of one of the most simple and solemn themes in the world – the conflict between the ideal and the real, the difference between principle and practice. A book of some twelve hundred pages, based on thousands of documents, needs a backbone; and it is on this score that so many biographies fail, even when the subject is distinguished and the writer is talented. Ward does not fail. And he was fortunate that the facts of the case permitted him to present an eventual resolution to the conflict. Newman's trials at the hands of authority did not last for ever.

To give a resolution to this long conflict – a conflict not so much between Newman and authority, as between authority as a principle and authority as a fact – Ward has two very different scenes. Obviously, whatever scheme the biography had followed, the cardinalate must have been a prominent scene in it; and it must have been viewed, as Newman himself viewed it, as the time when 'the cloud is lifted from me for ever'.[1] The amends were long in coming but they were ample, for Rome gave Newman the highest honour in its gift. This is obvious, and Ward's treatment gives full weight to it. But he stresses also the confused circumstances in which the offer was made, in which *The Times* printed a report that it has been refused, in

[1] *Life,* II 446.

which Manning was suspected (rightly or wrongly) of a wish to prevent Newman receiving the hat, and further suspected of a wish to deceive the Pope about the nature of Newman's reply. So the reader's impression here is a mixed one. Rome had changed. Leo XIII, unlike Pius IX, was a man capable both of recognising Newman's immense importance as a theologian, and of feeling that a great deal was due to those loyal sensibilities wounded so often over so many years. But England, that is to say, the England of the higher Catholic ecclesiastical circles, was still the same.[1]

In all this Ward did very much what most competent biographers would have done. It is in his choice and placing of the contrasting scene that he shows his quality. Ullathorne, Bishop of Birmingham, and Newman's diocesan for some forty years, is a prominent figure throughout the life. He is the most distinguished and sympathetic representative of the English Old Catholic tradition in the book. After some early misunderstandings, he emerges as a strong sympathiser with Newman and, where necessary, an energetic defender of his wrongly questioned orthodoxy and loyalty. It was he who wrote to Newman after the return to Oxford had been refused (19th August, 1867), 'I have no hesitation in saying it, as my complete conviction, that you have been shamefully misrepresented at Rome, and that by countrymen of our own'.[2] By 1887 Newman was too infirm to have written a very clear account of his meeting with Ullathorne; and though Ullathorne too was over 80, Ward was fortunate in having a clear and touching account from him as the following:

After speaking on Newman's failing eyesight, Ullathorne goes on:

As I was rising to leave an action of his caused a scene I shall never forget . . . He said in low and humble accents, 'My dear Lord, will you do me a great favour?' 'What is it?'

---

[1] I am speaking of Manning here solely as he appears in Ward's book. There is some reason to think that he behaved better to Newman in this matter than Ward thought. See Shane Leslie: *H. E. Manning – His Life and Labours,* chapter 16, and especially page 281 (Manning's letter to Cardinal Franchi).

[2] *Life,* II, 184.

I asked. He glided down on his knees, bent down his venerable head, and said, 'Give me your blessing.' What could I do with him before me in such a posture? I could not refuse without giving him great embarrassment.[1] So I laid my hands on his head and said: 'My dear Lord Cardinal, notwithstanding all laws to the contrary, I pray God to bless you, and that His Holy Spirit may be full in your heart.' As I walked to the door, refusing to put on his biretta as he went with me, he said: 'I have been indoors all my life, whilst you have battled for the Church in the world.'

Certainly Ward was fortunate to have such an admirable account to draw upon. But that in no way detracts from his long-drawn strategic skill in using it. Newman was never more completely true to himself than when he chose the motto *Cor ad cor loquitur*; and no official distinction, however august, could render otiose for him this more intimate scene. It was a scene full of paradoxes, and those paradoxes all pointing towards the heart of Newman's mystery. It was an assertion of submission to authority, and yet subtly at odds with the normal forms and rankings through which that authority is exercised. (If Newman had still been only Father Newman, and thus still entirely subject to Ullathorne's episcopal jurisdiction, would he have knelt still?) It was an act of homage paid by the thinker, aware of his majestic gifts, to the man of practical ability and integrity. It was deeply felt, yet formal, possessing something of the character of an acted parable. It was, like the man himself, humble, yet in a certain sense proud also. Above all, it was unexpected, bearing the mark of a distinct, unmistakable personality. It is in every way a fitting end to the whole subject of Newman's dealings with authority. Then there remained only the task of describing Newman's death; and here a simpler scene, but a touching one too, was provided by the incident of the silk handkerchief, which had been left as a present thirty years before by an unknown, poor man, which Newman asked as his last request to have by him. This, too, in its own way,

[1] The reason Ullathorne was tempted to refuse was that Newman, as a Cardinal, held a higher ecclesiastical office than himself, and therefore the blessing would be, in a certain sense, *ultra vires*. (My note.)

was an act of prostration of the intellect, not now before authority, but before the ordinary man.

It is time to speak more generally. Perhaps the most noticeable thing about the book as a whole is the sense of rhythm in life that it conveys. Preoccupied as he was with the inner consistency of Newman's career, Ward might easily have missed that variety of mood and fortune which affects every life. But no; he was careful to capture it. The end of Chapter **XXXII** may stand as typical of his method. Ward prepares for the chapter that was immediately to follow, the chapter that dealt with the cardinalate and the lifting of the cloud, with an account of the sadness of the years 1875 to 1879.

> His silence and depression were very noticeable to those who lived with him. The death of Ambrose St John cast a shadow which could not be removed, and it was deepened by the loss of other friends. What is there to look forward to? – was the thought that would come as years advanced and strength diminished. The solemn conviction that he must think no more of an earthly future, but prepare to follow his friends who had gone, was never absent from his mind. Yet what he had done as a Catholic seemed as yet so fragmentary, so incomplete, accompanied with so much failure.[1]

Then comes the arrival of a small personal present from the new Pope, Leo XIII, which gave a momentary gleam of interest, following upon the honorary fellowship of Trinity. But Newman 'soon relapsed into the sadness which had been for a while somewhat dissipated by these two incidents'. The chapter ends with these words:

> Working and praying, sad yet resigned, he awaited the great summons which he felt might come any day.

The great summons was to be delayed for more than ten years, and the cardinalate was the destiny immediately approaching. By means like these Ward is able to give a clear view of the actual variety and unexpectedness of life, while keeping the main lines of his interpretation unchanging. It is so too in smaller things. He shows the contrast and keeps the balance.

[1] II, 431–2.

He shows Newman's solemnity, but also his wit and light-heartedness. He shows that as a practical force in the world Newman was both effective and ineffective. He shows that he received unkind and unfair treatment, and yet that his failures were not an accident, but were in part determined by aspects of his character. He shows his pride and his humility; he shows his pessimism and his deep hopefulness.

APPENDIX

Biographical Summaries

✻

THOMAS ARNOLD, headmaster of Rugby (1795–1842); educated at Winchester and Corpus Christi College, Oxford; Fellow
of Oriel, 1815; ordained in Anglican chuch, 1818; headmaster
of Rugby 1828 till death; profoundly influential on future of
education in three different ways; by personal influence over
able pupils, including Arthur Clough, A. P. Stanley (q.v.), James
Prince Lee, C. J. Vaughan and others; by establishing abler
boys as praepostors (prefects) with onerous responsibilities; by
broadening curriculum; supported Catholic Emancipation in
pamphlet, 1829; bitter opponent of Tractarians; published
sermons and history of ancient Rome; regius professor of history,
Oxford, 1841; father of Matthew Arnold and of W. D. Arnold,
author of *Oakfield*; an Erastian latitudinarian, stressing always
comprehensiveness of Church of England.

THOMAS CARLYLE (1795–1881). Born in humble circumstances
at Ecclefechan, Dumfriesshire; educated at Annan Academy
and Edinburgh University; early friend of Edward Irving,
founder of Catholic Apostolic Church; studied hard and learnt
German; after brief period as schoolmaster, took to precarious
literary life; married Jane Welsh, 1826; came to live in Chelsea,
1834; published his most influential book, *The French Revolution*,
1837, after first version had been accidentally burnt by servant
of John Stuart Mill; published essay on *Chartism*, the precursor
of the industrial novels of Disraeli, Mrs Gaskell and Charles
Kingsley, 1839; *Past and Present*, which compares his own age
unfavourably with medieval times, 1843; *Oliver Cromwell*, a
vigorous defence of one of his heroes, 1845; rector of Edinburgh
University 1865–6; his wife died suddenly in London while he
was on visit to Edinburgh, 1866; stricken by remorse for his

treatment of her, prepared her *Letters and Memorials,* published posthumously; and his own *Reminiscences,* containing an admiring tribute to his own parents; refused various high honours of state; died lonely and disappointed, but was deeply influential on some of the leading men of his time, especially Ruskin, Dickens, Kingsley and his biographer, J. A. Froude (q.v.).

JAMES ANTHONY FROUDE (1818–94), biographer of Carlyle; son of Anglican archdeacon; younger brother of Hurrell Froude (1803–36), friend of Newman and co-founder of Oxford Movement; educated at Westminster, where he was bitterly unhappy, and Oriel College, Oxford; came for a short time under Newman's influence; Fellow of Exeter College, Oxford, 1842; published *Nemesis of Faith* (1849), which was publicly burnt as being subversive of religious orthodoxy; resigned fellowship; published his lengthy *History of England 1529–1588,* 1856–70; friend, disciple and eventually literary executor of Carlyle; published Carlyle's posthumous works, and produced his own life of Carlyle, 1882–4; regius professor of modern history in Oxford, 1892–4; strong imperialist and supporter of Protestant supremacy in Ireland.

WILLIAM EWART GLADSTONE (1809–98), son of wealthy Liverpool merchant with West Indian and slave interests; received evangelical upbringing; educated at Eton and Christ Church, Oxford; double first and outstanding scholar of year, 1831; Conservative M.P. for Newark, 1832, through influence of Duke of Newcastle; became adherent of Tractarian views; junior office under Peel, 1834; published *Church in its Relation to State,* embodying High Church and High Tory views, 1838; called by Macaulay (q.v.) 'rising hope of those stern and unbending Tories' when he reviewed this book; opposed opium war with China, 1840; resigned over Maynooth grant, 1845, but more to maintain consistency with earlier views than because he then opposed it; supported Peel at time of split with Disraeli, 1846, though out of Parliament at this time; M.P. for Oxford University, 1847–65; bitterly attacked Neapolitan tyrannies,

1851; opposed Ecclesiastical Titles Bill, Russell's reply to so-called Papal Aggression, 1851; Chancellor of Exchequer in Lord Aberdeen's 'Peelite' government, 1852–5; an acknowledged master of intricacies of finance and taxation; supported Crimean War, but resigned when Palmerston became Prime Minister, 1855; Chancellor of Exchequer under Palmerston, 1859–65; opposed Bill for removing University Anglican tests, 1865; M.P. South Lancashire, 1865–8; failed to pass Reform Bill, 1866; leader of Liberal Party in succession to Russell, 1867; Prime Minister, 1868; passed Irish Church Disestablishment Bill, 1869; abolished purchase in army, 1871; passed Ballot Bill, 1872; resigned leadership of Liberal Party, 1875, after Disraeli's victory in General Election of 1874; bitterly attacked Turkish outrages against Eastern Christians, 1875; published study of Homeric writings, 1876; conducted immensely popular and influential Midlothian campaign, attacking Disraeli's imperialism and Eastern policy, 1879–80; Prime Minister again, after refusing to serve under Lord Hartington, 1880; passed Irish Land Bills; supported military campaign in Egypt, 1882; passed Bill for extension of franchise to agricultural labourers, 1884; succeeded by Lord Salisbury as Prime Minister, 1885, but returned to premiership, 1886; defeated on Home Rule issue at General Election of 1886; Prime Minister again, 1892; second Irish Home Rule Bill heavily defeated in House of Lords after passing Commons, 1893; resigned 1894; his main periodical writings gathered in *Gleanings from Past Years*; famed throughout life for oratorial powers; close friend of Cardinal Manning, despite estrangement in 1851, when Manning left Church of England after Gorham case, and Gladstone, after some hesitation, remained; strong churchman, but admired and followed politically especially by non-conformists after 1868; disliked and distrusted Disraeli; disliked and distrusted himself by Queen Victoria; generally known in later years as Grand Old Man; lay in state after death.

THOMAS BABINGTON MACAULAY, first Baron (1800–59), son of Zachary Macaulay, leading member of 'Clapham Sect' and associate of William Wilberforce, Sir James Stephen, etc.;

educated privately and at Trinity College, Cambridge; Fellow of Trinity, 1824; frequent contributor to *Edinburgh Review* from 1825; M.P., 1830; member of Supreme Council of India, 1834–8; his minute on education profoundly influential in directing Indian higher education towards European model; M.P. again, 1839–47 and 1852–6; Secretary at War, 1839–41; published *Lays of Ancient Rome*, 1842; proposed and carried new copyright law, granting rights to authors for forty-two years; published first two volumes of *History*, the classic statement of Whig view of revolution of 1688, embodying glorification of William III, 1848; other volumes appeared at intervals till 1861, last being posthumous; immense popular and financial success; baron, 1857; unmarried.

JOHN MORLEY, Viscount Morley of Blackburn (1838–1923), biographer, educated Cheltenham College and Lincoln College, Oxford; freelance journalist from 1860; joined *Saturday Review*, 1863; friend of John Stuart Mill and George Meredith; editor of radical *Fortnightly Review*, 1867–72; agnostic in religion and sympathetic to English followers of Auguste Comte; published study of Burke, 1867; of Voltaire, 1872; and Rousseau, 1873; political associate of Joseph Chamberlain (in his radical phase) and Sir Charles Dilke; full-length life of Burke, 1879; editor of *Pall Mall Gazette*, which he changed towards anti-imperial policies, 1880; published life of Cobden, 1881; M.P., 1883; Chief Secretary for Ireland, 1886; strong supporter of Gladstone's Home Rule policy; edited *English Men of Letters* series; Secretary for Ireland again, 1892–5; opposed to South African war; published *Oliver Cromwell*, 1900, and *Life of Gladstone*, 1903, only five years after Gladstone's death, having been intimate with him in his years of retirement; Secretary for India, 1905–10, maintaining courteous disagreement with Viceroy's more Conservative views; Viscount, 1908; resigned from Asquith Government on outbreak of war, 1914; O.M. and Hon. Fellow of All Souls; published *Recollections*, 1917.

JOHN HENRY NEWMAN (1801–90), son of a London banker; educated at Ealing and Trinity College, Oxford; Fellow of Oriel by examination, 1822; vicar of University Church, 1828; travelled in Europe, 1832–3, and suffered a severe illness; returned to England just before Keble's assize sermon of July 1833; joined with Keble and Hurrell Froude in what later became known as Oxford Movement, which proclaimed Anglican Church as true portion of original undivided Catholic Church; author of many of early *Tracts for the Times*, published anonymously; strong in controversy on behalf of this view of Anglicanism, 1833–9; troubled by doubts of soundness of Anglican position, 1839–41; published *Tract XC*, which attempted reconciliation of *Anglican 39* articles with doctrines of Rome, 1841; convinced by storm of opposition to this tract in Oxford and throughout the Church that his views were unlikely to gain acceptance; retired with a few selected friends to Littlemore, near Oxford, 1842, ceasing to perform clerical functions or university duties; resigned as vicar of University Church, 1843; received into Roman Catholic Church, 9 October, 1845; published *Development of Christian Doctrine*, his most original and influential theological work, justifying what he had formerly supposed to be accretions of Rome, 1845; ordained priest, and became head of first English house of Oratorian order in Birmingham, 1847; published *Present Position of Catholics*, analysing 'Papal Aggression' scare, 1851; rector of Dublin Catholic University, 1854–8, publishing inaugural lectures under title *Idea of a University*; attacked as dishonest by Charles Kingsley, and published his most famous book, *Apologia pro Vita Sua*, in self-defence, 1864; honorary fellow of Trinity College, Oxford, 1877; created cardinal by Pope Leo XIII, 1879; brother of F. W. Newman, author of *Phases of Faith* and other books.

SAMUEL SMILES (1812–1904); educated at Haddington Grammar School; apprenticed to local doctor, 1826; studied Edinburgh University, 1829–32; editor of radical *Leeds Times*, 1838–42; railway administrator from 1845; propagandist for Manchester economics; published *Life of George Stephenson*, 1857; followed by many similar biographical works, all stressing power of individual to overcome circumstances, and identity of

enlightened self-interest with public interest; also *Self-Help,*
1859, a best-seller in many languages; *Character,* 1871, *Thrift,*
1875; autobiography, written very late in life, published posthumously, 1905.

ROBERT SOUTHEY (1774–1843); educated at Westminster
School, from which he was expelled for opposition to authority,
and Balliol College, Oxford; met Coleridge and was converted
by him to unitarianism and pantisocracy, married Edith
Fricker, sister of Coleridge's wife; visited Spain and Portugal,
1795–1800; soon abandoned early views and became Anglican
and Tory; extensive contributor to *Quarterly Review* for thirty
years from 1808; published life of Nelson, 1813; poet laureate,
1813; friend of Shelley for a short time from 1815, but bitter and
unreconciled quarrel soon ended association; published life of
Wesley, 1820; his *Vision of Judgment,* 1821, embodying apothe-
osis of George III, parody of which by Byron is better known
than original; friend of Wordsworth, his near neighbour in
Lake District; bore generously and without complaint burden
of Coleridge's undischarged family responsibilities; his mature
views on religion, politics and society best given in his *Colloquies,*
1829; compared by Macaulay (q.v.) to Satan in *Paradise Lost,*
'Following darkness'; later years strongly influenced by fear of
revolution; much admired as poet by good judges in his time;
but better known as letter writer in recent times.

ARTHUR PENRHYN STANLEY (1815–81); pupil and biographer
of Dr Arnold (q.v.); of ancient family of Stanleys of Alderley;
educated Rugby and Balliol College, Oxford; fine classical
scholar; Fellow of University College; published life of Dr
Arnold, 1844; canon of Canterbury, 1851; professor of Ecclesiastical history, Oxford, 1856; carried on latitudinarian tradition
of Arnold; wrote essays defending Jowett, *Essays and Reviews,*
and Colenso; dean of Westminster, 1864 till death; intimate of
Royal family and strong royalist; remarkable for learning,
impartiality and breadth of view with which he wrote of topical
matters of religious controversy.

SIR LESLIE STEPHEN (1832–1904), son of Sir James Stephen, noted colonial administrator, historian and leading member of 'Clapham Sect'; younger brother of great criminal jurist Sir James Fitzjames Stephen; educated at Eton and King's College, London, and Trinity Hall, Cambridge; wrangler, 1854; Fellow of Trinity Hall, 1854–67; ordained in Anglican Church, 1855; resigned fellowship because of developing agnostic religious views; wrote for *Saturday Review* and *Pall Mall Gazette*; editor of *Cornhill Magazine*, 1871–82; published anti-Christian *Essays on Free-Thinking*, 1873, and *History of English Thought in C18*, 1876; contributed to *English Men of Letters*, lives of Pope, Swift, George Eliot and Hobbes; editor of *Dictionary of National Biography*, 1882–91; published life of his brother James Fitzjames, 1895, and *Studies of a Biographer*, 1899–1902; married daughter of Thackeray; father of Virginia Woolf by second wife; devoted throughout life to athletic pursuits and walking; a pioneer of Alpine climbing.

GEORGE OTTO TREVELYAN, biographer and nephew of Lord Macaulay (q.v.) (1838–1928), second baronet; son of Sir Charles Trevelyan, notable Indian administrator and reformer of English Civil Service; educated at Harrow and Trinity College, Cambridge; private secretary to his father in India; M.P., 1865; enthusiastic supporter of Gladstone and member of his administration, 1868–70 and 1882–86; resigned on Home Rule question, 1886; but reconciled to Gladstone's Irish policy, 1887; Secretary for Scotland, 1892–5; published *Life of Macaulay*, 1876; *Early History of Charles James Fox*, 1880; *History of American Revolution*, 1899–1914; squire of Wallington in Northumberland; devoted later life to literary and country pursuits; father of three well-known sons, including G. M. Trevelyan, Master of Trinity, Cambridge.

WILFRID PHILIP WARD (1856–1916); biographer of Cardinal Newman; son of W. G. Ward (1812–82), author of *Ideal of a Christian Church*; educated at Ushaw College and Gregorian University, Rome; wrote account of his father's part in Oxford Movement, 1889; and in *Roman Catholic Revival*, 1893; life of

Cardinal Wiseman, 1897; became editor *Dublin Review,* 1905; life of Newman, 1912; in ultramontane controversy within the Roman Church, took side of Newman rather than that of his own father, and of Cardinal Manning.

INDEX

✳

NOTE: *BS* indicates biographical summary at end of volume

Adams, W. H. D., 55-6
Arnold, Matthew, 81, 88-9, 91, 99, 191, 209
Arnold, Thomas, 22-3, 39, 64, 80-1, 83-6, 87-104, 116, 214
  BS 209
Ashburton, Lady, 172-4

Bagehot, Walter, 79n, 80, 106, 123, 141, 143, 181
Bamford, T. W., 96n
Bell, Quentin, 11n, 75
Bonner, Mrs H. B., 53-4
Boswell, James, 11, 14, 17, 91, 101, 137, 143
Bradlaugh, Charles, 53-4
Bridgewater, Duke of, 117, 120-2
Briggs, Asa, 105n
Browning, Robert, 37, 97
Brunel, I. K., 114-15
Burke, Edmund, 175-6
Burns, Robert, 18, 25-9
Butler, Lady Eleanor, 33
Byron, Lord, 32-5, 40, 97, 214

Cardigan, Lord, 122n, 139-40
Carlyle, Mrs Jane Welsh, 30, 144n, 150-1, 159, 164-74, 209
Carlyle, Thomas, 14, 15, 16, 30, 38, 50-1, 56-61, 64, 86, 89, 93, 101-2, 143, 144-74, 210
  BS 209-10

Cavendish, George, 90-1
Cecil, Gwendolen, 126
Church, R. W., 69-70, 196
Clare, Lord, 33
Clough, A. H., 64, 81, 88, 209
Coleridge, S. T., 19, 25-6, 28-9, 61, 81, 110, 147-8, 214
Colquhoun, Archibald, 49n
Cottle, Joseph, 25, 28-9
Creighton, Bishop Mandall, 17
Creighton, Mrs, 17
Cromwell, Oliver, 46-7, 56-60, 148
Cross, J. W., 48-9

Derby, Lord, 183-5
Devonshire, Duke of, 40
Dick, Robert, 107
Dickens, Charles, 17, 23-4, 42, 44, 63, 64, 106-8, 111, 130, 147-8, 210
Disraeli, Benjamin, 11, 64, 71, 102, 106, 111, 112-13, 182-4, 187, 189, 209, 210, 211
Dryden, John, 11

Edward VII (as P. of Wales), 39
Eliot, George, 36, 64, 69, 70-1, 98, 225
Eliot, T. S., 13n, 128n
Ellmann, Richard, 11n

Firth, Sir Charles, 59

Foot, M. R. D., 179
Forster, E. M., 71, 75-9
Fox, Charles James, 142, 215
Froude, Hurrell, 81-2, 210, 213
Froude, J. A., 11, 12, 14, 15, 16, 86, 93, 99-100, 101, 143, 144-74, 186, 210
    BS 210

Gardiner, S. R., 59
Gibbon, Edward, 108, 154
Gladstone, W. E., 15, 30, 64, 69, 84-6, 88-9, 93, 98, 139-40, 147-8, 175-92, 215
    BS 210-11
Goethe, 47
Gosse, Edmund, 67
Grosskuth, Phyllis, 23n
Guiccoli, Teresa, 34-5

Hamer, D. A., 178n
Hardy, Thomas, 37-8
Hare, Archdeacon, 43
Hayter, Alethea, 29n
Henry VIII, 12
Hodson, Major, 44, 89
Hogg, T. J., 61-3
Holland, Bernard, 40n
Hopkins, G. M., 19
Housman, A. E., 57
Hughes, Thomas, 89
Hume, David, 57, 154
Huxley, Leonard, 54
Huxley, T. H., 54, 68

Irving, Edward, 30, 167, 209

Jeffrey, Francis, 151, 167
Jewsbury, Geraldine, 165
Johnson, Samuel, 11, 23-4, 49n, 55-6, 72-3, 91, 101
Jowett, Benjamin, 84, 214

Keble, John, 65, 80-1, 82-3, 85, 213
Kingsley, Charles, 42-3, 84, 92, 96, 186, 209-10, 213
Kingsley, Mrs, 13, 14n, 42

Lawrence, D. H., 11
Leo XIII, 202, 204, 206, 213
Leslie, Sir Shane, 65, 204n
Lewes, G. H., 47-8
Lockhart, J. G., 18, 25-9, 137, 148

Macaulay, Hannah (Lady Trevelyan), 130, 133-4, 135, 138
Macaulay, Lord, 64, 71, 72, 74-5, 86, 89, 93, 106, 116, 122-3, 125-43, 181, 210, 214, 215
    BS 211-12
Macaulay, Margaret, 130, 132n, 133
Maitland, F. W., 14, 38, 49, 78-9
Manning, Cardinal, 45-6, 65, 68, 200, 203, 211, 216
Manzoni, Alessandro, 49n
Maurice, F. D., 49-50
Mill, J. S., 17, 65, 80, 147-8, 149-50, 177-8, 192
Milnes, R. M., 61
Moore, Thomas, 32-6, 40
Morley, John, 15, 46-7, 60, 86, 93, 175-92
    BS 212
Murray, Archbishop, 197

Napoleon, 22, 111-13, 115
Nelson, Lord, 16, 25, 41-2, 214
Newman, J. H., 23, 30, 64, 65, 71, 80-1, 82-6, 89, 93, 96, 98-101, 147, 155, 186, 193-207, 216
    BS 212-13

Newsome, David, 23n, 75n, 131n, 180n

Oliphant, Laurence, 30-1
Oliphant, Mrs, 30-1
Origo, Iris, 34n

Palmerston, Lord, 182, 184, 211
Pater, Walter, 81
Peel, Sir Robert, 84, 112-13, 210-11
Pope, Alexander, 32, 115, 215
Prothero, R. E., 23-4, 91-2, 102
Purcell, Edmund, 45-6

Reade, Charles, 42n
Rennie, John, 112, 118-19, 120
Richardson, Samuel, 11
Roper, William, 90-1
Rosebery, Lord, 22
Ruskin, John, 14, 23, 74, 106, 164, 210
Russell, Lord John (Earl Russell), 186-7, 188, 211

Salisbury, Lord, 65, 126, 179, 182, 191, 211
Scott, Sir Walter, 25-6, 132n, 148
Shelley, P. B., 35, 61-3, 97-8, 214
Smiles, Samuel, 24, 86, 105-24, 144-5
    BS 213-14
Southey, Robert, 16, 19-20, 25-6, 41-2, 51-4, 62, 110
    BS 214
Stanley, A. P., 22-3, 39, 43, 64, 81, 84, 86, 87-104, 209
    BS 214
Stanley, Lady Augusta, 22, 39
Stephen, Fitzjames, 36, 51, 65, 71, 74, 75

Stephen, Sir James, 65, 76-7, 79, 215
Stephen, Leslie, 14, 20, 36-8, 49, 71, 74-6, 78-9, 127, 176
    BS 215
Stephenson, George, 117, 119, 213
Sterling, John, 50, 60, 157
Swift, Jonathan, 55, 215
Symonds, J. A., 23n

Taylor, Sir Henry, 74
Telford, Thomas, 114-15, 122
Tennyson, Hallam, 38-9
Tennyson, Alfred Lord, 38-9, 40, 47, 49, 87, 97, 148
Thackeray, W. M., 56, 72, 97, 215
Trevelyan, G. M., 125, 215
Trevelyan, Sir George Otto, 64, 75, 93, 125-43
    BS 215
Trollope, Anthony, 64, 79, 121n, 130
Trotter, L. J., 44

Ullathorne, W. B., 204-5

Vaughan, C. J., 23, 209
Victoria, Queen, 22, 87, 211

Ward, W. G., 194, 215-16
Ward, Wilfrid, 16, 79-80, 86, 93, 193-207
    BS 215-16
Wedgwood, Josiah, 108-9
Wesley, John, 19-20, 21, 51-4, 72n
Whateley, William, 82-3
Wilberforce, R. I., 29n, 71, 75, 81-2, 127, 131

INDEX

Wilberforce, Samuel, 29n, 71, 75, 127, 131
Wilberforce, William, 29, 65, 72-3, 74, 75, 81, 154, 211
Wiseman, Cardinal, 194, 216
Wolseley, Sir Garnet, 162-3

Woolf, Virginia, 65, 71, 75-9
Wordsworth, William, 17, 19, 81, 88, 90, 116, 147-8, 214

Yeats, W. B., 30
Young, G. M., 59, 113n